THE
AFTERLIFE

THE
AFTERLIFE

An Investigation into the Mysteries of Life after Death

JENNY RANDLES &
PETER HOUGH

LONDON   NEW YORK   SYDNEY   TORONTO

Permission to use copyright photographs is gratefully acknowledged to the following: *page 11* British Library/Bridgeman Art Library; *page 21* Topham Picture Library; *page 31* Peter Hough; *page 35* Dr Elmar R Gruber/Fortean Picture Library; *page 45* Fortean Picture Library; *page 53* Sunday Mirror/Syndication International; *pages 63 and 71* Mary Evans Picture Library/Harry Price Collection, University of London; *page 66* Michael Bromley; *pages 79 and 80* Mary Evans Picture Library; *page 84* Guy Lyon Playfair/Fortean Picture Library; *page 87* Dr Elmar R Gruber/Fortean Picture Library; *page 96* Hugh Gay/ Fortean Picture Library; *page 103* BBC; *page 109* Fortean Picture Library; *Page 110* Mary Evans Picture Library/Andrew Green; *page 111* Mary Evans Picture Library/Harry Price Collection, University of London; *page 114* Grafton Books; *page 123* Maurice Grosse; *page 125* Peter Hough; *page 130* Ken Webster/Fortean Picture Library; *page 137* Peter Hough; *Page 142* Peter Hough; *page 144* Fortean Picture Library; *page 147* Jan Zyniewski; *page 152* Fortean Picture Library; *page 155* Images Colour Library; *page 166* Ivan Spenceley/Rex Features; *page 169* Images Colour Library; *page 176* Oldham Evening Chronicle; *pages 182 and 183* Fortean Picture Library; *page 194* © Crown Copyright; *page 211* Dennis Stacy/Fortean Picture Library. Whilst every effort has been made to trace all copyright holders, the publishers apologise to any holders not acknowledged.

This edition published 1993
by BCA by arrangement with
Judy Piatkus (Publishers) Ltd
5 Windmill St., London W1P 1HF

CN 1728

Edited by Esther Jagger
Designed by Paul Saunders
Illustrations by Mark Oldroyd

Printed in Great Britain

CONTENTS

———◆———

INTRODUCTION

———◆———

In life, one thing is certain – our own personal physical extinction. No one escapes death, yet from the beginning man has hoped and believed in an afterlife – a realm of existence where the psyche survives, perhaps evolves, or is returned to Earth in a new vessel.

This belief is suggested by Neanderthal burials of more than fifty thousand years ago, ancient Egyptian mummification and pre-Christian pagan rites. But in our modern scientific world, belief is not enough. Proof is demanded, and is being sought by scientists from the disciplines of medicine and physics. The biggest strides in afterlife research are being made in the fields of past life 'memories' and near death experiences (NDEs). In particular, scientific examination of the NDE phenomenon, conducted by medical professionals since the late 1970s, presents very persuasive evidence that mind and body are separate entities, and that as a result mind can survive the demise of the physical self.

Even so, man at worst is a conceited animal, who, because of his superior intellect, finds it untenable that he should die and return to dust just like the lesser animals he exploits for his own pleasure and comfort. Is it 'racial' arrogance that demands an afterlife to preserve man's fragile ego? Or would it be arrogance to believe that we were outside the mechanism of the universe – a universe which seems to operate within a structure of cyclic renewal, a key component of some gigantic, unfathomable cosmic machine? Energy cannot be destroyed, only converted into another form. Is this what happens to us on physical death?

The pens of some of our greatest fiction writers from Bram Stoker and Algernon Blackwood to contemporaries like Philip José Farmer have postulated the indestructibility of the soul. Are such stories purely a product of invention, or imagination based on a concrete universal truth?

HOW YOU WILL WRITE THIS BOOK'S FINAL CHAPTER

What we have done is delve into the extensive literature dealing with the afterlife, and produced a broad cross-section of historical and contemporary material. We present in this book the beliefs, myths, human experience and research into life after death.

Much of what you will read is the result of our own personal investigations into haunted houses, reincarnation and out-of-the-body experiences. However, we are not on a crusade. We retain our objectivity and, we, like you, can only make judgements on the evidence. Both sides of the arguments are presented and summarised for you to ponder. In addition we offer you a simple method for arriving at your own personal decision.

At the end of each chapter we have given a summary of the main points for and against survival. After each chapter award a score out of 10, based on whether you believe the evidence you have just read supported survival or whether it favoured a more sceptical stance.

If it positively supported survival, award a high PLUS mark (as close to 10 out of 10 as you think it deserves). If you think it favoured the sceptics' view, award a NEGATIVE mark (anywhere between minus 1 and minus 10 according to how strongly you believe the case was demonstrated). If you really cannot decide, award a neutral score of 0.

At the end of the book you will have thirteen scores to add together. Tot up all the plus scores, then all the negative ones, and take the lower figure from the higher. The results will be a total (either positive or negative according to your scores) which will reflect how you judged the strength of evidence throughout the book.

At the end we offer a few guidelines as to what the total you have reached may represent. In doing this, you – in effect – will have written the last chapter of this book! Until unambiguous proof arrives, each of us must weigh up the circumstantial evidence and decide where it points . . .

A Universal, Global Belief

───◆───

Some of the greatest civilisations have evolved on the premise of a world beyond this world.

The belief in an afterlife is universal. It permeates time and culture, evolution and philosophical revolution. Some of the greatest civilisations have evolved on the premise of a world beyond this world, a dimension not of the physical but of the soul. Mankind's most celebrated philosophers have promoted the idea that there exists a place of spirit, a dimension of love and light, or, for some, a pit of suffering – a fiery Hell. Alternatively, this other world is a place of limbo, a staging post until the 'self' is reborn in flesh anew.

That the imagery is reasonably consistent and very widespread may be the most significant circumstantial evidence for its veracity. If these universal beliefs are not subconscious cultural awareness of some basic truth, then there has to be a powerful reason for their existence (presumably one linked to the survival instinct in a strictly animalistic and evolutionary fashion). This would surely demand that a society adopt these views to further its progress. Yet, in terms of survival, the view that life is short and can end very abruptly seems far more likely to promote alertness and reproduction of the species (so as to perpetuate it beyond the finality of death) than does the concept that this life is but a passing phase that leads to something better.

So why 'invent' such stories if we are merely animals and they are useless myths? If survival is real, then all of us will know this fact deep within our psyche. Global beliefs of this nature would then be a predictable response, even if there are cosmic reasons why full awareness is withheld from our conscious mind.

Even primitive man seems to have shared this fundamental belief that life did not end with the corruption of the flesh. Fifty thousand years ago, the Neanderthals were burying their dead. This may not sound unusual, but it takes effort to dig a hole, especially with inadequate tools, when every waking hour is needed to stock up the larder with fresh meat. It would have been easier, and logical, to have left the dead for predators to dispense with. Yet not only did Neanderthal man bury his fellow tribesmen – the task was carried out in a ritualistic manner.

Corpses were sometimes tied with ropes into a foetal position. Is this an indication of belief in reincarnation? That by forcing the body into its position in the womb, it would encourage rebirth? Or were the ropes intended to stop the reanimated dead rising from the earth and terrorising the living? Either way, it illustrates a reasoning that body and mind were separate entities, and that the ego survived and had power over the flesh: the ghost within the machine.

How does this belief manifest from culture to culture, age to age? Is there a uniformity of belief which might indicate a source other than the imagination? Has this fundamental tenet of man's philosophy something to do with Jung's 'collective unconscious'? Carl Jung, a Swiss psychologist, formulated the theory in the early part of the twentieth century. He suggested that apart from a personal unconscious, there also existed a racial or communal unconscious. This contains every thought, every emotion, every piece of information that mankind has ever experienced or brought into being. Each individual is linked to the collective unconscious, drawing from it as well as adding to its huge matrix.

On physical death each one of us could be absorbed into this super-mind – the actual place of the afterlife.

EGYPT

Egyptian religious texts inscribed on to the walls of pyramids at Sakkara are the oldest describing a belief in an afterworld. They form the basis for modern occult systems of magic. More than four thousand years old, each details the rituals necessary to transport the dead pharaoh from this world into the next. Spells and prayers were used to bring out the desired effect in ancient Egypt. In time these spells were also used by the Egyptian hierarchy, and eventually by anyone who had the money to buy them. Whether pharaoh or peasant, providing the spirit had a purity of heart it coexisted with the gods in the afterworld.

Different spells transported the deceased by different routes. The dead could fly like a bird or climb a ladder to Heaven. Once arrived, they would live in eternal happiness. This longevity was further assured by identifying the subject with Osiris – the god of fertility and of resurrection. To help, a guide called the *Book of the Dead* was buried with the body. It instructed the newly risen soul in the correct responses to tests that the spirit must go through before merging with Osiris.

Perhaps all this was meant to dispel any doubt that the deceased would

go to a place of bliss. The Egyptians believed that the soul was judged by the gods, then rewarded or punished. The Papyrus of Ani, dating from *c.* 1320 BC, contains an illustration of a heart being weighed against a feather – the feather representing 'truth'. This 'weighing of the heart' was recorded by Thoth, scribe of the gods.

The Papyrus Book of the Dead depicting a heart being weighed in a balance against a feather – symbol of truth.

The ritual of mummification had its roots in Egyptian mythology. The god Seth, or Set, later worshipped as Satan, dismembered Osiris in a fit of jealousy and scattered his body across Egypt. Isis, the wife of Osiris, collected all the parts, bandaged them together and breathed life afresh into him.

With the dead were buried some of their earthly possessions. Yet the Egyptians were not the first to bury 'grave goods'. One wonders what use material goods were supposed to be to an intangible spirit. In Germany and Scandinavia the dead were buried with their shoes on, to save their feet from stumbling painfully in the next world!

Royal tombs dated around 2250 BC at Ur in Mesopotamia (now Iraq) contained quantities of furniture, musical instruments and even gambling equipment. Weapons, wine and food have been discovered in graves, as well as the executed remains of soldiers and courtiers who were meant to continue serving their masters in the world beyond. Apparently these loyal servants died willingly, as no signs of violence or a struggle were found. However, the description of the sacrifice of a slave girl at the funeral of a tenth-century Swedish chieftain, written by an Arab traveller named Ibn Fadlan, shows that she was drugged beforehand.

The Egyptians believed that, while the body resided in the tomb, an ethereal 'double' grew from it and rose towards Heaven. At first it was thought that the afterworld existed beyond the iron dome of the world, but later its location was moved to the land where the sun shone at night – underneath the Earth. This heavenly land was known as the Field of Reeds, set within the Fields of Peace. There, the spirit lived in a beautiful house in the midst of a great estate, filled with fragrant flowers and vines heavy with ripe grapes.

The estate was managed by small statues, now given animation, which had been buried with the deceased. At the centre of this Heaven was the House of Eternity where all the gods resided; the resurrected men and women were able to move amongst them. It was a place of happy feasting and lovemaking.

GREECE

The underworld of the ancient Greeks was ruled by Persephone and her husband Pluto. These gods were powerful, beautiful, and yet in some ways sinister. Like the Egyptians, the Greeks believed there were many routes to this darkly wondrous place. Their evaluation of the afterlife was pessimistic: it is best realised in Homer's poems, particularly the *Odyssey*.

This great epic describes how the wandering hero Odysseus descends into Hades (Hell) to discover why he has been prevented from returning home after the fall of Troy. There he meets the 'shade' of his mother. When he tries to embrace this shadowy form, he cries out in frustration. She explains:

> 'This is the way decreed for mortals when they die. The sinews cease to hold the flesh and bones together; for they are destroyed by the power of the blazing fire, as soon as the life leaves the white bones, and the shade hovers about, then flits away.'

The 'fire' was a reference to cremation of the body; 'life' was *thymos* – the animalistic self which was destroyed with the body; and the 'shade', or *psyche*, refers to the very essence of self which then descended into Hades.

Homeric heroes were very physical. They fought, drank wine, attended huge banquets and made love incessantly. To them, the underworld, where the psyche was stripped from the physical self, was an insubstantial place of misery.

Homer also described a place situated at the end of the Earth, on the banks of the fabled river Oceanus. Elysium was where the righteous went after death, a land of perfect happiness and perpetual spring, ruled by Rhadamanthus. But there were places in the afterlife populated only by the élite. Such a place was referred to by the poet Pindar as the Isles of the Blest, which were inhabited by a noble hierarchy dominated by their king, Cronus.

In time these beliefs were assimilated by the Romans, formalised, refined and blended with their own myths. In the Latin epic known as the *Aeneid*, Virgil described Hades as a place of retributive punishment. Here, confessions for mortal sins were extracted, and the guilty punished by demons and writhing snakes. Great heroes such as Aeneas found pathways to the underworld, where they were able to converse with their dead ancestors before returning.

JUDAISM

It was not until the second century BC that the Hebrews formulated a belief in judgement after death. Before that they saw man as a psycho-physical being which was all but destroyed at death. What did remain was a 'shade', a thing of little significance. This shade descended into a deep pit below the foundation of the world which was called Sheol – a place of gloom and dust – and was inhabited by both the just and unjust. This idea bears some similarity to Greek mythological belief. Eventually a conceptual change took place which is marked by a brief passage in the Book of Daniel (12:2): 'And many of those who sleep in the dust of the earth shall awake, some to everlasting life, and some to shame and everlasting contempt.'

No one knows what brought about this change, but now a belief in resurrection and judgement of the dead became part of the Hebrew mythos. The idea gained support in Jewish literature, which included detailed descriptions of judgement by Yahweh (Jehovah). It was believed that there would be a Day of Yahweh, when God would punish the oppressors of the Jewish people. This was gradually transformed into the concept of the Last Judgement, and these refined beliefs were later taken on board by Christianity.

HINDUISM AND BUDDHISM

*Death is an absurdity ...
everyone and everything
has eternal life.*

The early Indians did not believe in reincarnation, but thought that man
lived only once. He went to a world of bliss shared with the gods if he was
good, and to punishment in Hell if he was evil. This belief was shared with
the Iranians. Zoroastrianism is the name given to the religion founded by
the Iranian prophet Zoroaster around the sixth or seventh century BC, by
which time a more complex religious system was emerging in India. This
was a fusion of Aryan, non-Aryan and Sumerian influences.

The Aryans, a nomadic tribal group from Europe, invaded northern India
between 1700 and 1200 BC. Their religion was based on sky worship,
which included gods analogous with Greek and Roman deities. Around
3500 BC the Sumerians settled in Babylonia and initiated a cultural revolution which formed the blueprint for social structure through to modern
times. Each settlement had its own individual deity. In time this created
a large pantheon of gods with complex interrelationships. Hinduism,
which grew out of all this, introduced a hierachy of gods, who were in turn
facets of a unitary principle, a force that is said to exist throughout nature
and in all men. Here, God is believed to be in every living thing. The
Indian religions are the only ones which postulate that after death the soul
loses its individuality and merges with a greater being.

Hinduism has no founder, but it does have a body of texts known as the
Veda – a word meaning 'wisdom' or 'knowledge'. The Veda set down the
belief in rebirth and transmigration – the idea that the soul of a man may
be reborn in the body of another animal. The reason for rebirth is the law
of Karma – that a soul must keep returning to mortal existence until it has
learned all the lessons of spiritual evolution.

Hindus are metaphysically minded. They spend a lifetime searching for
that unifying principle which they believe binds the whole universe: that
unknown something was termed 'Brahman', or occasionally 'Atman'. The
search leads to mystical states of mind, so strange that they are hard to
explain in words. This 'cosmic consciousness' has been described by one
modern practitioner, who said it shows ' . . . the cosmos as entirely imma-
terial, entirely spiritual and entirely alive, it shows that death is an absurdity, that everyone and everything has eternal life; it shows that the
universe is God and that God is the universe, and that no evil ever did or
ever will enter into it.'

Buddhism appeared in the sixth century BC, growing out of Hinduism.
It postulated a series of graded paradises, each more beautiful and sensual
than its predecessor. Ascent through these dimensions is dependent on
individual virtue and meditation. Yet in both religions the desire was not

for ultimate and personal pleasure, but for a release from the bondage of 'personality'. This pure spiritual state is referred to as 'Nirvana'. A soul may dwell in the levels of paradise for aeons, but ultimately it must leave to continue its pilgrimage.

In Buddhist and Hindu beliefs there is a 'Hell', too, where souls languish in suffering. But to be relegated there is not necessarily permanent. The Hindu god Krishna, for instance, visited the kingdom of the dead and released a favourite pupil. In Buddhism, Hell is often entered by a 'Bodhisattva' who then releases some of its inmates. A Bodhisattva is one who is highly evolved spiritually, and on the way to becoming a Buddha as a result of merit gained in previous earthly lives. The Chinese Buddhist goddess Kwan Yin turned a Hell into a Paradise whilst in trance.

According to the Rig-Veda – part of the Veda – the god of the dead is known as Yama. The son of Vivasvant – the first mortal to die and go forth to the afterlife – Yama became the judge of the dead in Chinese, Tibetan and Japanese Buddhism. He is depicted as a fearsome figure, presiding over Hell. Buddhist and Hindu beliefs in the afterlife are as complex and detailed as their own social structure here on Earth.

ISLAM

The prophet Mohammed founded the complex religious movement of Islam in the seventh century AD at Mecca in Arabia, when he was about forty. At this time he started receiving revelations from God, but it was twelve years before the movement became established with a large community of Moslems. Its beliefs and laws were set down first of all in the Koran, then additionally in a collection of material called the Tradition.

The Koran gives guidance on many matters, and summons man to submit to God and do His will or suffer the consequences. Those consequences are to be realised in the afterlife. The good were promised a garden of paradise filled with delights. The evil, however, were threatened with severe punishments in the hereafter.

After the dead have been buried and the mourners have departed, two angels, Munkar and Nakeer, are said to arrive and interrogate them. The dead are made to sit upright, and are expected to have a full knowledge of and belief in Islam. If the questions are answered correctly, then the deceased is allowed access to paradise through a door that opens on command from Heaven. However, if the questions are answered incorrectly, the infidel pays the price. A door to Hell opens, releasing heat and an

*A door to Hell opens,
releasing heat and an
odious wind. The grave
closes in on him, crushing
his ribs…*

odious wind. The grave closes in on him, crushing his ribs and leaving him suffering until the day of resurrection.

On that day, man is made to stand up before God and be judged. No defence is allowed – everything of each individual's past life is recorded and read from a scroll. Finally, the good deeds and the bad are weighed against each other to determine the fate of each person.

In the Tradition, there is also mention of a bridge over Hell. This bridge is said to be 'finer than a hair and sharper than a sword'. All must attempt to cross it: believers arrive safely, while unbelievers fall into the abyss.

CHRISTIANITY

The Christian religion originated in Judaea, and its first members were Jews. The initial expansion was into the Greek-speaking world of the eastern Mediterranean. It seems to have emerged as a religion recognisably different from Judaism around AD 64. As Christianity spread, divisions of religious practices and interpretation of holy texts arose amongst its adherents.

Christians argue that a benevolent God would hardly have given us life merely for it to end after a relatively short period of time with the demise of the physical body. The Christian doctrine taught that the human soul created by God was immortal. Once placed within the physical shell, the two were then inextricably linked until death, when the soul left the body. But the theory of organic evolution teaches that man was descended from the lower animals. If this is the case, at what point did man become immortal – or is all sentient life indestructible?

Jesus himself promised eternal life: 'I am the resurrection and the life; he who believes in me, though he die, yet shall he live.' Some, notably the sect known as the Gnostics, claimed that because the body is material and therefore intrinsically evil, Christ had been composed of a spiritual body and not of flesh and blood. However, when Jesus was resurrected from the cross he assured his disciples of his physical reality by eating a fish.

Some ecclesiastical ministers, such as Professor Roland Bainton, argue that this faith in the resurrection of Christ was the main creative force behind the formation of the Church; that, and the belief that he would soon return to Earth and set up a new order. Christ convinced his followers that it was possible to transcend death and defeat demonic forces.

Christ also promised a last judgement day, when the good would receive

The historical and cross-cultural belief in an afterlife is reinforced by Christ's ascension into Heaven after having risen from the dead.

eternal happiness and sinners perpetual pain and misery in the fires of Hell. After the last judgement the majority of souls were destined for purgatory, where they were to expiate their sins. At the Second Coming of Christ, the decomposed bodies of everyone who had ever lived would be reconstituted and their souls returned to them for the Final Judgement.

Mankind is perceived by Christians as a fallen race. Each baby is born with the blemish of Adam's original sin, and is immediately tarnished in the eyes of God. Heaped on this are the sins each individual commits during life. After death, even a newborn child has to make atonement to God.

In the Middle Ages, a terrifying picture of Hell was painted. Those who resided in Heaven were perceived gloating, watching from on high those suffering fiery tortures below. On the whole, modern Christians and Jews, whilst still firmly believing in an afterlife, view Heaven and Hell in a more diluted and philosophical form. Some reject the concept of Hell altogether; or agree that, if it does exist, it represents a place where the wicked are denied access to God. Conversely, Heaven is seen as a condition where the human soul is elevated to God's level and exists close to Him. The modern Christian fundamentalist movement, however, firmly believes in a dimension – places – of Heaven and Hell.

AUSTRALIAN ABORIGINES

The 'dream time' represents a kind of heavenly sphere. It is the home of the gods, psychic messages, spirits and ancestors.

The wildlife of Australia is in many senses unlike any other fauna on Earth. This huge landmass has been an island throughout most of geological time. In other parts of the world primitive animals migrated when the continents were linked together by land bridges at the dawn of evolution. As a result there was an even spread of species that have grown from a common set of ancestors. However, Australia's isolation allowed it to develop almost like another planet, creating the strange and unique animal life we see today.

Although it is believed that the original human inhabitants of the Australian continent migrated there, they have been largely isolated from other races as civilisation spread and intermixed in various parts of the world. Only relatively recent immigration by Europeans changed that. It is not surprising, then, to find that the Australian natives have a rich store of beliefs. Significantly, those beliefs feature a very strong concept of survival after death.

The 'dream time' represents a kind of heavenly sphere removed from time and space. It is the home of the gods, psychic messages, spirits and ancestors, and even today has an exceptionally strong part to play in Black Australian culture. Despite the growth of modern concrete cities – citadels of soulless Western capitalism – many aborigines still live their lives according to rules handed down for millennia in no more than a story and a song. This is especially true in the vast, near uninhabitable hinterland, or in the rainforest, plains and mountains of the far north, where 80 per cent of the population still lives in a way that many would consider primitive, but in fact has a definite sophistication.

On a 'walkabout' – a sort of wandering reverie into the searing heat and endless wastelands – the aborigines can commune with the dream time and engage in what can only be termed psychic pursuits. Many of them have an innate gift for meditation and ESP (extra-sensory perception), although they do not use terms of this kind. Several of the roots and medicines imbibed by tribespeople contain chemicals that create altered states of consciousness. The shaman (comparable with the medicine man in African tribes or amongst American Indians) is both a psychic medium who can 'tune in' to things and an important bearer of knowledge handed down through the generations. It is not uncommon to see an aborigine standing bolt upright in one place for a long time. In poor light, strangers have taken such figures for a rock or tree. These people are in an altered state where time and space have relatively little meaning.

Mythology tells of whole tribes responding to an inner call to move out of danger to another place.

There is also a strong sense of spiritual feeling attached to many of the decisions made by aborigines. They base their lives on intuitive hunches and the ability to empathise with the emotions and actions of others, even at a distance. Mythology tells of whole tribes responding to an inner call to move out of danger to another place, or of rescuers finding compatriots in distress who have issued a kind of 'psychic flare'. Whilst to some members of the 'civilised' world such peoples may appear primitive, in many respects they are far ahead of us. They have harnessed the powers that we may all possess at some level but which modern Western society has driven down into the deep recesses of the mind. We have become conditioned to assume that communing with spirits and sensing the oneness of all things is superstitious nonsense. Yet as a result we have lost touch with basic survival skills that may once have kept us alive in a hostile environment.

Paranormal researcher Bill Chalker has made a study of the claims and legends of the shamanistic culture of the aborigines. Many of their spirits, reflected in the spectacular rock art of the Northern Territory, seem to suppose that death is not the end.

Early students of aboriginal legend discovered the belief that the dead were 'taken to the sky' and eventually brought to Earth again. Those who were returned would do so in a trance, bemused by the mourning of their friends and relatives who thought them dead. They would be treated with reverence and many became shamans. Whether these were legends of survival or examples of near death experiences (see Chapter 13), one can appreciate the impact they made on aboriginal culture and the importance placed upon the view that we do have spirit and that it survives bodily extinction.

AMERICAN INDIANS

There are many native American Indian tribes, and most share a strong belief in the presence of spirits. Many of their rituals which persist today are based upon the idea that the dead exist in another dimension which has a form of interaction with the Earth. This other dimension was originally conceived as existing in the sky high above the Earth. The stars and bright planets were thought by some tribes to be the camp fires of the tribes which lived there, but later these celestial bodies were deified. The Indian afterlife was inhabited by the souls of men and animals, who co-existed without the need to kill one another for food.

The eagle's soaring flight and dominion over the world are for some tribes an intimation that it represents higher guardian spirits.

The Indians believed there was only a slight difference between men and other animals. Indians often apologised to the spirit of a bear after it was slain. For this reason creatures such as the bear and the eagle are sometimes held in great awe. The eagle's soaring flight and dominion over the world are for some tribes an intimation that it represents higher guardian spirits. Most tribes believed that spirit protectors in the form of animals could be acquired by young braves through rituals involving fasting and self-torture. The animal spirit was believed to inhabit the skin carried by the brave.

The growth of agriculture developed the Indian religion towards a personification of the forces of nature, which often decided the fate of their crops. Up until the late nineteenth century, the Pawnees were known to sacrifice young girls to the morning star – Venus. The victim, kidnapped from another tribe, was stripped and tied to a frame and then shot to death with arrows. In the days leading up to the sacrifice she was treated kindly and given beautiful clothes and good food. This was to ensure that her spirit would go to the star, which had great power, and intercede on their behalf.

After the white man had slashed and burned his way through the great forests of North America, and wiped out whole tribes of Indians, confining the rest to reservations where they could barely eke out a living, these once proud people were at last brought to heel and a strange religious metamorphosis occurred. For three hundred years or more the white man had been trying to convert the Indians to Christianity. In 1890, this white man's religion was absorbed into the native culture and manifested in the phenomenon of the Ghost Dance.

The Ghost Dance religion was founded by a Paiute Messiah called Wovoka. The ceremony itself, which spread across the reservations like prairie fire, starts off with a handful of Indians forming a circle and singing in a soft undertone. Gradually more join in – anything up to five hundred

– the song grows louder and the people dance, until many of them fall into a trance. During this state, the Indians claimed they left their bodies to visit the spirit world.

On 9 October 1890 a Minneconjou Indian called Kicking Bear visited Sioux chief Sitting Bull and told him of Wovoka, the risen Christ. Kicking Bear told Sitting Bull that the ghosts of all the Indians would return and inhabit the Earth. He had travelled to meet the Messiah and stopped at Pyramid Lake in Nevada. There a camp of Paiutes told them that Christ had returned, this time in the flesh of an Indian. The group joined hundreds of other pilgrims from many different tribes, gathered around Walker Lake. Three days later, the Christ appeared.

Wovoka preached that he had returned to bring about a new order. Next spring the earth would be covered with new soil which would bury all the white men, and the grasslands, forests and buffalo herds would return. The Indians would be protected by following the Ghost Dance. Their spirits would rise above the Earth while this transformation took place, and afterwards they would be reborn together with their ancestors. According to Kicking Bear, as he and his friends left the gathering Wovoka flew above them, teaching them new songs.

The Ghost Dance religion was founded by a Paiute Messiah called Wovoka. During the ceremony, Indians dance themselves into a trance. In this state they claim to leave their bodies and visit the spirit world.

Although the Ghost Dance was entirely peaceable, Washington ordered that the 'fomenters of these disturbances' be arrested. Sitting Bull was one chief who was to be arrested and, in blundering to do so, he was accidentally shot dead by an Indian policeman. A massacre of three hundred Indians – including many women and children – at Wounded Knee Creek was one of the atrocities which followed.

Tribes such as the Hopi of Arizona and New Mexico have a set of ecological beliefs that are quite modern in outlook. They consider that all life has an inner spirit and that the Earth itself is imbued with a collective consciousness formed from all living things. So to desecrate or despoil the planet invites wrath from the Earth Mother – a super guardian spirit. The aptness of the crises we face today is noted by some tribe members. We have raped precious minerals from the land and destroyed natural habitats. Now we face retribution as the ozone layer is thinned and greenhouse gases in the atmosphere threaten the basis of life itself.

The Indians live by balance and, they say, we have upset that balance in nature. Several leading researchers into the crop circle mystery have visited the Hopi because their shamans claim to recognise the symbolism within these circular marks found gouged into our Western grain fields. They interpret them as a warning from the Earth Mother spirit that we must make drastic changes in the way we live our lives or suffer the inevitable consequences.

This review of most of the main world religions and cultures illustrates conclusively that, from the dawn of man's reasoning, there existed an almost universal belief in a life beyond the material world. Whether pagan or Christian, African, North or South American, Asian or European the fundamental belief remains the same. The ghost in the biological machine survives its extinction and moves on to a place beyond the material world.

Is this belief unreasonable, merely wishful thinking, or is it based on an inner knowledge of that other place – a dimension, indeed perhaps dimensions, where spiritual energy, released from the shackles of the physical organism, travels? Is our existence here merely part of a long and complex learning process, so vast that we can sense only the merest whiff of its true nature?

TO BELIEVE IN SURVIVAL

Dr John Shaw is a fascinating man. Describing himself as 'not conventionally religious', he none the less has a spiritual outlook on life. He is also by profession a psychologist working at Manchester University and is willing to speak out in favour of the paranormal when this is justified. How do these things equate? And why is there such a worldwide belief in so many differing cultures that we do not die along with our bodies?

'People have experiences which require explanation,' Dr Shaw explains simply. 'It has been remarked, for example, that memories of reincarnation are more likely to be obtained in cultures that permit this as a belief. In cultures such as our own, where the Christian Church rejected it in the third century, then there tends to be a barrier and fewer spontaneous memories of that kind get through.'

But is this perhaps just an illustration of man's inherent desire to cheat death? Perhaps we want to believe in our own immortality so desperately that all tribes or societies foster some kind of concept. Dr Shaw comments:

Self-delusion is a human failing. People do sometimes engage in wish fulfilment.

'Undoubtedly self-delusion is a human failing, and it is one of the cardinal principles that all parapsychologists have to recognise. People do engage in wish fulfilment. They would like certain things to be true and so they tend to find evidence that makes them true. . . . But there is evidence. Even if you discount all those cases of, say, previous lives, that can be put down to cryptomnesia or other causes, then you are still left with a residue of significant cases; and the explanation for these must be that they offer some support for the survival hypotheses.'

However, as a scientist he is aware of the difference between supposition and evidence:

'In these areas I always make a distinction between personal conviction and scientific proof. Individuals who have had experiences and reflect upon them often come to conclusions that they will survive death, but so far as the scientific community is concerned and the obtaining of evidence that will convince everybody and will be sufficiently impartial and objective, then this is a different matter. I personally believe it will be many, many years before the scientific community accept much of this evidence and so leave us free to draw implications from that.'

So where does that leave him as a scientist with spiritual beliefs? 'It leaves me out on a limb,' he replied. For Dr Shaw, persuasion comes in a different way from how it does to science, which is a discipline with rigid rules:

'I don't go ghost hunting, but I have certainly had several apparitional experiences, particularly after a family bereavement, and I remember these clearly and they were significant to me. I understand the sceptic who would say that I was in a state of suggestibility. But for me, anyway, these experiences had a force and vividness which I can never forget and clearly are significant. . . . To be precise, I saw my mother-in-law about four or five weeks after she had died. I can remember how she was dressed and I can remember her appearance. From being someone who had been in a coma during the last month of her life she was healthy-looking and happy-looking, and to me that was significant.'

Since such experiences have occurred throughout the history of human life on Earth and we have always tried to reconcile them, it is no surprise to John Shaw that there is hardly a culture without some belief in survival of death. Cultural belief is formed from a distillation of human experience. The fact that this experience is largely anecdotal is relevant only to science, which rightly demands more rigorous standards before it turns belief into doctrine. But the anecdotal basis of this global belief does not mean that it is suspect and science prudent, or that it is wrong and science right. It is merely the outcome of a different philosophy of interpretation.

YOUR VERDICT : A SUMMARY

AGAINST SURVIVAL

- Belief may be a survival mechanism created by evolution to help human animals cope with the idea of death.

- As a race evolves and comprehends individual death, wishful thinking is perhaps inevitable as a means to retain sanity and ensure that progress continues.

- Darwin's theory of evolution demonstrates that man is descended from apes. If this is so, by what criteria do they enter the Hell or Heaven of the afterlife? On the other hand, why should men possess a spirit, while other animals do not?

FOR SURVIVAL

- Belief may represent a deep intuitive awareness of a universal truth common to all races at a level of inner consciousness.

- There is a remarkable consistency in the belief of a continuity of life after death, returning to Earth in other forms, and a one-ness of all things. If it is just myth, how have different societies and civilisations all independently arrived at the same, or a similar, scenario?

- Darwin's theories can be integrated into the belief of an afterlife. Some cultures, including those of the American Indians, believe that animals too survive physical death – that the life which animates biological systems does not die with them.

DEMONS AND ANGELS

—————◆—————

One of the laws of physics states that for every action there is an opposite and equal reaction. Could this also apply to metaphysics? Does a universal law of equal opposites exist? If so, the afterlife could be the natural antithesis of existence on the physical plane. Further, if good cannot exist without evil, then if there is a Heaven there must also be a Hell.

Taken at face value, near death experiences (see Chapter 13) seem to support this philosophy. Within the framework of a law of universal polarity, the stories of demonic and angelic entities are persuasive. These are believed to inhabit Heaven and Hell but are not confined there, as many witnesses will attest. If we are prepared seriously to consider evidence for survival after death, this must include reports of demonic and angelic entities. They are as much a part of the afterlife hypothesis as ghosts and spirit communications. Man has nurtured a belief in such beings since his formulation of the concept of an afterlife.

DEMONS

The term 'demon' is derived from the Greek *daimon*, referred to by occultists as 'daemon'. Originally it was a blanket term for supernatural beings, both good and bad; but the Christians branded all pagan spirits as satanic, hence the connotation with evil.

Demons are purely supernatural beings, and have never had human form. Their often frightening and repulsive appearance mirrors exactly the malevolence and evil intent they are said to favour as emissaries of their dark master – Satan. Christian fundamentalists believe that Satan is a real entity – the fallen angel of scripture – who sends demons into this world to cause misery and pervert the will of individuals in his fight with God. The literature of demonology is littered with the names and aspects of hundreds of demons; for instance there are the ghouls, who originated in the

Middle East and Asia – they are supernatural monsters who rob graves and feed off corpses.

Occultists have claimed down the centuries to be able to call up demons from the underworld using magical spells. The magician protects himself by standing in a magic circle, and conjures up the entity in a triangle. Necromancy, as it is called, originated with the Mesopotamians thousands of years ago, and is still practised today even in the most sophisticated of societies.

Thousands of occultists across Europe and the United States are involved in calling up demons. They follow in the footsteps of Aleister Crowley, dubbed 'the most evil man alive' during the early part of the twentieth century.

Crowley, born in Warwickshire, identified with the Beast 666 of the Apocalypse, referred to in the Bible. Through the use of ritual aided by drugs, alcohol and sex, he and his mistresses entered other worlds and contacted demonic intelligences. One such entity, named Aiwass, was contacted by Crowley during his time in Cairo. Aiwass dictated a short book to him during three consecutive days in April 1904. It was to be called *The Book of the Law* – a new order for mankind. Leah Hirsig, Crowley's 'Mother of Harlots', also communed with the entity.

But not all demons arrive on the Earthly plane by invitation. There are accounts in which such entities have arrived of their own free will. Did Shelley Robertson come face to face with a demon in the early hours of 25 June 1989?

A FACE AT THE WINDOW

Shelley Robertson is the manager of a Nottingham casino, happily married with two young children. On this particular night she arrived home from work at about 11.30p.m., had a cup of tea, watched some television and then went to bed. Her husband was already fast asleep.

At about ten to three, something woke her up. She decided to go to the bathroom, but as she prepared to climb out of bed she sensed that someone – or something – was staring at her. The feeling was intense, frightening. At that time, the couple slept with the bedroom curtains drawn back. Shelley turned her head to face the window, and was confronted by the head and shoulders of a strange and ugly being.

'The figure was human-like, but his head and face were hairless. He had large, protruding ears, a very short neck and a long nose. There were round dark eyes which were very close together, and a button chin. The head was egg-shaped, but more bulbous, and the skin a grey colour.'

Shelley Robertson's sketch of the strange entity that she awoke to find staring in at her through her bedroom window.

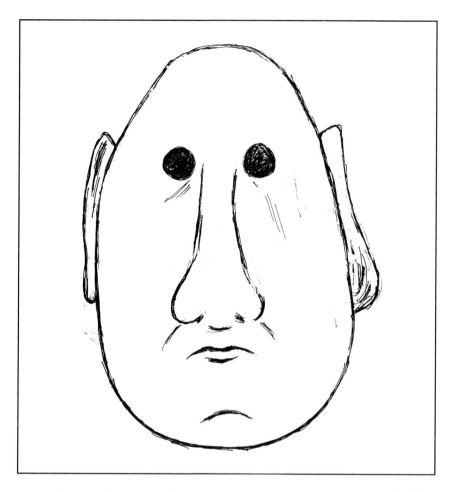

As she and the strange-looking entity stared at one another, Shelley tried to reach out to wake her husband; but a very high-pitched sound started up and she found she was paralysed. She felt a burning pain at the crown of her head, which became unbearable. All the time the face, which was human yet unhuman, continued to stare. Finally, Shelley lost control and screamed. The high-pitched sound stopped and the figure had gone. It was now 3.15a.m.

Despite the noise, her husband was still fast asleep. It took several minutes to wake him. When he did stir, and she told him what had happened, he said it must have been a bad dream. But Shelley is adamant it was not a nightmare.

'The face was solid, real. As real as if you were standing in front of me.'

Could it have been someone in a Halloween mask staring through the window? Hardly. The Robertsons sleep on the first floor – fourteen feet from the ground.

INCUBI AND SUCCUBI

One of the most common categories of demonic creature consists of 'demon lovers'. Referred to for centuries as the incubus and succubus – male and female respectively – they prey on human beings, often while a partner is in an unnaturally deep sleep beside them. The phenomenon is real, and very much alive today. It is 'real' in the sense that victims' experiences of the incubus/succubus match even in minute detail. Most victims are so ignorant of the phenomenon that they cannot even put a name to it. If it was imagination, one would expect descriptions to differ from case to case. The phenomenon may not be demonic, but it offers for study something more than subjective imagination. The majority of victims appear to be women, although this might be explained by the fact that women are more likely than men to discuss an intimate problem of this nature. Despite the subject's obvious taboo, we know of several contemporary cases. Here is the tale told by one victim who contacted us:

'I wanted to tell you about certain strange things that have happened to me. One thing I am really frightened of at present is that I have 'something' in my house. A friend has told me that this thing is called an 'incubus'. When the 'thing' comes, I also have an experience of leaving my own body at times. The whole thing is weird and I really don't know what I can do to stop it.

'These strange things started around 1985 or 1986. Since mid-1986 I have had 'the visit' from the incubus. It is not just in my bedroom but in other parts of the house too. It never hurts me or marks me, but I can assure you I am not some sort of crank. Both myself and my family have had strange things happen, but I have never known anything as bad as this. I really am frightened in many ways and I can assure you that I am neither dreaming nor imagining these things.'

Stephanie saw the quilt ruffle and felt a pressure on her chest.

Victims describe a pressure on the bed, on their chest and on other parts of the body. Some admit to experiencing full sex, usually against their will.

Another victim, whom we have interviewed, experienced an incubus on several occasions over a period of about four months. These visits always occurred after her husband had left for work, as she was preparing to get up. Stephanie saw the quilt ruffle, and felt a pressure on her chest. On the final occasion, she experienced sexual intercourse. Stephanie is 'psychic' in that she had sighted several apparitions, and it could be that one needs to be a medium in this respect to allow discarnate entities to manifest from the afterlife.

BLACK BROOK FARM

Black Brook Farm in Essex has been the focus for a wide variety of super-natural phenomena, but in particular several female members of the family have experienced an incubus. The family are not out for notoriety; we had to coax the details from them, and they wish to remain anonymous. To respect their wishes, we have used pseudonyms. This is what Jayne Bond told us:

'Both Mum and I have felt something in bed with us. Almost all of us have felt something sitting on our feet when there was nothing there. Mum's bed has vibrated, and all of us have felt our earrings pulled at night. It happened to me at least three times, although how it began is hard to remember.

'I would be asleep, and gradually wake up, bit by bit realising I was pinned to the bed. It felt like two fingers squeezing the top of my shoulders on either side of my neck, which hurt. I felt I was physically restrained, and when I tried to wriggle free my arms were stuck to my sides. I wouldn't say I felt paralysed, just totally restrained. My eyes were open but covered, and so was my mouth, but not my ears. I heard my muffled cries for help, but no one ever came to my aid.'

Far left: Fuseli's *Nightmare* – an incubus preying on its female victim. There are many contemporary accounts of 'demon lovers', as the authors discovered.

A bedroom at Black Brook Farm, where a teenage girl experienced a pressure on her chest and hands around her throat.

'I think it went on for a couple of minutes, but I really do not know. I remember once just giving up and waiting for it to finish. Suddenly it would stop, and apart from a pounding heart (I was very frightened while it was happening) I would be okay. Then I would just doze off.

'Recently, I awoke to feel something touching me through the duvet. It felt like someone playing the piano on my side. Feeling brave, I thought I would grab 'it', but when I went to move my arm, I realised I was totally paralysed – every part of me except my eyes. I had to lie there while it ran its 'fingers' up and down my body.'

Jayne's sister, Sandra, told an equally horrifying account:

'I had gone to bed and fallen asleep when I was awoken with a start to find I was being strangled. I remember being in pitch darkness. Unable to move, I felt pinned down, with additional pressure on my neck. I don't remember struggling, or how long the feeling lasted. Afterwards, all I do remember is a feeling of relief and peace before going back to sleep.'

'I felt I was physically restrained, and when I tried to wriggle free my arms were stuck to my sides.'

To say that the incubus is a physiological response to sexually frustrated individuals does not really explain the phenomenon. If that was the case, then judging by the letters of complaint on the problem pages of women's magazines there would be an epidemic! On the contrary, the initial approach of the incubus is not overtly sexual at all, and indeed many visitations like the above do not develop into full-blown intercourse. In any case, these approaches are largely unwelcome and frightening to the victim.

The incubus/succubus, which has been reported for hundreds of years, must have played its part in the emergence of the vampire legend. Vampires are said to suck blood from their victims to ensure their own survival. In truth, blood is a 'life force'. Demons are also said to take 'psychic energy' in order to manifest. Victims of the incubus/succubus have reported drifting back to sleep after the encounter – surely an unlikely thing to do unless they have been drained of energy?

Sometimes the incubus/succubus seems to be actively encouraged by a witness. One of the most convincing cases is that of investigative psychologist and self-confessed medium Stan Gooch. In his highly articulate book *Creatures from Inner Space*, Gooch describes the arrival of his own demon lover:

'I was lying in bed in the early morning, awake but drowsy, with daylight already broken. I became aware of another person in bed with me. For a moment I totally dismissed the idea. Then she – it was a she – moved a little closer, pressing me more urgently. With a sense of rising excitement, which I tried to control, I somehow knew this was a "psychic entity". I knew it was not a real person who had got into my room by normal means.'

Gooch relaxed and let the 'entity' take control. He sensed that it was a composite of all the women he had ever known, including his ex-wife. Yet it was not solely the product of his imagination, but 'its own creature', using his sexual memories in order to present itself to him. On this first occasion it gradually faded away, but on subsequent visits it actually made love to him. Gooch claims that, in some respects, sex with the entity is more satisfying than that with a real woman.

WHEN FANTASIES COME TO LIFE

A case which suggests that such experiences may be shaped by the human mind itself is that of the Ninja dwarf of Cheadle. In the summer of 1988 a group of youths met regularly in the grounds of Abney Hall in order to take part in martial arts classes. These involved the use of sticks and fierce poses to learn self-defence and channel their generated pent-up anger.

One July night the group were outside when a strange foot protruded from some bushes. At first it was thought to be one of their members larking about, but it soon became clear that this 'thing' in the bushes was not quite natural. One brave person went right up to it. Others said they could make out its form in the shadows, but he could see nothing at all even whilst standing right beside the phantom. Does this suggest that imagination was creating the monster out of patterns of light and shade with the addition of anticipation?

The encounters continued over several months, and the group started to play games with the 'demon'. As time went by, its structure became more solid. Eventually it was described as a dwarf-like creature wearing a dark martial arts suit. It would sit on rocks by a waterfall staring at them. Every so often it would drift upwards and loom over them, monster-like.

The phenomenon was now behaving in an increasingly supernatural way. It would dematerialise and move from place to place. There was a sinister feel to the air whenever it manifested. One of the female members of the team could 'sense' its presence in a sort of mind contact. It was not long before the attacks started.

One female student went into the bushes and saw nothing, but was approached by the 'thing'. The others saw this; then she screamed and fled in terror, alleging that she had been 'touched' by a force.

Matters grew worse when their instructor claimed to have been strangled by unseen hands and ran off in a panic, to be saved when he was on the verge of throwing himself into a lake. Then the 'psychic' girl attacked her boyfriend in a 'possessed' state, and four of the others had to pull her screaming from his throat.

By October almost all of them had experienced something. A man was thrown against a wall by an invisible force. One girl fell asleep on a bench; she awoke to experience the classic demon night terror sensation of a force pressing down from above, and saw the disembodied form of a hand reaching out from mid-air to grab her.

This was finally enough for the intrepid class. With the psychic girl in the group claiming that 'it' would 'prey on the bad part of everyone present' they decided to quit the grounds of Abney Hall.

Our investigation of the location found no real sign that the force was an actual phenomenon – without the group's presence, at least. We are left to ponder the way in which its form clearly emerged as belief in it grew. Initially it was seen much better by those who were 'believing' from a distance as opposed to those who challenged it in some way and went right up to it. Then it crystallised into full reality when a 'medium' was found to channel the belief and the energy.

Possibly most relevant of all is the form that the demon took. Phantom Ninja warriors are not exactly ten-a-penny spooks. Yet here was a group of people building up incredible mental, emotional and physical energies and releasing them in short bursts via their Oriental martial art form. In atmospheric surroundings, and with months to allow the belief in the demon to simmer, it took on a life of its own and became real – as a manifestation of the group's Oriental pursuit. Was it the result of negative psychic energy leakage?

Certainly in this case it looks as if the demon was a creation of the fantasy lives of these people. But it was no simple hallucination. It was not mere invention. Indeed, it ended up with a life of its own, much like Tibetan 'tulpas'. Tibetan monks are said to be able to create these entities through meditation. Initially the entity can be seen only by its creator, but gradually other people too become aware of it, perceiving the being as real. As it gains strength the entity takes on a life of its own beyond the control of its creator. Eventually, however, the thought form loses power and fades away.

Was the Abney Hall demon a product of strong belief which became more autonomous as this belief was shared? Modern 'chaos' magicians seek to allow the forces of chaos into this world, and believe that the demons they conjure up are sub-personalities of their own brought to temporary life. However, Christian fundamentalists violently disagree that demons are merely a product of the mind. Perhaps demons are real objective entities bent on mischief and destruction. Negative emotional energy released by mankind might power them in this world, bringing them through the veil. They may need this negative life force in much the same way that we need tanks of oxygen in order to operate in the environment of the ocean.

ANGELS

The term 'angel' comes from the Latin *angelus*. It entered the English language in very early times, denoting a benevolent supernatural being. In Hebrew and Greek it translates as 'messenger', first appearing in the Old Testament in the phrase 'angel of the Lord'. Angels were God's first creation, formed out of fire.

There are many accounts of angels appearing to people in the Bible, although they were not always immediately recognisable as supernatural beings. Contrary to the popular image in church windows and on Christmas

Is this a photograph of an angelic being? It was taken by a metal-bender in 1978. The photographer – a man called Silvio – was strolling through a wood after the death of his mother, when he saw a luminous ball. The resulting picture showed an angel-like image enclosed in a yellow circle of light.

cards, angels did not have wings. Wings were included in later representations of angels because they were able to 'fly' – therefore it was deduced that they must have wings.

These emissaries from God appeared in human form, theologians speculate, to communicate effectively with people. They carried messages to and from God as well as helping and guiding individuals and whole nations with their wisdom. Michael, one of the 'chief princes' of angels, was described in Daniel 10 and 12 as 'the great prince who has charge of your people'. The angel who brought this information to Daniel was described in the following way:

> I was standing on the bank of the great river, that is, the Tigris. I lifted up my eyes and looked, and behold, a man clothed in linen, whose loins were girded with gold of Uphaz. His body was like beryl, his face like the appearance of lightning, his eyes like flaming torches, his arms and legs like the gleam of burnished bronze, and the sound of his words like the noise of a multitude. And I, Daniel, alone saw this vision, for the men who were with me did not see the vision, but a great trembling fell upon them, and they fled to hide themselves.

Angels appear prominently in the New Testament also. The first angel appears in Joseph's dream telling him of the conception of Jesus, and later to a group of shepherds to whom Christ's birth is announced.

Angels were protectors, and everybody is said to have a guardian angel. In the afterlife, angels watched over souls. But not all angels were good. One angel, who rebelled against God, was to become Lord of all which was evil.

Some strange creatures flew in . . . small with waxen faces and coal-black eyes, but most notable for the beautiful and delicate wings that they bore.

'WE KNOW ALL ABOUT JESUS'

In the modern world, however, seeing angels or demons has an added drawback: the witness may not recognise their origin. That may well be what happened to Mrs Jean Hingley at Rowley Regis in the West Midlands early one morning in January 1979. She said that some strange creatures flew in through her open back door, making peculiar noises as they zipped around her house. They were small, with waxen faces and coal-black eyes, but most notable for the beautiful and delicate wings that they bore. These wings reflected colours as they inspected her room and spoke to her of peace and love, sympathising about her problems with the church and saying, 'We know all about Jesus'.

There is little doubt as to how these beings would have been evaluated a mere century ago – regardless of their odd behaviour in taking a mince pie when offered, and fleeing in terror when the witness lit a cigarette! But to most subsequent researchers these were 'aliens', not angels. In fact they had even arrived in a 'UFO' – an egg-like object which had reportedly landed in the Hingleys' back garden. Marks in the melting snow gave testament to the presence of something real in this extraordinary saga.

In 1978 a very practical man who is an engineer at one of the busiest airports in the world, Chicago O'Hare, saw a strange form materialise in the bathroom window at his home. It seemed to pass through the double glass and form as a white, round, angelic face on the surface. Unbelievably it said 'Boo!' to him and then simply vanished. We may be tempted to dismiss such a story, but it has to be seen in context. It is one of a growing number of such accounts.

A London woman on a coach tour of eastern Europe related what happened to her near Posen in Poland. Suddenly on the roof of a bus travelling in front of her own vehicle she clearly saw several 'gremlins', devilish green monsters the size of a seven-year-old child. Interestingly, she refers to them as 'not quite solid, yet not transparent'. They were playing in full view and yet nobody else (including the driver of her coach, who should have done so with ease) appears to have seen them. Does that mean they were a hallucination – and, if so, why?

HELP FROM BEYOND

In another case, from Bodmin Moor in Cornwall, a woman lay seriously ill in bed with her husband beside her, cradling her and unable to sleep. Suddenly a ball of light only a few inches in diameter entered the room and moved about the awestruck couple. It seemed to play soothingly on to the sick woman, and then disappeared.

In the past such lights have been given religious associations. Some say they are the souls of the dead departing. But here the woman made a dramatic recovery, so perhaps we might consider this a soul *from* the dead – such as a guardian angel – who had come back to effect a healing cure. Of course, it comes as no surprise to learn that most commentators have evaluated this 1980 version of an age-old story as the visit of a mini-UFO.

Peter Johnson of Colorado, USA, described how he met a strange woman at Poona in India. Her eyes were particularly noteworthy. She told him that he had work to do back home and that she was going to buy him an airline ticket back to the States. Peter assumed this was a joke: total strangers do not give away hundreds of dollars to one another. But she proved true to her word, and at the airport announced that she was working for the offices of his guardian angel – hence the need to ensure he got home quickly! Peter wrote in his letter to the American magazine *Strange* (1990) that he thought nothing of this until on returning to the USA he had a medical check-up. Here it was discovered that he was suffering from a serious blood disorder. Had he stayed on in India, his doctor told him, it is very unlikely he would have survived.

THE ANGEL IN THE SIGNAL LIGHT

The witness in this case is a hardy engineer, trained in practical reality and yet gifted with an artistic imagination, which perhaps is important. The incident occurred in 1957 when he was with another teenage friend beside the Crewe–Northwich railway line in Cheshire. They had been poaching and were relaxing from the tension and hard work, sitting beneath a bridge and staring along the track with their eyes unfocused.

In the altered state of awareness, the blurred light changed form.

In this direction was a signal light, blurred and out of focus. But then something very strange occurred. What we term the 'Oz factor' took hold: time stretched out, and their minds tuned to a different sensory reality. Peculiar sensations took hold of them, and all normal background sounds ceased. In their altered state of awareness, the blurred light changed form. It grew and blossomed into the full image of an angel.

The being was twenty feet tall with long, pale yellow hair, white wings and a centre patch that was a mass of delicate translucent light of multiple soft colours. There was no doubt that it emerged from the signal light, but there was equally no doubt that it was, to the two young men, very real.

Our witness fled up the embankment as the entity drifted towards him. Here he bumped into his friend. Although neither had said a word, they had independently seen the same phenomenon – both had observed an angel pour out of the light and fly towards them.

On the one level they knew this was a hallucination, in the sense that it represented an 'inner world' experience rather than total objectivity. At the same time they were aware that it must have some reality since they had both shared it so exactly.

Intriguingly, this stretch of line has a legend associated with it about the 'lady of the lamp' said to haunt the track bed. Although both witnesses had been told this story as children, they assumed it had been created to warn people away from the dangers of the railway line. But does it mean that others had experienced the angel before? Certainly, on that night in 1957, legend had turned into startling reality – but how?

OCCUPATION: GUARDIAN ANGEL

Jane Peartree from Perth in Western Australia was visited at 6a.m. one day by what she believes was a guardian angel. It was winter 1985, and Jane awoke to find chilled air entering her lungs. Suddenly she realised that the normal bedroom scene had changed. She was staring at the mirror wondering if it was a dream. Yet it felt so real, and was very different from any sensation she had ever known before. She watched in puzzled excitement as the mirror turned grey and a strange form began to draw near.

Dimly she became aware of a figure by her side. The entity looked like a normal man, almost six feet tall, with blond to brown hair and ordinary facial features. Yet he wore what seemed to be a ski-suit of a dazzling blue that fitted so tightly it might have been a second skin. He was talking to another person, at first unseen, who then entered the bedroom, appearing to check on her slumbering husband. The two spoke in loud voices as if oblivious to her presence.

The figure spoke in strange and almost brusque tones, which rippled through her mind.

She began to think of all those questions that her mind had pondered. Here was the chance to learn the secrets of the universe; to decode the riddle of life and death. Afterwards, all that Jane could recall of the conversation were two things. The 'angel' had responded, when asked, that he would call to see her again in twenty years' time. Then – when she enquired whether she was on the right track in life – the figure spoke in strange and almost brusque tones, which rippled through her mind.

'Yes – just keep on the way you are. But don't get mixed up in any hanky-panky!' This was not what she had expected to hear as wisdom from the life beyond.

The other being reappeared and the two conversed. They seemed to regard this visitation as a job to be done – if anything a bore, and certainly a chore.

Jane Peartree suspects they were not talking in any physical sense. Only she could hear them. The sounds were forming directly into her mind. At this realisation, the witness found that she was back in her bed totally bemused by what had happened. Logic told her that it all had to be a dream – but the experience had been so realistic and vivid.

She told us: 'I am intuitive, but I am not at all imaginative or suggestible. I have an open mind, but one that doubts before it believes. Neither am I a member of any religious group, nor do I consider myself to be "psychic".'

An illustration from a song sheet based on a fictional story which turned to 'fact' in the eyes of many people.

THE EVIDENCE AGAINST

It is still widely believed that in August 1914, during World War I, angels appeared on the front line to ensure that the Allied troops were victorious. Legend has it that thousands of soldiers during the brutal and bloody battle of Mons saw this angelic host in the sky and as a result were stirred on against terrible odds. Sadly, the so-called 'Angels of Mons' story shows only how myth and reality can become interwoven to a point where fact and fiction are almost indistinguishable.

The battle was a defeat for the Allies. They had to flee a fierce German onslaught, but fought with such bravery that at times they appeared to outnumber the enemy. In truth, the German forces were much bigger.

From this basis Arthur Machen wrote a short story called 'The Bowmen', in which he used the battle as a vehicle to express the fantasy that St George and a host of phantom bowmen had appeared on the scene to ensure a safe retreat. It was published in a London newspaper a few weeks after the battle. However, it was soon to outgrow its fictional roots.

According to sceptical researcher Melvin Harris, Machen was approached by many magazines requesting to reprint his story; they included psychic journals which asked if it was based on fact. Reputedly he told them it was not, but as the story circulated it took on new dimensions. Allegedly, the newspaper that had originally carried it had no idea that, when they granted reproduction permission, it was sometimes being presented as reality. One parish magazine asked for accreditation to prove that it was true!

As time went by, the story transmuted. The ghost bowmen became angels, and some eye-witness accounts (none of which were to prove true when checked out) appeared to support the legend. Pamphlets were sold and did wonders for morale and the war effort. There lies one of the key reasons why this story swept across the country as it did, and why its credibility was accepted so readily.

People *wanted* to believe in it. Much more than that – with most families having someone away at the war, and with no TV or radio to bring rapid news of what was happening, they *needed* to believe in supernatural protection for their distant loved ones. Perhaps too, the authorities saw the value for morale in encouraging the story.

It is fascinating to compare the way the Angels of Mons story grew from a humble fictional starting point with the manner in which the Cheadle Ninja dwarves manifested more than seventy years later. Perhaps the psychology and sociology of belief has a lot to do with these things; we need to pay more attention to the extraordinary way in which the beliefs of a large group can make something unreal become 'real' – at least in some fashion.

THE EVIDENCE FOR

Can we always assume that such cases have simple explanations? Stan Gooch believes his succubus is a genuine demonic entity which has absorbed the female attributes and personalities of real women stored in his own subconscious. Another psychologist, Margot Grey, sees demons in more clinical terms.

> 'I think there is a realm which has a parallel with the subconscious known variously as 'the watery depth', 'the moon' and 'the shadow'. There's also ample evidence in mythology of people going into 'the underworld' to encounter things there.
>
> 'As a psychologist I do a lot of work with people's 'monsters' situated

in the subconscious basement. These monsters always present themselves in some sort of archetypal form. Interestingly, shamans had to confront demons in the underworld before they could be granted various magical gifts; clairvoyance, healing, astral travel and so on. I believe they're actually overcoming a blockage stopping them from communicating with their higher consciousness.'

Noted New York research journalist John Keel has been chasing manifestations of all sorts of strange creatures since the 1960s, as testified in his many astonishing books. One of these, *The Mothmen Prophecies*, was reissued a quarter of a century after the amazing events on which it was based. Angelic and demonic visits to Ohio and West Virginia culminated in a prophecy about the collapsing of a road bridge, during which many people lost their lives. As is typical of such supernatural predictions across the centuries, the warning was so vague –indeed even partly incorrect – that nothing could be done to prevent the tragedy.

In May 1992, Keel reported to a Fortean Conference in Nebraska, USA. (The term 'Fortean' is applied to strange phenomena after an early twentieth-century collector of anomalies called Charles Fort.) Keel was concerned about a wave of what he called 'religious miracles' which were sweeping around the world. Angels and visions of the Virgin Mary were being seen in the most unlikely of places in prodigious numbers. This was particularly true of the former USSR, now the Commonwealth of Independent States. In the wake of glasnost and democratisation, which had demolished decades of anti-Christian suppression, there had been a sudden wave of visionary episodes. Keel even suggested that this had involved the crew of an orbiting space mission: the cosmonauts had supposedly seen angels alongside them in outer space!

It is hard to believe that such experiences are merely a psychological aberration, and not truly encounters with beings from the afterlife.

YOUR VERDICT : A SUMMARY

AGAINST SURVIVAL

- There is a long tradition of belief in supernatural beings which appeals to our imagination.

- The incubi and succubi show signs of sexual wish fulfilment.

- Psychology and sociology show how belief in something can make it take on a pseudo-reality where even a group can experience its manifestation.

FOR SURVIVAL

- Physical sensations and effects are involved in some cases. Can these be merely 'imagined'?

- How does one person share a hallucination with another, even without saying a word?

- Demons and angels could be objective entities which use negative and positive emotional energy in order to manifest in our world, their outward appearance being structured by our own expectations.

COMMUNICATORS WITH THE DEAD

◆

Was Jesus Christ nothing more than a highly developed medium with healing gifts and ESP?

THE RELIGION OF THE AFTERLIFE

Spiritualism is a movement and not an organisation, and considers itself to be a religion. Its basic belief is that, under certain circumstances, it is possible to communicate with the surviving personalities of the dead residing in the lower echelons of the afterlife. Spirits who have made little progress in the 'beyond' exist on these planes, finding it relatively easy to communicate with the living for a period. Much of the infrastructure of Spiritualist dogma is based on the content of such communications; hence the divergence of thinking by Spiritualists around the world. As the discarnate entities move upwards to higher planes, communication supposedly becomes more difficult.

In a sense Spiritualism has been with us since the dawn of man's awareness of himself as a spiritual, as well as physical, creature. There have always been shamans, seers – psychically gifted people – who claim, or believe, they are in contact with the dead. At various times these individuals have either been revered by society and elevated to positions of power, or hunted down and burned to death. It has been claimed that Christianity itself has its roots in Spiritualism – that Jesus Christ was nothing more (and nothing less) than a highly developed medium with healing gifts and ESP. There is some evidence that communion with the dead was practised in the early Christian Church, but had ceased before the third century. The modern Spiritualist movement, however, dates from 1848, with the emergence of the Fox sisters.

The Fox Sisters

It was in December 1847 that Methodist farmer John Fox, his wife and daughters, Margaretta aged fourteen and Kate aged twelve, moved into a small wooden house in Hydesville, New York State. For the first three months the family were kept awake by inexplicable raps and bangs. On

Friday, 31 March 1848, the family retired for the night as usual. Mrs Fox later described what happened.

Kate (left) and Margaretta Fox were the catalyst for the Spiritualist movement after contacting the spirit of a murdered pedlar in their home in New York State, during 1884.

'It was very early when we went to bed on this night – hardly dark. I had been so broken of rest I was almost sick. I had just lain down when it commenced as usual – the children, who slept in the other bed in the room, heard the rapping, and tried to make similar sounds by snapping their fingers.

'My youngest child, Cathie, said: "Mr Splitfoot, do as I do," clapping her hands. The sound instantly followed her with the same number of raps. When she stopped, the sound ceased for a short time.

'Then Margaretta said in sport: "Now do as I do. Count one, two, three, four, striking one hand against the other at the same time – and the raps came as before. She was afraid to repeat them.

'I then thought I could put a test that no one in the place could answer.

I asked the "noise" to rap my different children's ages successively.

'Instantly, each one of my children's ages was given correctly, pausing between them sufficiently long enough to individualise them until the seventh – at which a longer pause was made, and then three more emphatic raps were given, corresponding to the age of the little one that died, which was my youngest child.

'I then asked: "Is this a human being that answers my questions correctly?"

'There was no rap.

'I asked: "Is it a spirit? If it is, make two raps."

'Two sounds were given as soon as the request was made.'

The spirit subsequently identified itself as a pedlar named Charles B. Rosna, who had been murdered in the house by John C. Bell, a blacksmith. That summer the Foxes dug up their cellar, as instructed by the deceased, and found part of a human skeleton. Fifty years later, more bones were found – and a pedlar's tin.

The family became plagued by sensation seekers and people hoping to contact dead loved ones. Because of this, the sisters went to stay with relatives. Margaretta moved to her married sister's house in Rochester, and Kate went to friends in nearby Auburn. The rapping noises continued at the new locations, and before long the girls were tracked down by the public. The rappings were supposedly messages sent by the dead relations and friends of those present. People who came and witnessed the girls went back home and claimed that the phenomenon had followed them there too.

The press loved this new sensation. In 1849 the girls gave their first public performance in Rochester, then toured other towns in the eastern states. It was like a contagion. Other mediums joined the throng – the mainstay of this fledgling religion. Before long 'spirit rapping' had spread across the entire United States, then over to Europe and Britain. This was the genesis of Spiritualism – a movement built around the psychic abilities of two teenage girls.

Its rapid rise was due to natural curiosity. The first meetings, held in front parlours, were in the spirit of scientific enquiry. People set out to test the claims of psychic contact with the dead through holding seances. Those who had success joined with other groups, and permanent societies and churches began to develop.

In 1851, three professors from Buffalo University in New York State claimed that their investigations of the Fox sisters revealed that fraudulent methods were used to create the rapping sounds. The movement of knee joints, and an alleged confession by Kate that she cracked her toes, were said to be the cause. But this did nothing either to blight the reputation of the sisters or to stem the development of Spiritualism.

Spiritualism embraced other phenomena beyond spirit rapping. Telekinesis – the paranormal movement of objects, including furniture, was the most common. Occasionally, hands formed out of a substance called ectoplasm were seen manipulating objects. Indeed, entire entities were observed to be formed from such material, and they were able to converse with those present.

There were also 'direct voice' mediums. Here, the disembodied voice of the deceased could be heard in the seance room. Musical instruments would play themselves and levitate around the sitters. 'Spirit guides' became the vogue, too. Usually the deceased spirits of children or Red Indians, they took control of the medium. Whilst the medium was in a trance, the guide would take over the body and make use of the vocal cords. Many of the systems of communication with the afterlife developed then are still used by mediums today, although they tend to be less theatrical. The way that mediums work is described in detail later in this chapter.

SPIRITUALISM IN BRITAIN

The Spiritualist movement took off in Britain when an American medium named Mrs Hayden took part in a lecture tour in 1852. A short-lived craze ensued when other mediums followed in her footsteps. Many 'home circles' came into existence at that time – gatherings of friends interested in experimentation, or of followers attracted to individual mediums.

In the 1860s, these circles became more formalised and expanded. The new organisations spread out from two centres – London, and Keighley in Yorkshire. Indeed, outside of London the movement was most successful in Yorkshire and Lancashire. The first national organisation emerged in Darlington in 1865. The British Association of Progressive Spiritualists represented the first attempt to define the movement as an independent religion, but more conventional Spiritualists brought about its downfall by attacking its 'anti-Christian' stance and it collapsed only three years later.

In 1873, a further attempt was made to start a national organisation; but the British National Association of Spiritualists was also doomed to have its ambitions curtailed. There was little interest in it outside London, and in 1883 it was reconstituted as the London Spiritualist Alliance. In other areas of the country, societies were joining together and forming district organisations. The first was the Lancashire Association, which appeared in 1875. By 1912 there were fifteen such associations.

It was 1890 before the first effective national organisation finally succeeded. By 1896 the Spiritualists' National Federation had attracted fifty-eight societies, mainly from the north. In 1902 the organisation was reconstituted as the Spiritualists' National Union Ltd in order to obtain legal status.

Now on a firm footing, the movement stabilised and went from strength to strength, particularly in the period between the two world wars. Despite the critics, and the continual claims of fraud, there was no shortage of mediums nor of champions. Scientists Sir Oliver Lodge, Sir William Crookes and Sir William Barrett; Sir Arthur Conan Doyle, the creator of Sherlock Holmes; the writer Victor Hugo; and Hannen Swaffer, then editor of *The People*, were active protagonists of Spiritualism. In 1916 Lodge published a book called *Raymond*, which told of spirit communications with his son who had been killed during World War I.

Sir Arthur Conan Doyle

Conan Doyle practised medicine in Southsea until his fame as a writer rendered it unnecessary. His interest in the paranormal lasted almost half a century, and he devoted the last twelve years of his life to promoting the doctrines of Spiritualism. He added considerably to the literature, and held many sittings in his own home with Lady Doyle acting as medium. Messages were transmitted from the afterlife by 'Phineas', her Arab guide.

Is there a levelling out of age in the afterlife? Do those who have died old become young again?

Conan Doyle's son, Kingsley, died just after the armistice from a combination of pneumonia and war wounds. In his book *Memories and Adventures* his father describes how, a year later, he visited a Welsh medium where he heard the voice of his son, who communicated to him things which were unknown to the woman. Whilst attending a sitting with a different medium, Conan Doyle saw his mother and nephew 'as plainly as ever I saw them in life'. Two other witnesses attested to the materialisation.

Over a period of years, Conan Doyle developed a simple, some may say naïve, belief in the conditions of the afterlife. This philosophy was based on his own psychic experiences and the documented messages channelled through mediums. According to Conan Doyle, in the afterlife there was a levelling out of age. Those who had died old became young again, and those who had been young at the time of death grew up. Everyone was around twenty-five years old. Why physical age should matter in the afterlife is not clear, although the concept is accepted by a great many mediums. Most mediums believe that spirits grow up. Babies, for example, evolve from babyhood to about twenty at an accelerated rate. It may take them only a year or two to do this. Doris Stokes certainly believed in this concept of time and age.

Conan Doyle, a supporter of Darwin's theory of evolution, carried this logic on to the paraphysical level. He developed a theory of spiritual evolution. In the afterlife there existed a series of grades, or spheres, that the deceased inhabited according to their behaviour on Earth. Once graded, it was possible to aspire to other, higher spheres. This is all too reminiscent of the fundamental beliefs held in other religions (see Chapter 1). Indeed, it is plain to see that Spiritualism, despite its scientific, or, as some have said, 'pseudo-scientific' pretensions, was developing as a religion from its inception.

THE RELIGION OF SPIRITUALISM

The dawning technological age caused many people to turn away from Christianity towards a religion more suited to the times. Christianity seemed antiquated in an age where things needed to be tested and evaluated on evidence – not just accepted as some whimsical 'belief'. Spiritualism seemed to bridge the old and the new. It possessed the fundamental tenet of most religions – the belief in an afterlife; but, more than that, it presented material evidence which could be scientifically examined.

As a religion, it was based on philosophies expounded by the deceased, which were often contradictory. Ritual played its part too. Societies developed into churches with the development of Bible reading, hymn singing and prayer. This was believed to create an atmosphere conducive to contact with the afterlife, and also created a psychic barrier to the manifestations of evil entities.

This did not impress the Christian Church, which argued that the Bible forbade communication with the dead. The alleged spirits of the deceased were nothing more than demonic entities out to mislead people and ultimately enslave them on behalf of Satan. In recent years the Church has mellowed somewhat, although the modern Christian fundamentalist movement still talks in terms of fire and brimstone. The recent unproven allegations of Satanic ritual abuse first came to the attention of the media through the fundamentalist movement.

In 1928, attempts were made by Conan Doyle to Christianize Spiritualism, but he failed. Medium Winifred Moyes was more successful when she established the Greater World Christian Spiritualist League in 1931. Four years later it had 580 affiliated churches.

The Spiritualist movement not only suffered attacks from other, more established religions, the media and professional sceptics, but the weight of the law was occasionally brought to bear too. Such attacks were based on the Witchcraft Act of 1736. In 1945, a Spiritualist church at Redhill in Surrey closed as a result of legal threats. That same year controversial Scottish medium Helen Duncan became the last person to be prosecuted under the Witchcraft Act. Newspapers heralded it as 'the trial of the century'. The Fraudulent Mediums Act replaced this legislation in 1951. Now the onus was on the complainant to prove that a deliberate fraud had been committed.

Although there is no Spiritualist creed or bible, there is a book entitled *Spiritualist Teachings* derived from the automatic writings (see Chapter 4) of the Rev. William Stainton Moses. Generally, Spiritualists agree that the universe consists of seven planes of existence – the physical being the lowest. After death most souls travel to the first plane, known as the Summerland. This is similar to Earth, except that it lacks suffering. Here, souls can aspire to the higher planes. Those that reach the 'seventh heaven' are united with God.

Most Spiritualists abide by these 'Seven Principles':

- The fatherhood of God.
- The brotherhood of man.
- The communion of spirits and the ministry of angels.
- The continuous existence of the human soul.
- Personal responsibility.
- Compensation and retribution for all the good and evil deeds done on Earth.
- Eternal progress open to every human soul.

THE SPREAD OF SPIRITUALISM

Spiritualism sprang the boundaries of the United States and Britain in the 1950s and spread first across Europe. Most notable was its transition to South America. This was attributable to one man, and he was neither American nor British.

French doctor Hippolyte Léon Denizard Rivail was psychically informed that in a previous incarnation he had been a druid called Alain Kardec. Rivail changed his name to Kardec and became a prolific author. His books, largely ignored elsewhere, proved very influential in Brazil. The Brazilians have set up Kardec spirit temples, where mediums attempt to help the confused souls of the newly dead. In 1957 the Brazilian government officially endorsed the religion by printing Kardec's head on five million postage stamps.

THE MEDIUMS

The evidence for Spiritualism lies with the mediums. They are the focus, and it is through them that the central tenet of the religion has evolved – a bold, uncompromising belief in the afterlife. Evidence for this stands or falls with them.

Mrs Leonora Piper

American Leonora Piper discovered her psychic abilities during her mid-twenties, after visiting a healer because of a tumour. She became one of the most investigated mediums during the early years of psychical research, between 1885 and 1915. Psychologist William James, a founder of the American Society for Psychical Research, thought he could explain away her abilities in mundane terms, but came away convinced that she was 'in possession of a power as yet unexplained'.

Her details about deceased persons were so accurate that private detectives were hired to carry out surveillance to determine if she obtained the information fraudulently. She was never found cheating, although James did note inaccuracies and sometimes an obvious groping for facts.

James introduced her to Richard Hodgeson, who had already exposed several fraudulent mediums. Hodgeson was stunned when Mrs Piper provided him with some very personal information regarding his deceased relatives. He tested her with other subjects and she produced similar results. When Hodgeson died, he apparently communicated through her via automatic writing. Mrs Piper died in 1950 at the age of eighty-three.

Her details about deceased persons were so accurate that private detectives were hired to carry out surveillance to determine if she obtained the information fraudulently.

Daniel Dunglas Home

Born in Scotland in 1833, D. D. Home emigrated to America when he was nine years old. At seventeen, poltergeist activity dogged him after the death of his mother. Discovering that he could control the phenomena, he earned a reputation as a physical medium. In 1855 he left for England, and travelled across Europe displaying his abilities. No evidence of trickery was ever discovered during his seances, and he was extensively tested under laboratory conditions by Sir William Crookes.

Home did not do things by halves. He performed in well-lit rooms, causing raps to be heard, tables to levitate, musical instruments to play, and spirit hands to materialise. Sitters also felt something invisible touch them and tug at their clothes. Home became best known, however, for his own bodily levitations, witnessed by many people.

The most famous of these was his supposed levitation out of one window and re-entry through another. The room in which this phenomenon was performed was reportedly several storeys high, and the act was witnessed by Lord Adare, the Master of Lindsay and a Captain Wynne. In recent years some scepticism has been heaped on this alleged feat. Apparently it is not absolutely certain in which building it took place, although it is believed to be one of two. Outside the windows of one, a narrow ledge runs around the building, causing some people to speculate that Home actually walked from one window to another.

Rudi and Willi Schneider

The Schneider brothers are amongst the handful of physical mediums who have been seriously investigated. Born in Austria around the beginning of the twentieth century, they were tested in the 1920s by Baron Albert von Schrenck-Notzing, a German physician and paranormal researcher, and later by Dr Eugene Osty and a controversial figure named Harry Price (see p. 143). Willi was the first of the brothers to exhibit psychic powers; and when these waned, Rudi rose to the fore.

Rudi worked in trance, at the behest of a control called Olga. With the help of his spiritual companion, Rudi was able to make objects move and bring about materialisations. In one experiment, conducted by Dr Osty, items which Rudi was asked to move were surrounded by infra-red beams connected to an alarm system. If the beams were broken by a 'reaching device', or a human hand, bells would go off and a camera would record the fraud.

On several occasions the alarms did indeed go off – although, as the cameras recorded, caused by no visible agency. This coincided with Olga's announcements that she 'was going into the ray'. The experiments were repeated by other researchers.

Doris Stokes

Right: The late medium, Doris Stokes. She openly admitted to cheating twice at the start of her career. BBC journalist Mike Kiddey, who worked closely with her for a time, claims there were certain things she knew which were beyond rationalisation.

Mrs Stokes, who died in 1987, became well known as a clairaudient medium (see p. 58). Even as a child she experienced precognition, and 'knew' things which were not common knowledge; but it was after she married that her psychic abilities intensified.

During World War II, she was told at a Spiritualist church in London that her husband had been killed in action. Back home, in a state of shock, Doris had a bedroom visitor experience (see Chapter 5) during which her deceased father appeared. He assured her that her husband, John, was not dead, and that she would receive proof of this 'on Christmas Day'. Indeed she did. The War Office informed her that John was alive, although wounded and a prisoner of war.

Doris rose to fame in the 1970s during an appearance on Australian television which flooded the studio with mail and jammed the switchboard. As her renown grew, she openly admitted that on two occasions she had cheated. For short periods the spirit voices faded, and she would find herself in front of a packed audience with nothing to say. On one of these occasions she made a hash of it through trying to cheat, and on his sudden return her guide, 'Ramononov', admonished her for it.

Several 'autobiographies' were published in the 1980s, actually the work of professional writers. One such collaborator was radio presenter Mike Kiddey, who with his wife went on tour with the medium to gather material. He told us that it was possible to pick up some things from an audience, unconsciously, through body language, but added: 'Doris came out with some very specific facts about people. We were in a position to know that there was no way she could have gleaned this information through cheating.'

MESSAGES OF THE NEW AGE

Today channelling and the New Age have become topics of great importance. Allegedly this is no accident, but has been engineered by spirits in the land beyond who have banded together to get this vital message across. It is now being detected at an intuitive level by millions of people who respond in tune to what they recognise as a fundamental truth. The rise of the movement can be seen alongside the career of channeller Ruth Montgomery, whose books have sold millions of copies worldwide and who in many senses initiated the concept.

Ruth was formerly a successful political correspondent who knew and wrote about many US Presidents in her years in Washington DC. Her involvement in the psychic world began quietly and she had many experiences of the conventional kind, detecting spirits of the dead and passing on messages about them.

In her book with Joanne Garland (*Herald of the New Age*, Grafton, 1988) she tells how, upon hearing of the tragic death of the daughter of an acquaintance, she went to her typewriter and contacted her spirit guides in her own version of automatic writing. The girl apologised for her suicide, in words that contained several key phrases (such as the use of 'adieu' instead of 'goodbye'). These meant nothing to Ruth – who had not known the girl – but were immediately significant to her grieving family.

After developing her interest in ways like this, Ruth met a number of key figures in the psychic world such as medium Arthur Ford, and then wrote a series of best-selling books during the 1960s. These included one of the first serious studies of reincarnation (*Here and Hereafter*) and a biography of the celebrated medium Jeanne Dixon (*A Gift of Prophecy*).

Then her own abilities began to develop at a prodigious rate, and within hours of her friend Arthur Ford 'passing on' he joined a team of advanced souls led by a man named 'Lilly' who communicated daily with Ruth via her typewriter. In this way she began to channel messages of a universal nature. Here Ford offers impressions of God from the afterlife. 'God is the core of the universe from which all else flows forth. He is truth and energy. He is matter and spirit. . . . He is also the essence of our being . . . .'

Gradually the channelled communications began to warn about drastic and irrevocable changes in the late 1990s; they would be awful in the physical sense, but would usher in the golden 'New Age' as the twenty-first century dawned. Throughout the 1980s and early 1990s these channelled communications via Ruth Montgomery became more specific and began to take hold of others, which in turn produced a groundswell of lifestyle changes and psychic upheaval that has resulted in today's New Age movement.

It is worldwide and has many champions, but focuses on pockets of 'energy' said to exist around the planet. One of these is in Wessex, near the ancient stone circle sites of Stonehenge and Avebury in Wiltshire. Here UFO-like lights have long been seen; esoteric thinkers congregate; and since the late 1970s mysterious circular patterns have been gouged out in crop fields, acting as a magnet to 'believers' from around the world. They are seen as 'warnings' about the coming Earth changes or as concrete messages from the spirit world on a much grander scale than 'trivial' poltergeist outbreaks, and are felt to provide signs which nobody can ignore. They reputedly fulfil long-made prophecies by channellers that signs which the whole world would see on their TV screens would be set down on the Earth. Certainly the way they have gripped the imagination of humanity from the late 1980s is in itself a phenomenon – whether their origin is supernatural or not.

Another energy centre is in the beautifully barren Red Rock country of Arizona. Long recognised as a Hopi Indian focal point of magical power, this hot land rises out of the desert between the appropriately named city of Phoenix (symbolising rebirth from the ashes of fire) and the huge fissure of the Grand Canyon (representing the ripping asunder of the Earth which the coming cataclysm is supposed to bring). Now a whole New Age community exists here and has set up a thriving town called Sedona, directly beneath the place where, locals say, an unseen spiritual city beams down its power.

The communications coming from the numerous channellers at these focal points straddle the border between the mediums of old and the contactees of recent UFO folklore. These individuals who claim mental contact with aliens are largely discredited by the 'serious' UFO researchers, who do not trust any relationship between the psychic realm and their own.

Indeed, Ruth Montgomery was once again to be at the forefront of this. In 1979 her book *Strangers Amongst Us* had spoken of 'walk-ins', a concept that even psychic circles found odd, but in fact supremely logical if you think about it. Ruth alleges she was urged to investigate the matter – at a time when the phrase meant nothing to her – in a 'fan' letter which her guides were later to explain had in fact been written by a walk-in.

California, most of England, all of Holland and Japan and much of Hawaii are amongst places destined to vanish off the map in the very near future.

Just as an evil spirit is believed capable of 'possessing' a human, forcing the 'soul' out and taking over the body, so can a good spirit do the same, Ruth alleges. A walk-in is a highly advanced being who has earned the right not to have to reincarnate as a baby but can literally take over the body of an adult whose soul has agreed to offer vacant possession. Consequently, walk-ins occur in situations where a person has suffered a near death experience, or attempted suicide, or in certain other circumstances. They have come through the ordeal, seemingly a 'new person'. Formerly this remark would have been treated figuratively; now many people assume that the being literally is a new person because a walk-in has taken over.

These walk-ins are slotting into key positions in our society to guide the world through the aftermath of the cataclysm. The 1992 or 1996 US President will be a 'walk-in', Ruth insists. He will be free of party politics and espouse policies that speak to the whole community.

According to Ruth (by no means alone amongst channellers), we are seeing the signs of this looming disaster in increased earthquake and volcanic activity and dramatic changes in global weather patterns. Indeed, the Earth is preparing to 'flip over'. A build-up of polar ice triggers this phenomenon every few hundred thousand years and there is nothing to stop it. Once the quantity of ice crosses a certain threshold the earth topples in an instant, and within seconds the planet changes out of all recognition. The poles move thousands of miles, frozen lands become hot deserts and deserts fertile plains. It has happened before, and there are some signs in the fossil records that hint at this which puzzle geologists.

Earthquakes and tidal waves will sink entire countries. Only a few places are safe, and these do not include coastal areas or islands, most of which will vanish overnight. California, most of England, all of Holland and Japan and much of Hawaii are amongst those places destined to vanish off the map in the very near future. Australia, on the other hand, will grow in size and thrive as a result.

In 1985 Ruth Montgomery followed with *Aliens Amongst Us*, in which she advised that many of the walk-ins were actually spiritual beings from Sirius, Arcturus and other star systems. They were behind the UFO mystery and planned to rescue a few people in spaceships as the disaster approached. These lucky few would be held in orbit until the pole shift was over, then seeded back into the community to ensure that the New Age constructed in a shattered world would be far more enlightened than we are today.

Whilst this concept takes some swallowing, it has a surprising appeal. Threads do link it together. Crop circle patterns have been recognised by Hopi Indians in Arizona. Alien contact messages are oddly identical to channelled messages from spirit beings. And an undercurrent of intuition seems to be manifesting in the way in which environmental movements and humanitarian groups are battling to save a beleaguered Earth.

It is interesting, too, that several paranormal researchers in Britain have had the 'urge' to move from the English lowlands to the less populated and more mountainous areas. This is a trend that is mirrored in general population shifts. Whilst, so far as we know, nobody is citing New Age warnings of tidal waves and sinking islands as the reason for such a move, perhaps psychic alarm bells are ringing somewhere deep inside?

Some of the New Age prophecies are seemingly accurate to an extraordinary degree. In 1983 Jenny Randles wrote a novel on this theme, called *Children of the Armageddon*, after first mooting it in her 1982 non-fiction book *Alien Contact*. Although never published, her novel has been quite widely read and used the wave of prophecies to extrapolate events said to be looming. It predicted the fall of communism in eastern Europe, the spread of a new plague (AIDS) around the globe, and the joining together of the former cold war enemies in a battle against a rising force of evil in the East. This was not due to any personal predictive powers, but was solely a reflection of these growing New Age/channelling messages.

If these seem to have become vindicated in such a remarkable way and to the great surprise of most pundits, then how seriously should we take the messages that the channellers are still predicting and whose day is drawing very near? Is this why there is now such an upsurge of interest in the concept of survival after death and the spirit world?

WHAT MEDIUMS DO

Mediums see themselves as radio receivers tuned into a particular frequency which carries information from the afterlife. They generally split into two types – 'mental' and 'physical' mediums.

Mental mediums utilise ESP which enables spirit communications to take place. They receive mental impressions from deceased persons which they then try to interpret for the living. These impressions can be received 'clairaudiently' – spirit voices are paranormally 'heard'; or 'clairvoyantly' – sensed or seen. Sometimes these communications take the form of auto-

Doris Collins is one of the best known mediums in the world. She performs publicly in large theatres, establishing contact with alleged spirits of the dead.

matic writing and drawing (see Chapter 4). Mental mediums are much more prevalent than their 'physical' colleagues.

Contact with the dead can take place during normal waking, as in the case of Doris Collins (see below) and Doris Stokes, or in a state of altered consciousness. This latter state can be achieved by staring at an object such as a glass of water or a crystal ball. Sometimes the services of a hypnotist are used. Mediums in the depth of trance often appear to have been temporarily possessed by a spirit. The entity vocalises using the medium's larynx; voice, facial expression and gestures emulate those of the deceased in possession of the medium's body.

Physical mediumship was very prevalent up until the middle of the twentieth century, but has since declined. Here, the medium acts as a channel for psychokinetic (PK) effects initiated by the deceased. These can take the form of levitation of objects and persons, the playing of musical instruments and the sound of discarnate voices. The deceased themselves can occasionally manifest by shaping a substance called 'ectoplasm' (see p. 62) which extrudes from the medium's body.

A MODERN MEDIUM AND HER TRADE

Doris Collins is one of the best-known mediums in the world. She regularly packs the biggest theatres with her stage performances, during which she claims to establish contact with spirit entities and pass on messages for audience members. She told us how she learned that she had these powers: 'I was born that way so I've never known anything different in my life . . . . I see, I sense, I feel and hear – and all this collectively is knowing.'

Like the late Doris Stokes and many other high-profile mediums, she has often been accused of trickery. Sceptics and even serious but cautious researchers have reported allegations of audiences made up of invited guests. They claim that in some instances (though not to our knowledge with Doris Collins) these confederates are seated on the front rows and are the ones to whom the medium then goes, resulting in 'spontaneous' and 'amazing' successes. In fact, the medium already has some unstated foreknowledge of the people seated there.

The day we spoke to Doris Collins, a respected British newspaper had just carried some quite similar claims about her work. We asked her to comment and she forthrightly disputed these allegations:

'I never see a telephone directory or know anybody in that town.'

'I am supposed to research into people's background. I am supposed to look in telephone directories [to find individuals to invite]. Well – I am doing forty-three meetings in six weeks on this present tour and I go into a town and work the same day. I never see a telephone directory or know anybody in that town, so I don't know how this is supposed to work. I mean, it's absolutely ridiculous. I know nobody in my audience at all. I don't ask questions. I go directly to a person I am guided to. Usually someone [later] asks them, "Do you know Doris Collins? Have you ever met her?", and they say, "No." "Could the information that she gave you be investigated?" And they say, "No."'

Doris believes that the afterlife comprises a world that we partly forge for ourselves through our deeds in this world. We asked whether belief in survival – if ever established as a fact – might not act as a signal for all the evil people in the world to commit terrible crimes on the grounds that it did not matter because nobody ever really died?

'Of course it matters,' she adamantly replied. 'We pass to a state that we have understanding of. People who commit dreadful things in the world pass to a state that they have an understanding of. It must be terrible. Can you imagine the state that someone like Hitler has passed to? You see we don't go to Hell. We create our own Hell in the way that we have used the gifts that we received.'

This answer is one that mediums often give, and we wonder if it might not mask a deeper purpose. If this view of the afterlife is correct, then possibly it explains why we do not all consciously know the fact. It would take some of the burden for everyday choices from off our shoulders – which might not be part of any cosmic plan.

Of course, if true, then a search for proof of survival will be forever doomed to failure. Such proof would be counter-productive to the way the universe functions. We may simply be allowed only tantalising glimpses that at the end of the day will always depend upon belief. These may hint and imply the truth, but can never establish life after death with absolute certainty.

THE MISSING SISTER

Doris Collins offered us one of the most important proofs that she has come across in her work. It is a complex story, but the essence is as follows.

In 1985 a well-known journalist came to one of her meetings without her knowledge. Afterwards they met for tea, and she told him there was a message from his parents who had suddenly come to her in spirit. He confirmed that they were both dead.

The message was that he had a sister. He denied that this was true. Doris told him: 'Your mother says it is a private family matter. She says to me: "He has a sister and his father would like him to get in touch".' The journalist insisted that he had no knowledge of a sister, but later an image flashed into his mind that she might be in Australia – something he had no way of checking.

Later he was to confirm to Doris – and admit in an article – that he was wrong. He did have a half-sister. She had been born of a different mother from an affair involving his father. The woman had married and had indeed emigrated to Australia. He had established this through tracing the family tree.

Not long after he saw Doris Collins, his secretary telephoned him at home to say that she had (it is not clear for how long) a letter from a woman in Australia claiming to be his sister. He was naturally astonished and rushed straight over to collect it. The woman wrote about how she had followed his career, but had only recently had the urge to contact him. It was up to him whether he replied to her or not. The journalist phoned the woman right away and later they met. A very close bond developed.

This is indeed an extraordinary story that appears to be impressive proof of survival. It may be precisely that, but there are a few added pieces of information not included in this summary which may affect your opinion.

Firstly, it seems that when he met Doris the journalist was already interested in tracing his family tree and had already established that his father had had a child by another woman. He had never discussed it with his family, but this knowledge was at the back of his mind and therefore could have been picked up by telepathy if Doris Collins possesses ESP, as seems implicit from her clairvoyant talents.

It does not disprove that the real source was what she claims it was – the spirit of the journalist's dead mother or father. However, it establishes another option than outright fraud.

We asked Doris Collins if she might not have found out about the sister by the unconscious application of telepathy – reading the information from the journalist's mind without being aware of it, and then understandably assuming that this message came from another source. She was insistent: 'In what way could I have known? The journalist did not even know anything about his sister. [The message] had reawakened a memory he had never discussed.'

But if it was there as a memory, then some detail existed in his mind to be extracted. Telepathy – if it does occur – may not offer a complete explanation, but under the circumstances it cannot be ignored.

Perhaps more significantly, when the journalist phoned his long-lost sister she said that the urge to write to him was motivated by attending one of Doris Collins's meetings in Australia where a message had come through (presumably from their father)! Of course, Doris Collins says she had no way of knowing who the woman in the audience had been. She was just one out of hundreds to whom Doris must have relayed messages on that Australian trip alone.

It is perfectly possible that the discarnate parents of these two people forged a mental link through Doris Collins with both the separated half-brother and half-sister. Then, by subtle psychic pressures directed into the couple's minds, they ensured that they were brought together.

In the end we cannot establish the truth of this issue and, assuming (as we have no reason not to) that all parties are being absolutely sincere in what they report, the story still fails to prove survival. The sceptic will always seek more rational options which – in this case, as in most others – can never be completely ruled out.

ECTOPLASM

This is a whitish substance usually exuded from the natural orifices of the medium's body, such as genitals, breasts, navel, ears and eyes – although this is not always the case. Medium Eva C. produced the substance from her thumb. It was very common with the physical mediums who performed in the nineteenth and early years of the twentieth century, but as this type of mediumship has declined so reports of ectoplasm have almost vanished.

Ectoplasm has been described as alive, and sensitive to light and touch.

Ectoplasm has been described as alive, and sensitive to touch and light, whereupon it can shoot back into the medium's body, causing pain. Variously described as having the texture of muslin, liquid or paste, it is always cold, slightly luminous and with a characteristic smell.

Despite numerous witnesses and many photographs of mediums producing the substance, its authenticity has not been verified. The only documented instance of a scientific examination of ectoplasm took place at the Massachusetts Institute of Technology. Its composition was reported as being 'sodium, potassium, water, chlorine, albumen, epithelial cells and fresh red blood corpuscles'.

According to researcher Dr W. J. Crawford, lecturer in mechanical engineering at Belfast University, his work with physical medium Kathleen Goligher proved that ectoplasm was produced in some way by conversion of the medium's own body. After she produced ectoplasm, Goligher's weight had reduced compared with what it had been before the demonstration.

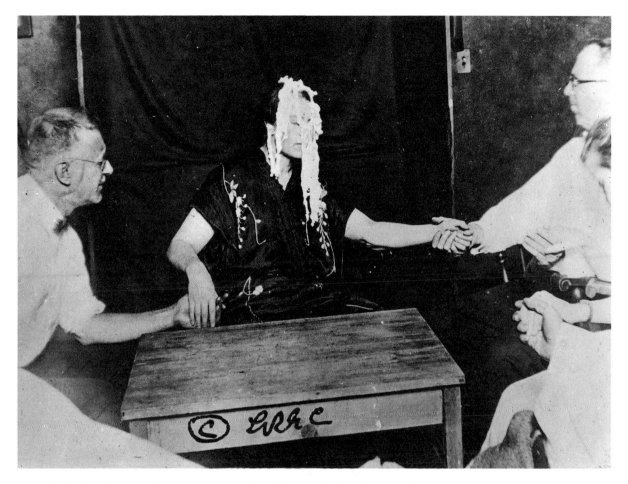

American physical medium
Margery Crandon producing
'veil' ectoplasm. She was later,
however, declared a fake.

Crawford also showed that the weight of a table which he observed levitating had temporarily transferred to the medium.

Ectoplasm is conceived as some sort of supernatural modelling clay. Once formed, it is used by spirits to manifest in our world. This manifestation can take the form of a face, hand or, very rarely, a complete figure. Although this is hard to believe, some very sincere witnesses have been convinced they have been confronted in the seance room by the figure of a deceased relative or close friend. The following story, as told to us, illustrates this phenomenon.

BACK FROM THE WAR

Professional artist Henry Thomson had a bizarre experience in 1956, which was rooted in World War II. During the war, Henry had served as a sergeant in the 8th Army. He fought in North Africa, and during this time befriended another young man called Alfie Hall. Alfie was very popular with his comrades, and Henry described him as 'a pretty good pal – almost like a brother'. They were marching through El Faiyum, in the north of Egypt, chatting, when suddenly there was an explosion. Corporal Alfred Hall had stepped on a landmine and was blown to smithereens. Henry could not have conceived that they would meet again, less than twelve years later.

In 1956 Henry and his wife, a medium, had moved to Blackpool. Henry had an interest in psychic experiences too, but he always looked for a logical explanation. When he heard that physical medium Jimmy Gardner was performing in the town, he decided to go along out of curiosity. Gardner had a reputation for bringing about the materialisation of spirits into temporary physical form.

The venue was merely a room over a shop, and the fee charged at the door would just about pay the medium's expenses. Henry was one of about fourteen people in the audience. Gardner arrived, so crippled with arthritis that he could only manage two shuffling steps. It was with great difficulty that his helpers struggled to get him and his wheelchair up the narrow stairs. The medium was wheeled to a corner of the room, and a black curtain was placed around him. This is necessary, mediums claim, to stop the ectoplasm drifting away before it can take shape.

Henry Thomson was amazed by what occurred during the evening. Six or seven figures materialised in the room, children and adults, all of them recognised by someone in the small audience. They were not a bit ethereal, but looked and acted as normal flesh-and-blood human beings, even holding conversations. But there was an even bigger surprise awaiting Henry. Suddenly, the tall, ginger-haired figure of Corporal Alfie Hall stepped from behind the curtain.

Still looking twenty-two years old, the uniformed 'man' strode towards Henry and held out his hand. His old friend took it and found it warm. For the next few minutes the two of them chatted about army life, Alfie reminding him of several things that even Henry had forgotten. Finally, Alfie assured his friend that he was very happy where he was, and turned to leave. As he moved towards the curtain his form had already become indistinct and transparent, and then it evaporated altogether.

SPIRIT GUIDES

As we have seen, most mediums do not communicate directly with the dead, but work through a spirit guide or 'control'. This is particularly true of trance mediums, who allow the control to take over their body. The phenomenon, like mediumship itself, is not new. The biblical Witch of Endor was possessed by a familiar spirit and the early Christians by a devil.

Controls range from Red Indians to Chinese sages and Arabian physicians, which are meant to be entities in an advanced spiritual state. When questioned, some of them make the most elementary factual mistakes about their backgrounds. Most mediums have one control, but some have several. Their role is to safeguard the medium's welfare and act as mediator, regulating the number of spirits attempting to communicate. Even so, occasionally a rogue spirit breaks through with information for someone not present at the seance. Sometimes the control, already in possession of the medium's body, will allow a spirit to take over – the medium now adopts the speech patterns and gestures of this new deceased. This is how shaman Michael Bromley described to us his relationship with his spirit guide.

A CELTIC SHAMAN

Michael Bromley is a Celtic shaman who spent seven years in America working with Indians. 'Shaman' is a very old word which originated in Siberia, although it is usually associated with the Red Indian medicine man. It is very likely that the connection is due to emigration from Siberia to North America when the two landmasses were connected by ice at what is now the Bering Straits. Shamanism is based on the ancient belief that there are many levels of 'spirit' both in the spirit dimension and on the Earth plane. There are shamans around the world, who are essentially healers and teachers. Michael has worked with brain-damaged children, and claims to have cured a woman of multiple sclerosis. But he has not always been a shaman. Twenty years ago he did not even realise he was psychic.

'I was working for the Gas Board. One of my colleagues retired and went off to set up a spiritual healing centre. I was invited to go, but left it a few weeks. Then, as usual, curiosity got the better of me and I went along. A medium told me I was a healer and a psychic. I thought they were weird and wanted nothing more to do with them. But over the next year I returned. Another medium told me things only I was aware of. I thought: "How did she do that?" I was determined to find out. I joined a development circle and learned about Spiritualism. Eventually I started running my own group, and it snowballed from there.'

Before becoming a professional psychic, Michael led a wide and varied career. 'My life has been very much like that of a gypsy. I've travelled the world absorbing. I was brought up a Christian, but I've been involved in Islam and Buddhism along the road to Spiritualism.'

British shaman, Michael
Bromley, who spent seven years
with North American Indians.

Several mediums told him that he had a Red Indian spirit guide. One of them, psychic artist Coral Polge (see Chapter 4), even painted a picture of the entity in pastels. He was openly sceptical at first. 'Of course, every medium is supposed to have a Red Indian guide!' Neither was he impressed by the picture. 'I expected a majestic head-dress, but all he had was one feather at either side of his head, fastened to the tips of his long hair.'

Coral Polge told him the Indian was called Great Eagle. 'Great Eagle and I built up quite a rapport. One day he told me he wanted to go back to his homeland. I said, 'Fine, you go!' He said, 'You're missing the point – you have to come with me.' Within a few weeks, a whole set of circumstances combined and I made a trip to America, intending to stay for two months. I made the most amazing contacts. Instead I stayed for seven years!'

It was while working in Los Angeles that he met Cheyenne, Lakota, Potawatomi and Chumash Indian medicine men. In particular he worked with Wallace Black Elk and his adopted son, Potawatomi medicine man Don Perrote. Wallace is a Lakota Indian and a leader of the Indian nations. Michael introduced them to 'crystal consciousness' – the idea that crystals are a powerful life force in their own right.

During their initial meetings he asked them the significance of the name 'Great Eagle'. They told him the eagle stands for strength and determination, and 'great' in the Indian language translates as 'sacred'. They also told him that the eagle has one 'power' feather in the tip of each wing.

'That clinched it for me,' Michael said. 'I was convinced. I knew my Indian guide was not imagination.'

After a time, the Indians asked him what he was. He said, 'A psychic, of course.' The question cropped up again, and he gave them the same answer. This time they replied:

'Michael, why don't you honour your spirit and call yourself a shaman, because that's what you are.'

He said he was British, so how could he be a shaman?

He said he was British, so how could he be a shaman? But after two years of meditating on the problem, and understanding what it meant, he accepted.

'I felt very privileged and honoured,' he said. 'The Indians work with feathers and animal power. I use a shaman's staff, wand and drum. The drum is a way of communing with spirit on a vibratory level.'

A PSYCHOLOGIST'S OPINION

Some psychologists suggest that recourse to unproven psychic abilities is not even necessary. They say that mediums utilise ordinary principles of human behaviour to extract information from their clients unconsciously. Mediums' belief that they are in contact with the dead is just a fantasy which reinforces Spiritualist dogma and transfers the responsibility for the messages elsewhere.

This is a not uncommon psychological process. It is true, for instance, that it could also be applied to so-called channellers – space age mediums who receive usually glib and generalised messages via the minds of extra-terrestrials. Just as mediums often have spirit guides from exotic races with strange and unpronounceable names, channellers allegedly communicate with alien beings bearing improbable names like Zookan and Maximus, which seem to have their genesis within the pages of science fiction pulp magazines of the 1940s. It is hardly surprising that these parallels suggest to psychologists that both are really the same phenomenon but interpreted differently.

Here is a typical message, attributed to a being called 'Marcus': 'The world is in a process of spiritual revolution. Purification is a necessary thing in the cosmic order.' Could you tell whether this was a speech from a higher spirit in Summerland or from an alien being orbiting in a UFO? It is allegedly the latter, but in truth could be either, and that is the problem.

Professor Alan Smithers is a psychologist at Manchester University. After studying several mediums in operation he told us:

'Mediums can tell us an awful lot about human consciousness. What seems to be emerging is that the bit of ourselves that we know about is only a small part of our brain functions and it is directly linked to our speech centres. Because our self-awareness is only a small part of our brain, a number of things come in which are surprising to us, and some of these filter through into consciousness. So we sometimes think we know things that we haven't worked out coolly or rationally. We need stories to show how these things come about. It's a natural function, but something we don't think much about.'

'Once you look behind the superficial attractiveness of much of Spiritualism's evidence you find that, whilst intriguing, it is nowhere near as conclusive as it appears to be for those who accept it as a matter of faith.'

We might cite 'intuition' as an explanation for statements like 'I knew you were going to phone me', or perhaps we tap into the subconscious in dreams to solve scientific puzzles or write literary masterpieces. There are many examples of this – for instance the discovery of the form of the benzene molecule and the writing of *Dr Jekyll and Mr Hyde*. We might attribute these things mythically (to a muse), rationally (to data transfer from our own mental store) or spiritually (from dead scientists or writers passing on their guidance). The point is not that any of these interpretations are right or wrong, but simply that there are other interpretations available. Once you look behind the superficial attractiveness of much of Spiritualism's evidence you find that, whilst intriguing, it is nowhere near as conclusive as it appears to be for those who accept it as a matter of faith. Professor Smithers continued to explain.

'There is a basic rule in psychology that we can never *not* communicate. We may be sitting frozen in space staring ahead, but all the time we are giving off messages. Some people are good readers of books. Some people who are 'psychic' are really very good at reading body language. They read people very well but are unaware of this. So they talk in generalities and one can fit stories to what mediums say that make sense. The medium presents a general framework on to which the client fixes specific meaning.'

As an illustration, consider this imagined exchange between a medium and an audience. It is typical of what often happens.

Medium: 'I have a B. . .Beatie or Bill. . . .' (Looks around)
Sitter: (*Reacting with some surprise*): 'Bill – yes, my father was called Bill.'
Medium: (*Fixing on this person*): 'Yes, he says hello. You did not expect me to get through, did you?'
Sitter: (*Laughing*): 'No, I didn't. The old so and so . . . .'
Medium: 'He was your father and a difficult man – but he says he has mellowed now.'
Sitter: 'You are so right. He must be there with you.'

Note that the medium reported getting a 'B' and offered both a male and female name. In any audience of even the smallest size someone would probably be thinking of a 'Bill' or 'Beatie'. As soon as one person gave the game away through their eyes, the medium might unconsciously 'home in' on them and use little cues in their responses. For instance, in just a couple of sentences here the sitter was telling the medium that Bill was his father, implying he was a bit of a rogue and so on, offering titbits of information which the medium might subconsciously absorb and incorporate into further responses.

So the process might go on. There need not be any trickery involved, no deliberate fraud. The medium might believe they were receiving the data from 'Bill', the sitter's dead father. Psychologists would say they were simply reading it from events . . . or could the medium really be using ESP?

One delightful Lancashire medium called Totty, who we believe is 100 per cent genuine in her claims, was admirably honest about her experiences and her attendance at hundreds of sittings with other mediums. Whilst she believes that she is a channel through which information passes, sometimes decoded correctly, other times not, she accepts some of what Professor Smithers says: 'A lot of tommy-rot is spoken about a 'Bill, Ben', etc. You can say 'yes' to it – but it doesn't mean a thing. However, there are times when you can say – 'How did the medium know that?' I don't care who the medium is – known, unknown or the so-called famous. They are only as good as their last message.'

'I don't care who the medium is – known, unknown or the so-called famous. They are only as good as their last message.'

THE EVIDENCE AGAINST

When Spiritualism popularised 'contact with the dead', turning it into an entertainment, it attracted several types of 'performers'. There were the sincere, the sincerely deluded and the out-and-out frauds.

Believing that information entering the mind comes from a realm where dead spirits reside is by no means the same thing as proving that it does. There are other sources from which such 'voices' might emerge and, although genuinely 'heard' in the mind of the medium, the mistake could be in giving them an external origin.

For instance, mediums might be psychically tapping into the mind of the sitter. Inevitably, at the back of his or her mind, a person in the company of a medium is almost bound to be thinking about people he or she once knew who had died and who might conceivably 'come through'. If the deceased then appears to 'communicate', might it not be just as likely that the mind-to-mind communication was between the medium and the sitter, rather than between the medium and a mind from a world beyond death? The only way to rule that out is to obtain information that the sitter could not possibly know or ever have known.

The fraudsters saw there was a fast buck to be made and employed conjuring tricks which took advantage of both the sensation seekers and the freshly bereaved looking for consolation and 'proof' of an afterlife. There were many sceptics who successfully exposed fraudulent mediums, but one seeker after proof was the conjurer and escapologist Harry Houdini.

Houdini, who rose to international fame at the beginning of the twentieth century, was so adept at escaping from sealed boxes and intricately locked manacles that some people thought he used supernatural means. One of them was his friend Sir Arthur Conan Doyle, who speculated that Houdini was a natural medium, capable of dematerialising from his constraints and then rematerialising elsewhere! Indeed, Houdini was intensely interested in Spiritualism, but his investigations usually ended with the discovery of yet another fake medium.

One of these was an American woman named Mrs Mina Crandon. Under the name of 'Margery' she produced the full gamut of the physical medium – raps, table-tilting, moving lights, materialisations and the 'direct voice' of her deceased brother, Walter. At one point, Walter even left his thumbprint in some wax.

Houdini was one of a committee of five psychical researchers appointed by the magazine *Scientific American* to investigate Mrs Crandon. He declared her to be a fraud, but final proof did not emerge until 1932 when

Right: Magician and escapologist Harry Houdini spent many years searching for proof of survival beyond death. Here he demonstrates how 'spirit' hands can be made from wax.

a Boston dentist confirmed that he had innocently made the thumbprint for Mrs Crandon.

Many of the full materialisations were accomplices of the medium, or indeed the mediums themselves, disguised. The wife of Mexican medium Luis Martinez was exposed in this way by W. G. Roll in 1964. Martinez had been performing since 1933, and some of the photographs of materialisations produced during this period are far from convincing. Ectoplasm oozing from ears and mouths looks more like cheesecloth, and ghostly faces resemble crudely painted papier mâché.

THE EVIDENCE FOR

The vast majority of mediums are quiet, inoffensive people prepared to use their gifts to bring piece of mind to the bereaved – often without a charge. They offer very specific information which they could not have known beforehand. Despite the fakers, there is a hard core of mediums who have been intensively investigated over long periods and have never been caught cheating. The feats of physical mediums have been captured on film. If those feats had been specially set up for the camera, the fraud would have included very many people over the years.

Despite the fakers, there is a hard core of mediums who have been intensively investigated over long periods and have never been caught cheating.

Spiritualism did not invent mediumship, but gave it a name and brought it before the public and the media. Psychic contact with the dead has always been around in one guise or another. The phenomena which occurred during seances are no different from poltergeist activity (see Chapter 6). Modern mental mediums are so confident in their accuracy that they encourage sitters to tape-record the spirit messages, to study in detail later.

Contrary to popular belief, not all stage magicians are antagonistic towards claims of mediumship. Some are actively involved in paranormal research. Professional American magician and psychic researcher Larry Auerbach told us that debunkers like James Randi are not actually in the majority. The late David Nixon admitted that it was not possible to duplicate all of the feats of Uri Geller through the use of trickery.

Auerbach is an adjunct professor teaching parapsychology at John F. Kennedy University in California, where he gained a master's degree in parapsychology; he also has a BA in cultural anthropology from Northwestern University. As a magician, he was creative consultant to the television series *The Magic of David Copperfield*. Together with illusionist Christopher Chacon, in 1980 Auerbach set up the Office of Paranormal Investigations. It looks into claims concerning the paranormal and acts as a resource centre for the media, business people, scientists and law enforcement agencies.

In a recent survey of magicians in California, Auerbach discovered that approximately three-quarters claimed that paranormal incidents had occurred during their acts. When tricks had gone wrong, paranormal phenomena had taken over to make them work!

Larry Auerbach also made some claims regarding Harry Houdini. He pointed out that Houdini's investigation of Spiritualism was undertaken to find proof of the afterlife and not to debunk mediums. Further, according to Auerbach, Houdini did finally discover a medium who provided him with unambiguous proof of life after death. Details of this are contained in private documentation that the sceptical camp of magicians are trying to suppress. He claims that there is an underground battle taking place to force these documents out into the open.

Three-quarters of surveyed magicians claimed that paranormal incidents had occurred during their acts.

EXPERIMENTAL PROOF?

Jenny Randles set up a test with a medium as a means of establishing whether any bona fide information could be gleaned from a sitting. The session was arranged with the help of university psychologist Dr John Shaw. Professor Alan Smithers was also in attendance as the subject of the trial. The medium was Dorothy from Manchester. The events of 17 June 1986 were tape-recorded and retained so that the psychologists could check their accuracy later.

Dorothy claims to be in contact with a very advanced spirit who has not incarnated on Earth. This concept forms a very curious bridge between the mediums who say they communicate with the recently departed and the channellers who receive messages from aliens. She offers interesting evidence in that much of it supposedly refers to the future of the sitter. Time is not linear in the spirit world apparently.

The test with Professor Smithers was deemed a total failure. Dorothy says he was 'blocking' her reception, something that he agrees was very probable. Of the many vague statements she made, he later refused to concede that any of the reported events took place – although he agreed that he could have made some fit if he tried. Only one very specific premonition was given. When he asked the medium if he would get a research grant he had just applied for, she said yes. This proved wrong!

However, immediately Jenny met Dorothy the medium offered a message about a pain in the stomach area that must be dealt with urgently. Later, this message was repeated. At the time it meant little, but after the session with Professor Smithers Dorothy insisted on doing a 'reading' with Jenny. A careful record was made of the results.

Some fifty statements were made. These ranged from names to a couple of vague remarks that were uncheckable. Perhaps significantly, that night Jenny had one of the most vivid out-of-the-body dreams she had ever experienced.

Of the names, two could be made to fit, but were rejected; five meant nothing; and only two (interestingly, the very first two given) were significant. One was the name of Jenny's only sibling, and the other that of a school friend whom she had not thought of for years, but who had died in a terrible accident the year after both left school. Later, she discovered that the medium lived only a few hundred yards from where her friend had lived some fifteen years before.

The medium offered a message about a pain in the stomach area that must be dealt with urgently. Three months later stomach pains led to a diagnosis of cancer. Coincidence or proof?

All the other statements were brief sentences that were semi-specific and could be said to be either a direct hit or a miss when tied in with past or present events. They were checked one year later. Of these, some fifteen (about 40 per cent) could reasonably be said to apply to Jenny's life. A couple referred to the past, three to the circumstances at that time but most to the coming six months.

Whilst some of these might have been too vague to score fairly (for instance, 'I see a doctor's certificate – someone is going to go on the sick' – not a startling prediction in most families) even some of these, especially this one, may be more accurate than it seemed at the time.

There were some startling successes. Dorothy described an old woman carrying a Sunday School banner – what she said matched Jenny's grandmother well. She offered a link with a police station in central Manchester. Jenny had once briefly worked there as a fingerprint detective.

So much for the past; what of present circumstances? There were several hits such as the reference to a cancelled appointment on a Thursday. That very week she had had to cancel a trip to Exeter scheduled for that day and, most incredibly of all, the bizarre statement (laughing) 'Have you recently had a dispute with a bus?' The day before this session Jenny had been involved in some 'past life' hypnosis experiments (see Chapter 11) in which a young woman had 'relived' a life in London in 1920. As Jenny knew a few things about buses, she had in fact had a healthy dispute with the hypnotised subject about the colour of the bus that she chanced to report meeting on the London streets!

Startling as something like this may be, such information could be said to have been accessible from Jenny's mind by way of ESP. It was not established that the information came from any other source. However, data about the future could not be obtained via 'simple' telepathy.

There were several hits. Possibly most dramatic was the remark: 'Watch where you are going – it will be called a *close*, not an avenue or road. It *will* be called a close.' Just a couple of weeks later Jenny was unexpectedly invited to the set of the TV soap opera *Brookside* to interview an actress about her ghostly experiences. The interview took place in a house on the real street used in the series – probably the most famous 'Close' in the British Isles!

The strangest of all predictions related to the 'doctor's certificate'. This could be coupled with the repeated comment about the need to act quickly on the stomach pain and with another comment which emerged during the session – 'There will be a Sunday when things will not go as planned. If someone wants to stay in bed on a Sunday, they're not feeling well. There will be something wrong.'

Jenny's mother did indeed stay in bed one Sunday some three months later – which was most unlike her, even if she was feeling unwell. Jenny remembered Dorothy's remarks when a pain in her middle area was described. Despite her mother insisting that she would be all right, Jenny called the doctor. He sent her to hospital, where after some tests it was discovered that she had cancer. A hysterectomy was necessary, but luckily the disease had been caught in its very early stages and she pulled through. The doctor later told Jenny that had there been a delay of even a few weeks in seeking treatment the cancer could have spread. Also, the type of cancer her mother had developed was often very difficult to diagnose in its early stages. Although from that time onward she was given continuous doctor's certificates and was really 'on the sick', she had in fact been very lucky.

Then again, had she? If Dorothy had not received that urgent warning, and Jenny had not acted swiftly as a result of the session, would her mother have delayed seeking treatment, exactly as Dorothy's message had feared? Was this luck or someone else's judgement?

YOUR VERDICT : A SUMMARY

AGAINST SURVIVAL

- There are rational means by which much of the data offered by mediums could be obtained.

- Mediums are remarkably akin to New Age channellers of messages from extraterrestrials. Are both groups right in their interpretation, or does it prove a psychological explanation?

- Much of what a medium offers is generalised and non-specific. It rarely contains things that only the deceased spirit would know.

- As science became more sophisticated, physical mediumship went on the decline. Fakers knew it could not stand up to modern scientific testing.

- Sincere mediums could be just deluding themselves, encouraged by gullible people who want to believe they have made contact.

- With so much waffle being spoken by mediums, the law of averages state that they are bound to strike lucky occasionally.

FOR SURVIVAL

- Since Spiritualism confronted the world of science, many mediums have been exhaustively tested. Often the results are ambiguous, but enough positive results have been achieved to convince some very prominent figures of its authenticity.

- Mediums are largely sincere people who lack the ambition to achieve fame or make money from their abilities.

- Spiritualism is merely Victorian packaging for the timeless belief in gifted people able to communicate with the dead. If it all was purely psychological it would have fallen by the wayside centuries ago.

- Despite the waffle, enough of the information is so accurate that it is untenable to put this down to mere coincidence.

- There is a large body of empirical data built up over many decades which authenticates the paranormal phenomena created by physical mediums.

- Some genuine mediums put under the spotlight do get tempted to cheat due to pressure to achieve results.

SKILL SURVIVAL

———◆———

Can genius cross the boundaries of time, space and even death? There is plenty of very persuasive evidence to suggest that skills of all varieties – literary, musical and artistic – can indeed do just this.

A Texas woman has begun to receive images in her mind of life in the Old West. The source is allegedly Jesse James.

AUTOMATIC WRITING

Recently we were contacted by a woman from Texas who made an extraordinary claim. She was not a medium in the traditional sense of the word, but had begun to receive images in her mind of life in the Old West. That may not seem much of a surprise, given her location. But things took an odd turn when she found herself writing long manuscripts in a peculiar handwriting. Even more unusual was the fact that these made sense and purported to be from the spirit world. Allegedly the source was Jesse James, the old gun-toting outlaw, keen to right wrongs and tell the real truth about his life and times. One of the strangest 'autobiographies' may soon appear on the bookstalls as a result!

This process is known as 'automatic writing'. The popular view of the sceptic is that the mind is a largely untapped source of information, and that if one puts the body into a state of reverie – idling and submitting conscious control to a back seat – strange things can happen.

Indeed, we all have evidence of doing this ourselves in our day-to-day existence. If we had to *think* about the process of breathing we probably would not be able to do it. It is a complex affair which requires the control of many muscles and processes that have simply become automatic. We go from minute to minute never giving it any thought and yet doing it all of the time thanks to the systems built into our subconscious.

Is that how automatic writing works? Do we simply let these hidden skills come to the fore and control the hand muscles and transcribe what is pouring freely from within the mind? If so, what is the source of the material that emerges? Is it imagination, as sceptics would believe, or can our minds at this deep inner level tap into the consciousness of others – even after death?

Former clergyman and medium William Stainton Moses filled twenty-four notebooks with automatic writing during the latter half of the nineteenth century. Some pages were signed by the spirit communicator. One of these was the composer Mendelssohn.

Dr J. B. Rhine was one of those sceptical researchers who believed that automatic writing was a subjective phenomenon. He dismissed it as spontaneous 'motor automatisms'. Rhine believed that conflicts, repressions and obsessions normally locked away in the subconscious were released on to the written page when the guard of the conscious mind was subdued. However, he admitted that some cases, such as that of Patience Worth, were not so easily explained.

Patience Worth was one of the most prolific post-mortem authors in the

Former clergyman William Stainton Moses filled twenty-four note books with automatic writings during the latter half of the 19th century.

An extract from one of Stainton Moses' note books.

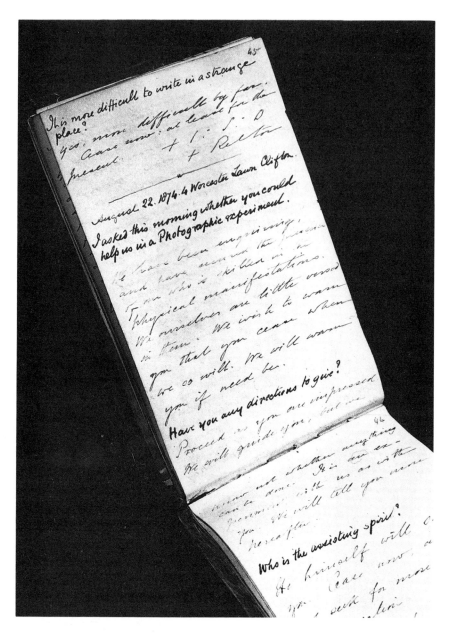

history of automatic writing. She first emerged as 'Pat-C' on 13 May 1913 in the southern United States where two women were experimenting with a ouija board. 'Pat' returned on 22 June and spelt out to Mrs Pearl Curran a few lines of prose which were remarkable for their beauty and philosophical clarity: 'Oh, why let sorrow steel thy heart? Thy bosom is but its foster-mother, the world its cradle and the loving home its grave.' On 8 July the messenger signed herself 'Patience Worth'.

Patience often spoke in rustic English which Mrs Curran had difficulty in understanding, so she asked her for clarification. It emerged that Patience had been born in Dorset during the seventeenth century to a Quaker family. Not long after they had emigrated to America, she was killed by Indians. But full details of the spirit's earthly life were not forthcoming. She seemed more interested in embarking, through the medium of Mrs Curran, on a literary career. After a while Mrs Curran gave up the ouija board for pen-held automatic writing. Then Patience began to communicate directly into her host's mind – speeding up the writing process. Her style moved towards a more modern form of English. Patience's output was prodigious by any standard. Between 1913 and Pearl Curran's death in 1938 she dictated millions of words which were realised in poems, novels and plays. One evening alone she wrote twenty-two poems, and in five years she produced 1,600,000 words. This was not gibberish, or even of average worth. Much of it received literary acclaim in America and Britain.

Her novel *Hope Trueblood* was published as having been written by Patience Worth, with no explanation of the bizarre circumstances surrounding its creation. The book described the life of an illegitimate child surviving in Victorian England. It received favourable reviews. But another of her novels established her as a best-selling author. *The Sorry Tale* was dictated at a rate of around three thousand words an evening. In 325,000 words it told the story of a contemporary of Christ who ended up being crucified beside him as one of the thieves.

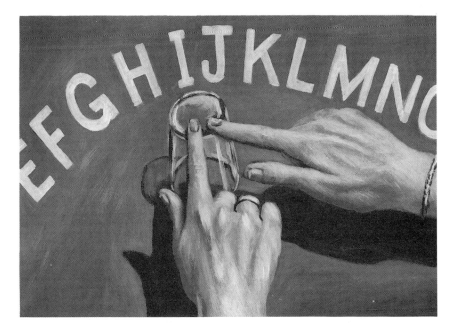

The personality of Patience Worth communicated itself initially through the medium of a ouija board. Two American woman experimenting with the device were contacted on 13 May 1913. The board, however, proved too slow for the entity, who seemed intent on embarking on a literary career. Eventually she controlled the hands of Mrs Pearl Curran, producing thousands of words of critically acclaimed poetry and prose.

Apart from its inventiveness, the novel was remarkable for its political and historical accuracy. In the normal way of things extensive research would have been necessary before a single word of the story could have been set down. Literary critics were asking who the real author was. Was it the surviving spirit of a Quaker girl, or Mrs Pearl Curran? Both possibilities have their problems.

How could a young girl from the 17th century possess the necessary knowledge to produce literature set in Victorian England?

Mrs Curran had had only a very basic education, and was not even interested in reading, much less in carrying out months of research for a novel allegedly penned by a surviving spirit. Up until the emergence of Patience Worth she had been just an ordinary housewife, who, if she had one at all, had a talent for singing. Her lack of education and interest in literature must rule out cryptomnesia (see chapter 11) as an answer. However, the explanation that the written material really was from a deceased Quaker girl also has problems. How could a young girl from the seventeenth century possess the necessary knowledge to produce literature set in Victorian England? How did she have access to accurate background material for *The Sorry Tale*?

Is this proof that spirits continue to evolve in the afterlife? Do they have access to some sort of spiritual computer matrix that holds all knowledge, all human experience? Was Patience Worth, through Pearl Curran, pursuing a literary career denied her on Earth due to a premature death? Is there really any other answer?

ART FOR ART'S SAKE

To everyone who has met him, Matthew Manning is a remarkable person – kind, unassuming and by no means a stage-struck medium. Yet his career and books (starting with *The Link*, written when he was still a teenager) span twenty years, demonstrating some of the most amazing and probative paranormal phenomena.

Manning first noted messages appearing suddenly on walls in his old house, and he was later able to channel these through automatic writing. They claimed to be coming from deceased entities using him as a 'link'. He moved on from there to become a channel for the most incredible artwork, reproduced in the style of countless dead painters such as Arthur Rackham, Aubrey Beardsley, Beatrix Potter and Pablo Picasso. The pictures range from exact copies of famous works to new productions that compare well with the efforts of deceased artists in their corporeal state. Their range and breadth of styles, in ink, charcoal and colour, is stunning – although apparently most of the 'spirits' are confused about using colour, as if colours are a different concept in the afterlife. This makes sense when we consider that colour is primarily a visual phenomenon. If the mind does survive bodily death, perhaps over a period of time – centuries even – then without continued visual stimulation it loses the definition of colour, existing as it must in a non-physical reality.

Matthew Manning makes no claims about the source of the phenomena, taking on board criticism and sceptical ideas with modesty and interest and merely reporting what takes place. He leaves it for others to judge what it all means, although he does note clues that could be significant. For example, the artists who sign their work all have distinctive personalities. He says of Picasso, for instance, that the artist's fire and energy really tire him as he works furiously through the young man's hands.

Whether the dead really are passing on their latest works in this way, or it is a derivative skill from his own inner resources, the phenomenon is no less incredible. If Manning is sincere – and there is no evidence to suggest otherwise that we are aware of – then his work is all the evidence one needs of something remarkable.

To his great credit, Manning has not sought to make a career out of being a medium or communicator of psychic art work. Once he learned to control the flow of 'energy' passing through him, he saw its potential for healing the sick. As a consequence he has devoted many years of his life to being a healer and keeping out of the limelight.

Manning is not alone in his ability. Brazilian Luiz Gasparetto has produced new work by Renoir, Cézanne and Picasso. He works in a trance, usually in the dark, often producing two paintings at the same time – one with each hand! During an edition of the BBC programme *Nationwide* in 1978, Gasparetto produced twenty-one pictures in seventy-five minutes.

These psychic artists, allegedly directed by the surviving spirits of famous painters, require no preliminary sketching and produce completed masterpieces in a matter of minutes or hours. Art experts argue over the validity of this work, but at the very least the results are stunning.

During an edition of the BBC programme Nationwide Gasparetto *produced twenty-one pictures in seventy-five minutes.*

MUSIC OF THE SPHERES

The idea that we might soon be able to hear Beethoven's tenth symphony, despite the fact that he only wrote nine, might seem a bit ridiculous. But one woman claims it as a real possibility.

Rosemary Brown has a limited musical background, but from her London home she has produced music transcribed to her by dead composers. British composer Richard Rodney Bennett commented: 'A lot of people can improvise, but you couldn't fake music like this without years of training. I couldn't have faked some of the Beethoven myself.' Concert pianist

Brazilian trance artist Luiz
Gasparetto has produced new
works in the style of many
deceased painters, including
Cézanne.

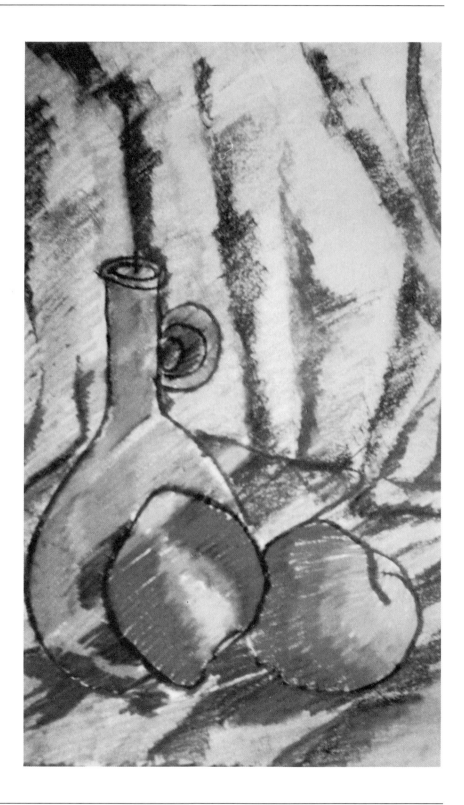

Hephzibah Menuhin remarked: 'I look at these manuscripts with immense respect. Each piece is distinctly in the composer's style.' Nevertheless, sceptics have remarked that the new music is reminiscent more of the composers' earlier work rather than his mature output.

But the pieces seem way beyond Rosemary's talents, and she believes they are dictated to her by the great composers from their new home in the afterlife. As with automatic writing and psychic art, the works are composed at a very fast rate.

Her first 'visitor' appeared when she was just seven: an apparition forewarned her of what was to come. Years later she saw an old painting of Franz Liszt and realised that it was he who had visited her. Gradually more and more composers contacted her, including Brahms, Chopin and Stravinsky. Remarkably, Debussy has channelled paintings rather than music through her, as this is supposedly his new interest.

Rosemary alleges that musicians pass on full compositions, already written, including some scored orchestral works. As they come she chats with the spirit (unseen by others) as if it was a normal joint authorship arrangement.

Years later she saw an old painting of Franz Liszt and realised that it was he who had visited her.

Her claims have aroused great interest within the orchestral community. When Leonard Bernstein met her, he was convinced by her unassuming sincerity and take-it-or-leave-it attitude. He particularly liked a piece that Rachmaninov supposedly wrote for him that day: the ghost had told Rosemary specifically to give it to Bernstein. He was most impressed with the music.

According to the spirit of conductor Sir Donald Tovey in communication with Rosemary Brown, the group of composers are interested in passing on their work for more than pleasure. He reputedly said to her: 'It is the implications relevant to this phenomenon which we hope will stimulate sensible and sensitive interest and stir many who are intelligent and impartial to consider and explore the unknown of man's mind and psyche.'

British concert pianist John Lill, winner of the prestigious Tchaikovsky award, believes that his playing is inspired by the ghost of Beethoven. It began when Lill was practising in the Moscow Conservatoire for the Tchaikovsky Piano Competition. He became aware of someone observing him, dressed in strange clothes. Lill recognised the man as Beethoven, and has since held many conversations with the apparition.

Another musician who believes he is in contact with the dead is Clifford Enticknap. Handel, his teacher in a previous incarnation, communicated to Enticknap a four-and-a-half-hour oratorio, parts of which have been recorded by the London Symphony Orchestra and the Handelian Foundation Choir. The music has been critically acclaimed, but the words have been derided.

Italian medium 'Anita' uses her left hand during automatic writing. The pen is held loosely, and the messages contain information she is not consciously aware of. Note the difference between the 'spirit' writing (top) and her own handwriting (below).

Some sceptical paranormal researchers, whilst ruling out conscious fraud, postulate that the musical communicators might be making the same mistake as other sensitives. They receive images from the subconscious which have no obvious source and so ascribe them to the ghost of the composer, which then obligingly visualises.

What other sources might there be? As in the case of automatic writers, there is talk of some great cosmic store of knowledge which some call the Akashic records or the Book of Life. Again, perhaps latent creative talents are being stirred into action. But why would such an elaborate piece of theatre be needed? Why could the mind not simply accept these oblique sources as reasonable enough? Would such a pretence – even an unconscious one – really be necessary?

One way of testing the theory might be to see if Mrs Brown or others like her can reproduce material from *living* composers, or even contemporary rock musicians. Could she conjure up something from Mike Oldfield, Jean Michel Jarre or Paul McCartney, for instance? Has the spirit of John Lennon been inspiring his son, Julian?

'THIS IS JOHN LENNON, LIVE, EXCEPT, OF COURSE, I'M DEAD!'

It is an eerie experience listening to 'John Lennon' talking about the day he was murdered, but that is what medium Bill Tenuto claims to provide. The mid-height American with a distinct New Jersey accent in no way resembles the Liverpudlian rock musician who was killed in December 1980. Yet from his lips come words in a voice that is at least passably similar to Lennon's, commenting on all manner of things about the afterlife. These are parts of a posthumous book the singer 'says' he is putting together, entitled *Little Pearls from John Lennon*.

This technique is known as direct-voice mediumship, a not unknown but relatively obscure phenomenon these days. It can be most impresive for those who knew the person claiming to speak through the medium.

In Bill Tenuto's case, you can certainly see a hint of Lennon when 'he' says: 'This is John Lennon, live, coming to you across the airwaves, except, of course, I'm dead! But that doesn't matter. I'm still here.' Or when he bemoans the fact that he cannot drink in his disembodied state or has to vacate the medium's body 'because it needs to take a leak'.

However, it is impossible to decide if this is merely clever mimicry on a subconscious level. As with psychic art and music, it may be that someone sufficiently skilled might be able to 'tap' a storehouse of creativity and produce imagery in the style of Lennon, rather than actual communications from Lennon himself.

Certainly, Lennon's wives (Cynthia and Yoko Ono) are apparently not happy about such claims. The medium told us that Yoko did not want him to send out his tapes to us. When Jenny Randles tried to get Cynthia to listen to the recordings and comment on how authentic they appeared, she seemed genuinely concerned about people exploiting John, which is understandable.

Of his murder, Tenuto/Lennon is strangely ambivalent. He regards it as a pay-off from a past life and something that was meant to be. Indeed he says: 'I died at just the right time I was supposed to, so I could take the next step.' He is now part of a group (just like those great composers) known unofficially as the 'White Brotherhood'. They are attempting to prove life after death by concerted effort, because in the 1990s the Earth is set to go through a major spiritual transformation.

'When everybody gets the message there won't be any bombs.'

In words spoken long before glasnost and perestroika took hold in the old USSR, Tenuto/Lennon told of 'a lot of turmoil. But there's going to be a lot of miracles too. It's all coming out now. Nobody is covering it up. There's a lot of purging going on.' He speaks of 'evolution and revolution' and warns: 'Get the bloody message, won't you! Do what you came here to do. And when everybody gets the message there won't be any bombs. There won't be any battles and everybody will get what they want. There's an infinite supply of everything.' One aim is to prove his survival in a remarkable way by materialising on live TV! 'I will do that. So mark it down on your little paper there!'

In 1982 he claimed to be channelling music through Julian, his eldest son. Certainly Julian has developed a career based on respected and inspiring music that has a style of its own, but in which some commentators clearly see his father's influence. Of course, that is hardly surprising, and we need see no paranormal factors in what is Julian's own work. For what it is worth, one of his songs, 'The Left Eye' – written after the Tenuto message – has lyrics that reportedly refer to a possible life-after-death bond with his father.

We simply cannot know whether Bill Tenuto is a clever imitator or somehow deluding himself into thinking that his own creativity is actually coming from Lennon. Or does Lennon's spirit really live on?

People can only make their own judgement and decide how to categorise the words from the lips of Bill Tenuto, spoken in a Lennonesque voice with its Liverpudlian accent: 'If you have faith in peace, you have peace. And we will have it. I know that.'

THE EVIDENCE AGAINST

Noted paranormal researcher Arthur Ellison believes that up to one in three people could produce automatic writing if they tried. But – as he put it – 'the results would be mostly gibberish'.

All that is needed is a pen, a blank sheet of paper, somewhere comfortable to rest it on and a chair in which to relax. Let your mind wander, doze into a light state of semi-consciousness and forget all about the experiment. Then see what happens. It may well be that your hand will write what your subconscious mind is telling it to.

Psychologists have known about this possibility ever since split brain surgery was first attempted by Dr Roger Sperry during the 1960s. The human brain consists of two hemispheres – one controlling conscious, rational, deductive, mathematical thought, and the other subconscious, imaginative, artistic imagery. Normally the two are linked by a network of electrical and chemical connections. However, in some patients who suffer from severe problems drastic surgery is performed to sever the link and so confine any problem, such as proneness to severe epileptic attacks, to just one hemisphere.

This can now be done without harm, although it is not without side-effects. Whilst both hemispheres remain undamaged they tend to act independently, almost as if two separate minds were contained in one skull. Show a rude picture to the right eye which feeds into the artistic side of the brain, and it will tell the muscles of the face to smile. Ask the person why he is smiling and he will not be able to answer, because the information has not transferred across to the other side of the brain where language and deductive thought are controlled. Of course, if both eyes see the picture, both sides of the brain receive the information and the individual responds as normal.

In exactly this way the subconscious can feed information it detects into direct human responses – such as writing or painting – which the conscious, rational mind may not know anything about. The outstanding question is whether the information transmitted by the subconscious is brilliant imaginative fantasy or psychic data picked up from elsewhere. On present evidence it seems it could be either.

THE EVIDENCE FOR

What would constitute acceptable evidence of the survival of genius?

If the spirit of the author George Orwell, contacted by Doris Stokes on

The colour drained from the photo-journalist's face. Seemingly Rosemary had just given her a perfect description of the complete stranger's dead mother.

1 January 1984 as some bright spark's idea of a good news story, says that his predictions in the novel *1984* were proved correct. ('Computers are ruling your lives now . . . and it will get worse . . . . You have got to refuse to be counted.'), do we regard that as proof? If William Shakespeare returns through medium Hester Dowden – as he did in 1947 – to answer the age-old riddle by stating that the famous plays were written by *four* people – do we accept this at face value?

It is doubtful that many would answer 'yes'. We would expect more. At least, in the art and music offered by Brown, Manning and others, we do seem to get that. But is it enough? One remarkable story is told by Rosemary Brown.

A German had come to interview her and expressed scepticism at her claims. Mrs Brown calmly announced that Liszt was in the room with them. Thinking quickly, her visitor spoke to 'him' in rapid German, which the medium apparently cannot understand at all. Indeed, she alleges that she occasionally has to remind Liszt of this fact as he tends to lapse into his native tongue when in the throes of composing!

Evidently understanding what the visitor had said, Liszt vanished and returned soon afterwards with a woman. Rosemary Brown explained to her visitor what had happened and described the woman to him. The colour drained from the sceptical photo-journalist's face. Seemingly she had just given a perfect description of the complete stranger's dead mother. He had just asked Liszt to go and bring her – but in words Mrs Brown claims she had no way of comprehending.

If true, then this clearly surpasses any rational explanation and seems only to support the claim that deceased, but somehow surviving personalities, were in that room on that day and only Mrs Brown could see and hear them.

YOUR VERDICT : A SUMMARY

AGAINST SURVIVAL

● There are psychological explanations of where creativity can emerge.

● The products are not widely considered superior, or even equal, to those created by the alleged artist during life.

● Split brain surgery suggests that data from the subconscious can emerge without being recognised as such.

FOR SURVIVAL

● The products of these sensitives are well beyond the normal artistic creativity level which they possess.

● Many experts say that the results are undoubtedly 'in the style' of the supposed originator.

● No substantive evidence has ever been produced to suggest that the mediums involved are anything other than sincere.

● Complete new 'masterpieces' appear on canvas sometimes in minutes, without any preliminary sketching and drawn *in the dark*. This is something much more than a latent talent buried in the subconscious.

GHOSTS

◆

Whenever anyone thinks of life after death there is one subject that instantly springs to mind – *ghosts*. The possibility that we do survive beyond death might best be demonstrated by those stories where the spectres of once living people are supposedly seen after they have 'passed on'. Surely if anything proves that we live on in some form then this must be it? Of course, things are never quite so simple as that.

There are three types of ghosts which need to be considered: spooks in the most traditional sense (once living people who are seen when they are indisputably dead), secondly, 'crisis apparitions' – that is, spectres of someone who is at the point of death, but not actually dead at the moment when seen. But most unexpectedly of all, there are 'living' ghosts – apparitions which to all intents and purposes are the same as other phantoms but with one major problem – the person whose 'ghost' is witnessed is very much alive and well.

It is the existence of these latter two categories of ghostly encounter which has opened up the debate. Once it was assumed that if people were not lying or obviously deluded, then a reliable ghost sighting could only be attributed to the surviving spirit on its way to the afterlife or trapped in a limbo world and confined to a location that it perpetually 'haunts'. The hit British TV sitcom *So Haunt Me* presents this amusing but now rather outmoded concept in a modern guise.

Other possibilities are now in the melting pot, and it is accepted by paranormal researchers that ghosts could be 'real' without them being surviving souls of the dead.

The majority of apparitions are characterised by their solid, three-dimensional 'reality'.

WHAT GHOSTS LOOK LIKE

It is a popular myth that ghosts are semi-transparent entities or even glowing white forms that float in mid-air and can be mimicked by children placing sheets over their heads. Although this is a feature of certain sightings, by far the majority of apparitions are characterised by their solid, three-dimensional 'reality'. Many witnesses claim that the spectre they saw was initially mistaken for an ordinary person and only recognised for what it was when it did something 'supernatural', like disappearing, or was later identified as someone who was known to be dead.

An interesting account of this nature involved Mr F. H. Whiting, who runs a hotel in the West Country. In early 1981 his wife died from a protracted illness. Then in September of that year the following occurred.

Mr Whiting was sitting gazing at the floor with his mind idling (probably of great relevance, as we shall see). He suddenly realised that somebody was standing in front of him. When he looked up, he saw that it was his dead wife. Her form was 'perfect' but she wore clothing that he had

The ghost of Mr Whiting's dead wife disappeared from view in a most extraordinary way. The apparition split into a matrix of oscillating pieces which gradually faded away, leaving an empty space.

never seen her wear in life, and she seemed somewhat upset. None the less she walked around Mr Whiting, put her hand on his shoulder and then kissed him on the forehead. He felt both the hand and her lips.

Throughout this she said nothing, but then her solidity began to alter in an altogether novel and untypical way. As he vividly put it: 'She went into one big matrix made up of pieces that were oscillating. There seemed to be three sizes. The small ones gradually faded away, then the larger ones and finally the very big ones. This was not hurried, but they just slowly drifted away, and ultimately left the space clear again. I could not see through any of this whilst it was happening. It was solid.'

SEEING THINGS THAT ARE NOT THERE

There – seated on a chest – was an absolutely clear image of a girl wearing a grey dress and an old-fashioned cap.

The sceptic's most common interpretation for such cases is that they occur on the edge of sleep. A detailed investigation conveyed to us by Norman Hatt, of the Redhill and Reigate Phenomena Research Group in Surrey, demonstrates this.

The incident occurred in late 1986, in an old Victorian house in Reigate. The occupants had spent a quarter of a century in the building without incident. One night the wife of the family was awoken from sleep by a 'loud rumble' like a heavy farm wagon, plus a 'tinkling' noise like glass rods knocking against one another. The noise was without obvious cause, although a milk float is one option. As this faded, the woman clearly heard sobbing in the corner of the bedroom.

In order to see that part of the semi-darkened room the witness had to sit up firmly in bed, dispelling any thought that this was a dream. There – seated on a chest – was an absolutely clear image of a girl aged around sixteen, wearing a grey dress with white puffed sleeves and an old-fashioned cap. She seemed to be in the uniform of a scullery maid and was absolutely solid in form. So complete was the apparition that the bare arms of the girl stood out noticeably. Her face expressed sadness, but it was not oppressive – more as if she had just been reprimanded and was a little put out.

Interestingly, and in keeping with most other cases, the witness did not feel great fear. It is as if this normal emotional response is suppressed. Instead she felt sorry and wanted to try to help the dismal figure. Curiously, but again as commonly found in other cases, the woman never seems to have considered the girl to be an intruder, but instinctively sensed that she was a ghost.

The apparition disappeared when it seemed to become aware of the witness. It climbed upwards at an angle of forty-five degrees, and then 'melted' into the wall and ceiling.

Certainly the house was large, and may have had servants in its early days. But why would such an apparition be 'trapped' here? Norman Hatt told us he was interested in applying the theory of hypnagogic imagery to this case as a possible solution. We discuss this more fully later in the chapter.

JUST AN ILLUSION?

In the case of the scullery maid in the Reigate house, Norman Hatt was intrigued by an old painting of a woman in an old-fashioned dress on the wall in more or less the position where the 'ghost' was sitting. Although unconvinced by the idea that this was the ghost, he wondered if the picture might have somehow precipitated an optical illusion.

We have certainly known a number of cases where sincere witnesses have reported that they have filmed 'elves' in tree foliage. When these are examined and the 'little people' are pointed out to us, all that can be seen is a combination of shadows that vaguely resembles a strange entity. It seems that human imagination and the desire to see order within chaos has resulted in the subconscious mind of the percipient transforming mundane stimuli into far more exotic ones. In fact it is by this very process that we all see shapes in clouds, especially when we allow our mind to wander.

This is something that occurs in the paranormal right across the spectrum of phenomena. We have investigated many UFO reports where the witness was adamant that he or she saw a 'spaceship', and drew it in graphic detail. Afterwards, it was proven they had seen nothing more than a balloon or the full moon.

Recently there has been controversy over a 'face' that appears on some NASA shots of the surface of Mars. Believers claim this must be a huge sphinx placed there by extraterrestrials to attract our attention. Sceptics say that we read this non-existent pattern into a combination of light and shade with the help of a healthy injection of wishful thinking.

There is also a classic photograph of the Loch Ness monster (see p.96). Can you spot the long, sinewy body thrashing about? Now look at the different interpretation of this photograph we offer in the caption that accompanies it. Without deciding which conclusion is correct – if either – you can immediately see how a 'monster' can emerge from a still photograph which, at the very least, is open to a different evaluation if looked at in a slightly different way. The 'monster' may be at least as much a product of our mind as it is of reality.

These are all examples of how optical illusions operate in the

The long sinewy body of the Loch Ness Monster threshing through the water. At least that is how this photograph is usually presented. But look closely. Do you now see a dog swimming along with a stick in its mouth, blurred due to motion? Once you do see this you can never interpret the picture any other way. Whatever the truth (monster, dog or neither) this is a perfect illustration of how the brain sees what it expects to see. Our perception of reality – even in a photograph – depends upon processes taking place inside our mind.

context of the supernatural. We should not be at all surprised if some ghosts owe their origin to this mental process rather than to a paranormal mystery.

AT THE POINT OF DEATH

The traditional view of ghostly encounters is that they represent spirits of the dead somehow trapped in our world, as explained at the beginning of this chapter. However, ghosts can also appear at a time when death has not yet taken place.

In one case at Wallasey, on the Wirral, in 1970, a man and wife had just climbed into bed and turned out the light when they both saw 'hovering at [their] side a head, body, but no face . . .'. The woman screamed, but her husband calmed her down by assuring her that he could see it too. As soon as they switched the light on it disappeared.

This incident occurred on a Monday night. On the Tuesday the woman dreamed that her grandmother had died. She dismissed this as just a dream, but on the Wednesday a caller arrived with a letter for them which announced that her grandmother had indeed passed away – at what appears to have been the same time that they both saw the apparition.

Most people who believe in life after death would say of this 'crisis apparition' that it shows an attempt by the spirit of the grandmother to say goodbye to her granddaughter. But is it quite as straightforward as that?

Noted medium Rosalind Heywood told a fascinating story of how in 1918 she was in the Aegean whilst her lover was in Paris. One night she saw him appear, as large as life, in her tent at precisely the same moment (as they later discovered) that he 'saw' her in his room. Neither assumed the other to be a ghost, believing at first that the person was really present and had travelled to be with their partner. When it was realised that this was not so, they wondered if they had each hallucinated out of a longing to be together.

Yet why – and how – had they shared such a 'hallucination' in that one special moment of empathy? It seems that an emotional link is significant in such cases, and possibly it is a necessary requirement for an apparition to occur. If the ghost is a stranger, rather than a loved one, does the percipient need to 'tune in' to the emotional wavelength of a real objective entity?

Oscar-winning actor and TV star Cliff Robertson reports a not dissimilar experience. It occurred when he was a young man playing on stage in New Hampshire just after World War II.

The actor had been raised by his grandmother, who was then in La Jolla, California, some three thousand miles away. At about 3a.m. (eastern time) Robertson was asleep when he had a vivid dream in which his grandmother appeared; she told him her life was ending, but he should not grieve as she was ready to go and at peace. He pleaded with her not to go, and after a protracted debate she agreed to try to stay.

The actor awoke in a sweat from the nightmare, but there was no phone from which to call California. Instead he paced up and down, unable to get the dream from his mind. At 6.30a.m., a telegram was delivered. It came from an aunt in California and reported that his grandmother had been taken very ill at midnight (which – given the three-hour zone difference – was just at the point of his dream). She was not expected to survive – could he fly back west?

Robertson went into the nearest town to phone La Jolla. He learned that his grandmother had rallied after the telegram was sent. She was now through the critical period and seemed to be growing in strength. The doctor was surprised, but she did pull through.

Evidently the same sort of 'bonding' occurred here but, possibly because Robertson was deeply asleep, the mind-to-mind link was able to convey more specific information. One can readily see how, if he had been awake, perhaps with his mind 'idling', the urgency of the situation would have probably required something dramatic to take place. A simple 'message' in one's head would be likely to be written off as imagination.

If there is a mechanism in our subconscious capable of detecting a psychic 'signal' from someone else, and it had to get through to the conscious mind, which was awake and not docile, how would it do it? Would the actor have had a realistic vision of his grandmother superimposed on the background of his room – so vivid that he would have had to take note and ask himself what it meant?

It seems a fair supposition, based on the growing evidence that this might be how it works. Does that mean that ghosts are just extreme forms of vivid hallucination – 'messages' picked up by the subconscious mind and visualised when an urgent 'kick' is needed to alert the waking self? On the other hand, crisis apparitions might demonstrate that we are indeed capable of leaving our bodies and crossing vast distances.

THE LAST GOODBYE

Sheila Mendoza is a charge nurse who works in the intensive care unit wards of a large hospital in Texas. She has watched many people die, and admits that she has become rather hardened to the process. However, nothing prepared her for one night in 1982 when the most remarkable event that she has ever witnessed was to take place.

Sheila was on night shift, paying special attention to a man who had been in hospital for some days. Although under close care, he was not thought to be in any danger nor very seriously ill.

At about 8p.m. he began talking very lucidly about a loved one whom he longed to see. Sheila could not tell who this person was, but it was obvious that the man had not seen her in many years and never expected to do so again. The impression is that she must have passed away some years before. The man then slipped from this mumbling into a restless sleep.

At about 9.30 he began to talk about this person again, and his vital signs also began to fail. Fearing the worst, more medical staff were brought in; but the man slid into a comatose state.

Then the patient became wonderfully alert, as some people do very near the end. He looked to one side, staring into a vacant space. As time went by it was clear he could see someone there whom nobody else in the room could see. Suddenly, his face lit up like a beacon. He was staring and smiling at what was clearly a long-lost friend, his eyes so full of love and serenity that it was hard for those around him not to be overcome by tears.

Sheila says: 'There was no mistake. Someone had come for him at the last to show him the way.'

Minutes later the man died, in a state of sublime peace and happiness.

From that day Sheila Mendoza looked upon her dying patients with new eyes and dignity. Like so many others who care for the terminally ill, she had witnessed that precious moment when life slips all ties to a battered, broken body and moves on towards who knows where. Whether death is an extinction or a transition, Nurse Mendoza saw in the experience of this one man that it is not a frightening or sad occasion but a remarkable journey embarked upon in tranquillity and near intoxicating joy.

GHOSTS THAT FORETELL

It is not difficult to accept that ghosts can have mundane explanations on some occasions, especially if a witness merely sees a strange figure in a darkened room when emerging from an altered state of consciousness (be it sleep or reverie). Rather more difficult to account for are situations when the ghost seemingly possesses knowledge that the witness could not logically have access to – as with Cliff Robertson. This is illustrated by a decidedly weird case from Folkestone, Kent in 1964.

Mr Milton and another teenager both joined the Merchant Navy at the same time. While his friend was still on board ship, Milton returned home on leave. One night, whilst sitting in the outside brick-built toilet in the yard of his house, he was suddenly confronted by a flash of light and the figure of a Zulu warrior in full dress!

The terrified sailor ran indoors and was greeted by his mother, who accused him – not surprisingly – of being drunk. However, later that night as he went to bed, and was in the act of switching out the light, the warrior reappeared. Mr Milton cried out, asking what the phantom wanted, and immediately switched the light back on. There was nothing there. A few days later a letter arrived to inform Mr Milton that his friend had died after falling overboard off the coast of Africa.

The question here is: just exactly what was this apparition? We might conjecture that the spirit of a Zulu was trying to warn Mr Milton of the impending (or perhaps already occurring) tragedy. Or – on a somewhat more oblique approach – that Mr Milton picked up the image of his friend

He was suddenly confronted by a flash of light and the figure of a Zulu warrior in full dress!

being drowned off the coast of Africa, and that his mind attempted to relay that information in the visually dramatic form of something plainly linked with that continent.

Of course, the sceptical approach is to assume that this was just a hallucination and that its form was unrelated to the death of the young man. Either coincidence or subsequent colouring of the memory in an unconscious and unintended manner made the 'ghost' appear more relevant.

LIVING GHOSTS

Theories which attempt to explain ghostly apparitions as mind projections do seem necessary for the less straightforward cases. For example, Leonard Toohill recalls a fascinating experience he had in London in 1976. He was with a friend with whom he was trying to discuss a business deal, but she was clearly distracted. He met her at a dance, remarked on the blue dress she was wearing, but noted: 'She also seemed very strange, as though her body was there but her soul was miles away.'

The next day, as he passed the place where she worked, Leonard felt a very powerful emotion, 'as if I was in contact with eternity'. Brushing this off, he returned home, but instead of going inside he stood on his front doorstep, gazing idly at the sky and pondering. Again, he was in that state of reverie which seems so fundamental to certain paranormal experiences. Then it happened.

He suddenly saw it change into a Picasso-style 'broken' picture...

'I glanced down, and there to my astonishment, walking up the pavement past my house, was a semi-transparent figure of this lady. I knew immediately I was seeing a ghost, although I had never seen anything like it in my life before. It was certainly recognisable as her. Very distinct was the blue frock she had been wearing the day before . . . but it could *not* have actually been her, as she did not know where I lived, and I could see the houses through it.'

Leonard felt awed by this, but not a bit frightened. The somewhat anomalous reaction he reports is that he was concerned for her wellbeing. She simply disappeared.

Two days later, at around midnight, he was looking at a magazine with a woman's face on the cover when he suddenly saw it change into a Picasso-style 'broken' picture. He looked away, then looked back, but the effect was the same. He rationalised it as a hallucination, but even so he could not override his perceptions.

The following day he called a mutual friend and learned that the woman had had an acute mental breakdown in which she had started to receive a flood of mental communications in her mind. This had begun on the Friday when he had seen her apparition, and she was taken into hospital at about the time of his magazine cover experience. The woman was not dead, and did recover. The 'living ghost' in this case may perhaps have been a telepathic image that Leonard conjured up after detecting her distress, or perhaps under pressure she did in fact leave her body.

A RATHER JEALOUS GHOST

If we survive death, do we still have human emotions in the afterlife? The experience of Diana Christianson from Essex may well suggest we do. This experience defies a subjective explanation because some of the phenomena were shared by the woman's second husband, and the manifestations spilled out into other parts of the building.

A bird seemed to fly over her head as she lay in bed, although no bird was in the room.

The trouble started in 1967 when her husband Len died suddenly from cancer whilst he was still in his thirties. He was cremated and his ashes brought to rest in her home. But they did not rest in peace. As soon as Diana made the funeral arrangements, things began to happen. At first these were minor incidents. There would be the sound of furniture moving in the dead of night. A bird seemed to fly over her head as she lay in bed, although no bird was in the room. Then the apparitions arrived.

A white glow emerged from the wardrobe and began to drift towards her before disappearing. Mrs Christianson was terrified. Another time she saw an amorphous white figure kneeling at the foot of her bed.

It did not occur to Diana that her husband might still be present. But one day something happened to change her mind. During life Len had possessed a habit of sneaking up behind her and standing on the bathroom scales when she was weighing herself – this made her appear to weigh far more than she did. Some months after Len's death the same thing happened unexpectedly. She was standing on the scales and the pointer began to climb up and up until it reached an impossible level.

'Stop it, Len!' she cried aloud. The scales returned to normal and she was never bothered in this way again.

The episodes were growing so frequent that it became a worry to the family. Her brother suggested that keeping the ashes in the house was possibly the cause of the problem. It would be better if Diana were to bury them. Reluctantly she agreed that it might be for the best, and a burial ceremony was organised. Perhaps now both she and her late husband would coexist in peace.

Looking optimistically ahead, Diana remarried in 1972. She had put the past behind her and was looking forward to a new life. Unfortunately, things were not to work out quite as expected.

She had not been married for very long and her new husband was unfamiliar with the strange things that had plagued the house. As they slept one night, their bed began to rise into the air as if pushed up by a gigantic balloon inflating underneath it.

Diana and her husband awoke in horror. But it was less of a shock to the former Mrs Christianson, who sensed what was going on. Len was back – and it seemed as if he was not altogether keen on her new relationship!

'What is happening?' Diana was asked through gasps of astonishment. The bed slowly lowered itself down on to the bedroom floor.

'Don't worry,' she explained calmly. 'There's nothing to be frightened of. It's just my first husband. He comes back sometimes.'

Their bed began to rise into the air as if pushed up by a gigantic balloon inflating underneath it.

Later that day Diana arranged to meet her new husband to do the shopping, but when she arrived in town he did not turn up. With mounting apprehension she returned home. As soon as she turned the key she knew what she would find. Her husband had left. He could not cope with sharing his life with the jealous ghost of his wife's first love!

Diana has since remarried again and things have become happier, but she explained that life may never be quite normal: 'There is still a presence in my house, especially the bedroom. My eldest daughter never comes round because she says my place is haunted and I should have it exorcised. One day a religious picture which my husband had bought fell off the shelf and landed in front of the front room window. I called the police because I thought someone had been trying to get in.'

Did the police help? It seems not. After she had explained her experiences they politely advised Diana that this was a job for ghost, not crime, busters.

BEDROOM VISITORS

It should be obvious by now that most ghostly encounters occur to individuals who are in a state of altered consciousness. By far the most common state is that of being on the edge of sleep. As this occurs more often in the bedroom, apparitions in this context are termed 'bedroom visitors'.

In this condition, the stranglehold we normally have on our waking perceptions is relaxed. This might allow genuine visitors from beyond to manifest to our senses, or it could mean that the entire affair is purely internal. This latter assumption is challenged in the few cases where more than one person is witness to the phenomenon. Often though, a witness awakes to discover a figure standing at the bottom of the bed. Despite the fact that he or she is in pitch darkness, the witness is able to describe in detail what the figure looked like. Even more incongruously, there are many examples of witnesses unable to awake their slumbering partners lying next to them in bed while the experience unfolds. Here is a typical bedroom visitor experience.

SPIRITUAL HEALING?

Tommy Steele is a famous singer, dancer and actor, naturally gifted and a favourite of children across several decades. His musicals, such as *Half a Sixpence*, have entertained millions. Yet long ago he had an experience which confounds all understanding.

At fifteen Tommy ran away to sea and joined the Merchant Navy. But he was not to serve on a ship for long. He became very ill – so ill, in fact, that he had to be flown back to England right away. In a London hospital the terrible illness of spinal meningitis was diagnosed. It did not seem that he could survive for long, and his family were called to his bedside.

By morning he was still fighting for life, paralysed from the waist down but clinging on. The doctors suggested that he be left alone. Screens were put around the bed and young Tommy was allowed to rest in peace.

As he lay in a semi-conscious state the teenager became aware of a young child's laughter elsewhere in the room. Then a brightly coloured ball sailed over the screens and landed on the bedclothes just out of Tommy's reach. Not wishing to deny the child his toy, Tommy summoned up the energy to reach out and grab the ball and throw it back over the screen. Moments later it flew right back again, this time landing even further from his grasp.

Exhausted, with his head supported on the pillow, Tommy made the effort to reach the ball and throw it back one more time. Shortly afterward it happened yet again. And again. In fact it occurred several times over the next hour or so.

On each occasion great willpower and energy were needed to give the ball back to the unseen child. Tommy always managed to do this, and, almost without realising it, found that he was gaining strength and feeling better in the process. He could now move his legs.

The medical staff and Tommy's family were amazed. The fever was subsiding and the paralysis easing. He would now pull through.

As the doctors tried to understand the near miraculous cure, Tommy explained that they should thank the young boy who was his companion

Tommy Steele, the celebrated entertainer and movie star, who tells a remarkable story of his fight for survival and the implication of a possible life after death of a loved one.

in the ward. If he had not kept throwing the ball on to his bed, then he would never have found the strength to recover. This was what had saved his life.

'What young boy?' he was asked.

The screens were cast aside. And, of course, there was no young boy in the room. Nor had there ever been.

Baffled, Tommy described the ball that he had seen. His parents' eyes shone with sudden recognition.

'Don't you remember?' they asked.

The ball was exactly like one that Tommy had given to his younger brother Rodney as a Christmas present. The boy had loved it. But it was the last present Tommy had ever given him, for Rodney had died tragically soon afterwards at only three years of age.

What happened here? Had Tommy Steele's subconscious mind conjured up this image to give him the will to fight towards a full recovery? That is one valid way of looking at this story.

Of course, another possibility is that Rodney's spirit was repaying his brother's kindness with the precious gift of life.

AN INNOCENT CHILD

Neal Anderson's family were struck by tragedy in 1972 when his five-year-old sister died of a sudden illness. They were all devastated by the snatching of this young innocent life but, owing to a religious quarrel, the paternal grandfather would not attend the funeral when it was held in Bedfordshire. This created an even deeper rift within the family, which did not diminish over the ensuing decade.

In 1982 Neal's paternal grandmother died. Because he could never forgive her husband his act of using a child's death as a weapon in an argument Neal refused to go to the funeral, but he felt very guilty afterwards.

A few nights later, still nursing this guilt, Neal awoke from a deep sleep to see an image of his grandmother in the bedroom. She looked fit and well and was smiling. She told him that she understood and forgave his actions and that he ought not to worry about the incident.

Not surprisingly, Neal argued with himself that this was just a dream conjured up by his mind to exorcise his guilty feelings. However, it had seemed much more vivid and real than any normal dream and completely removed all his worries about the incident. Yet there was still that nagging doubt that perhaps it was just his over-active imagination.

But then his mother shared something that she had never told Neal before. In 1972, only a few weeks after his young sister had died, Neal's brother had come home from school with a matter-of-fact announcement. He said that he had seen 'Tricia'. When asked to explain which Tricia he meant he replied, 'our Tricia.' They had played together for a while.

His mother stared at the boy, unable to take in what he had been saying, but it was obvious that to this six-year-old there had been nothing remotely strange about seeing his sister. He knew she had 'gone away' to 'Heaven', but had probably not been able to grasp that this meant he could never see her again. And so he had seen her again.

The matter was broached with the local minister. He confirmed the apparent honesty of the boy and told his parents to accept it, saying that nobody could prove it did not happen. Twenty years later, Neal's now adult brother still insists he was visited by his sister shortly after her death.

HYPNAGOGIC IMAGERY

There is a stage that we all go through when falling asleep and when waking from sleep. During this stage various forms of imagery that are not part of any dream can often be experienced, but usually this is fragile and gets forgotten when full consciousness returns. The imagery may involve distorted human figures and is described as very realistic by about 5 per cent of the population, according to research carried out by psychologists.

These stages are termed 'hypnagogic' (falling asleep) and 'hypnopompic' (awakening) imagery. The mind is neither awake nor asleep, but resting in a neutral state. Some dream researchers feel it may allow stored up images deep within the subconscious to overlap into the real world environment of a bedroom and appear in a very vivid way. As a result a 'being' might seem to form.

Hypnagogic imagery (this term is usually applied to describe both states) is more than simple hallucination. It is also distinct from sleeping dreams. The imagery is never shared by others who may be in the same room at the time, but can form part of a possible answer to the bedroom visitor anomaly. Some statistical findings were tabulated as far back as 1925 by a researcher named Mrs F. E. Leaning.

Almost two-thirds of percipients questioned had not recognised the hypnagogic imagery as familiar. Virtually every witness remarked on the life-like nature of the images. Most were of figures and landscapes and triggered extreme emotions. Many percipients had no control of the imagery, although a small percentage claimed otherwise, akin to the manipulation exerted by lucid dreamers.

THE LIVING OR LUCID DREAM

One teenage girl told dream researchers at the Oxford Paraphysical Laboratories of a fascinating experience. She dreamed that she had woken up and gone to school one morning. As the event unravelled, she was absolutely certain of its reality. However, a loud banging noise 'heard' on the school bus suddenly shocked her into 'awakening'. She found that she was back at home in bed. Bemused, the girl got up and repeated her routine to get ready for school, eventually travelling there and reaching the school yard. Then someone threw a book at her in a playful manner. The blow made her suddenly appear back in bed, and she was waking up yet again!

These experiences are called 'false awakenings', and approximately 35 per cent of the population report having had them at some time or another. In fact they are common forms of what are called lucid dreams, which in their full-blown status are reported by only about 10 per cent of people (women slightly more often than men).

'Lucid dreaming is like starring in your own film with limitless special effects.'

In a lucid dream the scenery is so vivid and realistic that the person mistakes it for reality. There are usually smells, tactile impressions and all the normal sensations to add to the mundanity of a dream. Yet at some point the percipient recognises that it *is* a dream, and at that stage is usually shocked into awakening. However, if he or she does not awaken right away the lucid dream proper unfolds and the person is now literally unleashed within a magical dreamscape. They can control what happens, make themselves fly. Indeed it is like starring within your own film with limitless special effects. Throughout all of this the vivid realism of the lucid dream is its most remarkable feature.

Lucid dreams have been studied in depth at Oxford by Celia Green. More recently a team consisting of London psychiatrist Dr Morton Schatzman, Dr Keith Hearne, a noted dream specialist, and Dr Peter Fenwick, an expert on the workings of the brain from St Thomas's Hospital in London, have devised a method whereby a person who is prone to fairly frequent lucid dreams (as are about 2 per cent of the population) can signal the outside world.

The technique involves electrodes attached to the eyelids of the 'dreamer'. As soon as the dreamer realises that he or she is in a lucid state, the subject tries to move them and this triggers an electrical signal. When this was first successfully tested in 1975 Dr Hearne likened the message from a dreaming consciousness to the receipt of a communiqué on Earth that was sent from another galaxy. Attempts are now under way to allow the dreamer to convey more detailed information about the totally realistic and yet completely illusionary world within which the subject is operating, or even to let the experimenters impose some outside control over what takes place.

That the borderline between dreams and waking consciousness is much less concrete than was once imagined may suggest solutions to the mysteries of the bedroom visitor experience. However, can it always do so? There may be occasions where, whatever state of mind the person may be in, information was channelled by the experience which was beyond any obvious means of communication. Then something apparently supernatural takes place.

SAYING GOODBYE

Mrs Davies lived on the Welsh coast near the holiday resorts of Rhyl and Llandudno. On the night of 6 August 1982 she was awoken by a piercing scream, which sounded like a young child crying out. As this noise thrust her into full alertness the bedroom door burst open with terrific ferocity. The wind could not have caused it, she insists and their cat would not have had the strength. Mrs Davies climbed out of bed, but all was now quiet. The clock revealed that the time was 12.50a.m. Her husband had remained undisturbed. Shaking off the experience, she returned to sleep.

At 6a.m. the telephone rang. Receiving calls at such an hour always brings a slight chill: good news can wait; bad news normally cannot.

Mrs Davies followed her husband down the stairs and watched him pick up the receiver. It was a call from the holiday village camp site where he served as a warden.

'Oh, God – no!' she heard him say. Then he put down the phone and told her, 'There has been a terrible fire.'

An hour later her husband returned from the camp site in a state of deep shock. One of the tents housing families had caught fire during the night. Two young children had been trapped and burned to death. Even worse, it involved people they knew – a family that had visited the town every year, and which the couple had befriended.

As the news slowly began to sink in, and that dreadful feeling of uselessness that comes with a bereavement gradually emerged, a few things came into Mrs Davies's mind.

She had clearly heard the scream of a child in the bedroom just a few hours before. There was nobody present in the house to make such a noise. The door that had been flung open in the middle of the night was also odd. How had it occurred? Right beside the door was a photograph on the dressing

The bedroom door burst open with terrific ferocity. It was as if in their moment of departure from this life the two children had paid one last call on their friends.

table. It was a picture of Mr Davies that had been taken by the father of the children who had died.

'What time did the fire happen?' Mrs Davies asked.

Her husband was able to find out. It had been 12.50a.m., exactly when the scream had split the night and the door had been flung open.

It was as if in their moment of departure from this life the two children had paid one last call on their friends – perhaps drawn by the photograph that had been taken by their father. Even if we were to rationalise and say that Mrs Davies merely had a lucid dream or experienced some form of hypnagogic imagery, that nevertheless fails to resolve such a highly unlikely 'coincidence'.

PHOTOS OF GHOSTS

The objectivity of ghosts might also be suggested by photographs. It is true that photos of ghosts do exist. There are a number of them snapped in old churches and large stately homes, for example, where an image has simply turned up on the film when it is processed. Usually nothing was seen by the photographer at the time.

One always has to be wary. It is possible that 'fogging' on the negative may look vaguely like a human figure. Whilst we have come across this effect on several occasions, there are sufficient puzzling photographic cases which require a more esoteric explanation. The image is quite obviously a figure.

Several photographs spring to mind which remain puzzling to this day. A figure unknowingly captured on film in Arundel church in West Sussex is clearly not a fault. Better still is the unambiguous image of a ten-foot-tall hooded figure which appeared in a photograph taken by the vicar of Newby in Yorkshire near the altar of his church. The picture has been scientifically examined and yet no rational explanation can be suggested. Another remarkable photograph, clearly showing a figure, was unwittingly produced by another clergyman.

On 19 June 1966 the Reverend and Mrs R. W. Hardy from White Rock, British Columbia, on holiday in England, were visiting a stately home called the Queen's House at Greenwich in South London. They took a photograph of the Tulip Staircase, designed by Inigo Jones in 1629. Back home in Canada, when the film was processed the couple were astounded to see a shrouded figure clutching the stair-rail. Examination of the negatives by the British Ghost Club ruled out double exposure. Kodak confirmed that the negative had not been tampered with, and that no obvious trickery had been employed.

Further examination showed that both hands were *left* hands, leading the investigators to conclude that there were *two* figures on the stairs – one pursuing the other. The couple were adamant there was no one on the staircase at the time. Ghost hunter Peter Underwood said it was the most remarkable photograph he had seen in half a century of investigation.

In 1964 Anglia Television filmed a documentary at a reputedly haunted house in Norfolk. When it was transmitted, several people contacted the studios to say they had seen a 'ghost' in the background during one scene.

Photo taken by the vicar of Newby church, Yorkshire, clearly showing an extremely tall hooded figure. This picture has been extensively examined and seems to exhibit a genuine ghost.

A phantom figure in the pews at Eastry church in Kent taken by a bank manager in 1956. It is thought by some to be the ghost of an old vicar who had been seen in the church before.

Far right: A priest or monk turned up on this photograph of the altar at St Nicholas's church in Arundel, Sussex taken by a local lawyer in 1940. Nothing was seen at the time.

On re-running the film, researchers found nothing. But when it was transmitted again, more viewers called in to confirm that they had seen a monk, an old woman or a hooded skull. On careful inspection it turned out to be a patch of damp on the stone wall in the background, which had faint human shapes in it. Imagination plus expectation did the rest.

In cases where film records what the eye does not see, it has been suggested that ghosts can shift into a frequency range such as infra-red which is beyond the range of the eye, but which can still affect film emulsion. However, this is a long way from being established.

In 1983, the Association for the Scientific Study of Anomalous Phenomena (ASSAP) received ghost photographs from around the UK. Jenny Randles collated them for study by Dr Vernon Harrison, a professional photographic analyst. More than a dozen cases were studied. Harrison said, 'I live in hope', but added, 'I could not accept any of them as genuine.'

Amongst them was another damp patch on the wall, 'seen' as a ghost; an 'ectoplasm' form that turned out to be the camera strap out of focus, dangling in front of the lens; and a semi-transparent full-figure ghost photographed in a castle on Jersey by a startled couple. This looked promising. Unfortunately, after analysis it was found that they had simply filmed the reflection of a waxworks model on the sheet of glass through which they were taking pictures.

Nevertheless there are a very few cases that do not seem to fall into these categories and which still defy explanation. Given the number of cameras that people own, surely ghost photography should be growing more commonplace? In fact it seems to be happening less often than it did. Why? Could it be that today's technically advanced equipment is less likely to allow faults like fogging to occur? For those who believe there is a grand overall plan by an omnipresent creator, perhaps apparitions are just camera-shy. Are we meant to be tantalised by the evidence for life after death, but not wholly convinced until the time is right?

THE EVIDENCE AGAINST

It is likely that on at least some occasions ghosts owe as much to the percipient as they do to any hypothetical visitation from the realm of the dead. At times they may have their roots in optical illusions or anomalies of perception. The will to believe can often provide its own persuasive evidence.

Extremely realistic hallucinations can occur, as recent studies have shown. Morton Schatzman studied 'Ruth', an American woman who was plagued by the frequent images of her father. If the man had been dead, her spontaneous sightings and all other sensory experiences – which included touch and smell – would have been regarded as a bedroom visitor type of ghost encounter. But the man was alive and well and living in the USA throughout all Ruth's experiences.

Dr Schatzman was able to help Ruth control this ability to 'create' realistic hallucinations. Eventually she was able to produce three-dimensional talking images of other people. She could even create a second Dr Schatzman to sit alongside the doctor in his office, and she found it hard to tell real from fake.

In an experiment with Dr Peter Fenwick, Ruth conjured up the hallucination of her father and made it stand in front of flashing lights which were tuned to interact with her brain rhythms. The eyes would, of course, still see the lights unless something real and solid – such as an actual person – blocked them from reaching her senses. If the eyes *did* see the flashing lights, Ruth's brain waves would react. This would demonstrate that her conviction that she saw nothing, because her father's image was standing in the way, was wrong.

Intriguingly, the woman's brain reacted as if it really was no longer seeing the flashing lights. It was exactly as if a real person was blocking out the light rays, despite the fact that nothing but a hallucination seen by Ruth alone was 'standing' there. When asked to get her apparition to turn on a light when the room was in total darkness, she reported being able to do this successfully, and 'saw' the room as if illuminated. Yet she could not now read a newspaper or a book, because her perception that there was light could not overcome the physical reality.

These tests show that the brain is capable of 'seeing' something that is not there in such a realistic way that it can fool certain perceptual responses. However, it does not allow impossible things to take place, proving that nothing more than a hallucination is involved. Given these facts, there is reason to suspect that apparitions could at least at times be very vivid hallucinations.

FANTASY-PRONE PERSONALITIES

Psychologists use the term 'fantasy-prone personalities' to account for some 4–8 per cent of the population who have such vivid imaging capabilities that they find it hard to distinguish reality from imagined perceptions. The term was coined in 1983 by American researchers Theodore Barber and Sheryl Wilson, who found that such people fall into very distinct categories. They had a very rich dream life – dreaming lucidly, and dreaming

She could even create a second Dr Schatzman to sit alongside the doctor in his office, and she found it hard to tell real from fake.

of flying more often than most. They can easily be put into a deep hypnotic state, tend to be very gifted artistically, and as children often have detailed and credible imaginary playmates, who remain as realistic companions for unusually long periods.

There is significant evidence that these people have more psychic experiences throughout their lives. As many as 92 per cent claimed this – three times more than groups of non-fantasy-prone personalities. Almost half who have been studied report that, when driving alone, they have had to stop the car because they saw a figure on the road which ultimately proved not to be real. Quite often they had regarded these figures as ghosts. Paranormal experiences within the bedroom were also found to be very common.

But they are not suffering from any pathological condition; indeed, they are often of above-average intelligence. During 1986 and 1987 Steven Lynn of Ohio State University and Judith Rhue of the University of Toledo in Ohio reported that many such people had either been very lonely as children or had suffered severe physical punishment in one form or another. That appears to have been the case with Ruth, given her clinical history as published by Dr Schatzman. It is speculated that the individual develops extreme visual creativity as an 'escape mechanism' from the horrors of physical life, thus allowing an inner focusing or distraction to help him or her through.

Does this mean that those who perceive apparitions are merely highly imaginative, and cannot distinguish reality from imagination as most of us believe that we can? Entertainer, researcher and admitted psychic Michael Bentine told us that he thinks imagination and psychic experience could simply be one faculty: 'Someone will say to me: "It's just your imagination!" I agree, of course it is. They should realise that imagination is the ability to create images or integrate images from memory or impressions you have received from *elsewhere*.'

An interesting experiment in Canada involved a group of sitters who met regularly for a year and, as explained in their book *Conjuring Up Philip*, invented a cavalier phantom which they gradually came to know very well. So realistic was their creation that it eventually took on a life of its own (see Chapter 3), manifesting paranormal effects such as table raps.

In 1970 researcher Frank Smyth, whilst working on a magazine dealing with myth and folklore, decided to fabricate a ghost. He made up a complex life history for the spook of a clergyman from a house in London's docklands. He then wrote it up as factual, and sat back waiting to see what happened.

Within a few years many cases had been reported of people who had

Entertainer Michael Bentine who has had many natural psychic experiences and has written eloquently about such phenomena.

seen the ghost, describing it as an old man in clerical clothing. When Smyth admitted the fraud, stories still poured in from people who claimed they had really seen the spectre. One even tried to convince him that he only *thought* he had made it up – that a *real* ghost had been in contact with his mind.

Psychologist Gareth Rees, who believes that 'psychic energy' is the explanation for supernatural healing, is sceptical of standard interpretations of ghosts for just that reason. He told us: 'There has always been a better explanation. We all experience many different states of consciousness, and very often the person on the receiving end does not realise their change of state.' He confirms that 'an awful lot' of ghost encounters 'occur in the period between sleeping and waking. Of course, you cannot exclude the possibility that this [state of consciousness] is the best one in which to see a ghost.'

However, he finds it more likely that in such circumstances of reverie the mind is 'turned inwards' and visualises imagery from the subconscious. This is in opposition to more normal waking states, when it is 'tuned outwards', perceiving only the objective world. One of the reasons for his scepticism is that apparitions are always wearing clothes. Why? he asks.

'It seems very unlikely that when somebody dies they are going to be equipped with a ghost body with clothes or even ghost ornaments. So when somebody sees a ghost it is unlikely to be the traditional idea of the person from the dead visiting them. We have a great tendency to see things in terms of what we already know. So if somebody comes across something they have never experienced before, they are likely to see it in terms of a human figure. There may indeed be something behind it that is genuinely paranormal, but we have no need to believe that it is what the person ends up seeing.'

THE EVIDENCE FOR

During the nineteenth century the Society for Psychical Research conducted a census of reported hallucinations. In 1905, J. G. Piddington assessed the results. It was well known that pathological hallucinations can occur – for instance, when people are on strong pain-killing drugs. Piddington compared such pathological apparitions with those reported to psychic researchers by people under no drug treatment at the time. He found significant differences.

Medical cases frequently occurred at the edge of sleep, in a hypnagogic state, and were almost solely visual in nature. They featured shapeless masses or lights, rather than concrete images or recognisable people. Quite the opposite was true of non-medical cases. These occurred as often during the day as at night, and were far more vivid and specific in nature. They never appeared dream-like but were usually termed 'real' by witnesses (unlike drug-induced hallucinations, which had a dreamy quality). Figures seen were mistaken for real people.

A more modern study by Celia Green and Charles McCreery at the Paraphysical Laboratories in Oxford extended these findings, noting that apparitions tend to occur across the spectrum of the senses. Not only are they visual but they involve sounds, smells, touches and other sensations. In medical hallucinations, experiences other than visual phenomena are considerably rarer than this. This suggests that bedroom visitors may be different, possibly acting as dramatisations of information detected by the subconscious mind and picked up from some external stimulus whilst the person is in an altered state.

There are cases where an apparition seems to convey information that the percipient could not have known. Martyn Jones from Berkshire reports an odd happening when he was aged eleven. Awakening from sleep in the middle of the night, he saw a shadowy figure standing beside his bed. Nevertheless he was able to take in much detail, most notably that it only had half a left arm.

Some weeks later Martyn told his mother about the visitor. She explained that from his description it could only have been his grandfather, who had died before Martyn was born. The boy had never seen a photograph of his grandfather, but the old man had sworn that he would 'somehow' see any future grandchildren from Heaven! This was a story Martyn says he had never been told.

The question is, why the severed arm? For most of his grandfather's life it had been whole and was amputated only weeks before his death when he was riddled with cancer and doctors were fighting to save his life. Why – in the afterlife – would he still have this arm missing years later? More significantly, if a ghost is in any sense the spirit of the dead person, in what form would someone blown to bits in an explosion return – as a few scattered, disembodied pieces?

This really follows on from Gareth Rees's point. However, first of all it has to be remembered that a ghost is supposed to be the mental essence of someone who has died, and not physical flesh and blood. The witness could indeed be perceiving a surviving intelligence that presents itself to us in a way that we would find acceptable. A clothed figure would be part of that acceptance, as would a largely recognisable image of its former physical self.

The old man had sworn that he would 'somehow' see any future grandchildren from Heaven!

Mrs Waverton from Hertfordshire told us what happened to her in 1967. She awoke one night completely paralysed and unable to call out. A golden beam of light was pouring through the bedroom window. Standing in the beam was her teenage son, saying: 'It's all right, mum. I'm going to be all right.' She awoke, terrified that something was wrong. But her son was in his bedroom sound asleep.

Two days later the teenager decided to go out on his motorcycle, but came back soon afterwards saying there was a problem with the brakes. Recalling the 'dream', Mrs Waverton begged him not to go out but could not say why. So he went. A few hours later came the phone call which she had dreaded. Her son had been rushed to hospital after a terrible accident.

The youth was very badly injured, but survived, even though he required four operations. The first words he spoke to his mother in hospital that night were exactly those she had heard him say in the 'dream'. However, Mrs Waverton's premonition (if that is what is was) is not the end of the story.

Her son reported that his life was saved by a further paranormal happening. Just seconds before the accident, he heard the voice of his dead grandfather cry out loudly: 'Go home, Terry – go now!' The familiar voice and its message, just before a car came out of nowhere, probably enhanced his reactions enough to make a crucial difference.

One supernatural event is unusual, but two connected with a single accident is intriguing. Yet is it anything more than suggestive of survival after death? The grandfather might, of course, have triggered both experiences. Or, again, the warning to save the young man from premature death may have been 'dressed up' in a way to give the message more impact. Even so, who – or what – knew of the impending danger and sent the message to begin with?

An Essex woman was talking on the phone when her husband, who had died two months previously, suddenly appeared at the top of the stairs, descended and stood right next to her. She made an excuse about 'reflections', put the phone down and watched as he stood there and vanished. He reappeared several times after that and she could see every detail, 'even the pores of his skin'. He looked ten years younger. The only thing he conveyed to her during these visits was, 'There are plenty of supermarkets where I am!'

There was the young woman from Middlesex whose best friend was brutally assaulted and murdered in 1983. She reappeared many times and they held conversations, as if they had never been separated by death. But what did the ghost say?

She expressed no interest in identifying her uncaught murderer (unlike

Does the perfect ghost story remain in the realms of fiction?

the fiction of the later glitzy film *Ghost*). Instead, she led her friend on an 'out-of-the-body' trip to Heaven (see Chapter 12), where she showed off her new house and new boyfriend – just as she might have done in life. The dead girl pointed skyward and said her grandmother lived there, and she would move up in due course. As the two friends passed down a 'long corridor', the visiting girl asked to stay in Heaven too. She was told she had to go back to Earth, but would return before too long. Then she was back in her body in bed, feeling a terrible sense of loss mixed with happiness.

It is intriguing that this phase of the story should trace the same route as the classic near death experience (see Chapter 13) whilst actually being a ghostly encounter. Does this offer evidence that the NDE is the doorway towards life after death, as many suppose, or is it yet more indication of a consistent type of 'hallucination'? If not, why is the information conveyed in these cases so meaningless? Why was the murderer not identified by the victim? Was there nothing more interesting for the husband to report than the presence of supermarkets in the afterlife? Or is it that ghosts have a sense of humour?

The indisputable case would involve a person seeing the apparition of someone they did not know to be dead, and receiving information which later proved correct, but which they had no way of knowing – indeed which nobody living had any way of knowing at the time. It should be something that only the dead person could have known.

Elements of this ideal have been exhibited in some cases, but the perfect ghost story remains in the realms of fiction. As a result, we can only make a value judgement on the existing evidence as to how well phantoms support the reality of life after death.

YOUR VERDICT : A SUMMARY

AGAINST SURVIVAL

- There are encounters with 'ghosts' of people who are very much alive.

- Optical illusions and wishful thinking can explain some cases.

- The experiences nearly all occur in an altered state of consciousness, favouring a psychological explanation.

- Photographs of ghosts are decreasing in numbers for some reason.

- Apparitions often fit the belief system of witnesses.

- They commonly occur on the edges of sleep when imagery is strong.

- There is a major lack of back-up witnesses or physical evidence.

- Experiments show that 4–8 per cent of the population are 'fantasy-prone', finding it hard to distinguish dreams from reality. Such witnesses have been found to experience hallucinations so vivid that they can fool the conscious mind into believing them to be real.

FOR SURVIVAL

- Ghosts on the whole look three-dimensional and real, not ethereal.

- Genuine information seems to be conveyed, to which the percipient could not have had access in the normal way.

- Crisis apparitions can occur when people are on the point of death, but the percipient has no way of knowing that to be the case. This illustrates that the soul is capable of leaving the body.

- Some ghost photographs have not been explained away and remain very puzzling.

(box continues)

- Apparitions are nearly always of dead, not living, people.

- All senses are stimulated by the experience, not just vision as in pathological hallucinations.

- Studies have revealed significant differences between drug-induced or medically triggered hallucinations and spontaneously reported apparitions.

POLTERGEISTS

◆

WHAT IS A POLTERGEIST?

The term 'poltergeist' is German, and means 'noisy spirit'. Some of the earliest recorded cases, not surprisingly, are German. In AD 858, for instance, falls of stones, loud noises and knockings were reported near the town of Bingen on the Rhine. But it was not a uniquely German phenomenon. William Nott was convinced that his home in Wales was infested with spirits who tore up clothing and tossed clumps of dirt. That was in 1184. Gerald of Wales, a scholar of the twelfth century, recorded incidents of mud flinging, spirit voices speaking in aggressive tones, and holes maliciously cut in garments. Such incidents were thought to be the diabolical work of demons, or due to natural causes. These included outright deception, death watch beetles, shrinking timbers and underground streams. Contemporary sceptics still cite these explanations.

Poltergeist activity is really the ultimate haunting manifestation. Yet it is distinct from usual hauntings, because poltergeist phenomena are not confined to a certain locality but seem to be drawn to a particular individual. The effects can be mischievous or malicious and terrifying. An intense variety of unexplained events can occur during a finite timespan of weeks or months, but not usually more than a year. The degree of intensity varies, as does the number of components in each case. These characteristics consist basically of the following:

1. Auditory effects such as rappings, rustlings and knocking sounds.

2. Movement of objects from one room to another, observed and unobserved.

3. Disappearance of objects, such as jewellery and other personal effects, which usually turn up weeks or months later.

4. Materialisation 'from thin air' of 'apports' – small items ranging from coins to rusty nails, for example – which do not 'belong' to the location.

Gerald of Wales, a scholar of the twelfth century, recorded incidents of mud flinging, spirit voices speaking in aggressive tones, and holes maliciously cut in garments.

5. Appearance of writing by an unknown hand, sometimes on walls (see Chapter 4).

6. Vandalisation – for instance, where drawers are emptied and their contents are scattered about.

7. Destruction of objects by smashing (such as crockery) or by fire.

8. Rearrangement of things in neat, child-like patterns.

9. Very occasionally, the slaughter of animals.

10. Effects directly associated with a supernatural entity, such as footsteps, voices and the appearance of human and non-human-looking apparitions.

11. The throwing of stones at a building.

12. Violence against the individual – where a person is pushed by an invisible force, for instance.

Each case exhibits some of the above, but rarely all of them at once. Binbrook Farm, near Market Rasen in Lincolnshire, suffered various phenomena for two months early in 1905. They included the movement of objects, items thrown about rooms, things bursting into flames and the killing of animals.

The fires were easily put out, but one of them terribly injured a serving girl who was in the kitchen. According to the farmer, Mr White, the fire in the grate was very small and in any case protected by a guard. He came across the girl standing in the middle of the kitchen, sweeping the floor, apparently unaware that her back was ablaze! Her employer put out the flames with wet sacks and she was taken to Louth Hospital.

White was just as concerned about who – or what – was killing his chickens. By the end of the manifestations, out of 250 birds only 24 remained alive. They were all slaughtered in the same bizarre fashion. The skin around the neck, from head to breast, had been pulled off, and the windpipe tugged from its place and snapped. Even when Mr White kept an all-night vigil outside the henhouse, by morning another four or five birds were discovered dead. And no one ever heard a thing.

THE ENFIELD CASE

One of the most famous contemporary cases occurred in Enfield, north London, during 1977. The events revolved around the Harper family,

comprising four children and their mother, who was separated from their father. It all began on the evening of 30 August when the beds of two of the children began to shake. The following night the same children and their mother heard a sound like someone shuffling across the carpet in slippers. This was followed by four loud knocks and the observation of a heavy chest of drawers moving across the room. A neighbour searched the building, and when more knocks sounded the police were called. They could, of course, do nothing.

The following evening marbles and Lego bricks were thrown about the house by an invisible agency. One of the marbles was found to be burning hot. The *Daily Mirror* became involved, and through them the Society for Psychical Research. An investigation by Maurice Grosse and Guy Lyon Playfair ensued.

There were many witnesses to the movement of furniture and appearance of apports. At one stage, the disturbed spirit of a little girl who had

Psychic researcher Maurice Grosse wrestles with the mysteries of a house in Enfield, Middlesex, reputedly invaded by a poltergeist. All manner of strange forces were involved, including an alleged levitation of one young girl. The controversial case was linked by some observers to surviving energies connected with an old man whose earlier death in the location was traced.

The investigators recorded an amazing four hundred incidents, including the appearance of a pool of water on the kitchen floor in the shape of a person.

been suffocated by her father in a nearby house was suspected. Some of the furniture from that place had been brought to the Harpers' house, but it was discarded when the disturbances began. A medium was brought in, who contacted several entities allegedly responsible for the haunting. The medium said they were feeding off negative energy leaked by one of the children – Janet aged eleven – and her mother, who admitted feeling very bitter towards her estranged husband.

The activities stopped for a few weeks, then began again in October. The investigators recorded an amazing four hundred incidents, including the appearance of a pool of water on the kitchen floor in the shape of a person. As with most poltergeist cases, the incidents ranged from the mundane to the potentially dangerous. An iron grille landed near one of the children; then the gas fire itself was torn off the wall where it was cemented. As the poltergeist got into its stride apparitions were sighted, and messages were left on pieces of paper and on the walls after a visit by Matthew Manning.

More phenomena became centred around Janet, who went into convulsions and was on one occasion hurled out of bed. She went into trances and produced a drawing of a woman with blood pouring from her throat, underneath which she wrote the name 'Watson'. Apparently the Watsons had been the previous tenants of the house, and Mrs Watson died of throat cancer. It was not clear whether Janet could have known this or not. In December a strange voice began communicating, claiming it was Joe Watson. The voice sounded masculine and electronic, producing each word with difficulty. Later it claimed to be various other people, including an old man buried in a nearby graveyard.

Some members of the SPR were convinced that the children were involved in a fraud – a conclusion that the two investigators did not agree with. It is very difficult to see how they could have been responsible for more than a fraction of the incidents. The haunting died out during the summer of 1978.

A MISCHIEVOUS PHENOMENON?

A recent case which demonstrates the child-like attributes of the phenomenon occurred near Manchester during 1990 and 1991. The manifestations actually began at a house owned by a couple named Farris, who had bought a corner shop and were busy renovating it. When they moved out of the house to live over the shop, the poltergeist activity really hotted up.

Some of the things were sinister, such as several cigarettes which were discovered burned in their unmarked pack, even though there was no

Poltergeists can be mischievous, and sometimes sinister. This one in a shop in Stockport, Cheshire, arranged five tubes of mints on the counter – all with the labels facing uppermost.

obvious source of ignition. Mrs Farris kept visualising a little girl aged about eight, dressed in Victorian clothing, and some of the things which subsequently occurred could be put down to the tricks of a child.

On several mornings the couple, who have no children living with them, got up to find that things had been interfered with in the shop. Several rolls of Polo mints were taken from their display box and laid on the counter in a neat row – with labels uppermost. Half a dozen small coffee cups were also found in a neat line, with handles all facing the same way. Something had removed several cans of soft drinks, and similarly lined them up on the floor. At that time there was a further incident, which amused rather than frightened Mrs Farris.

'Terry had gone to work, and I shut the shop for twenty minutes while I went out on business. When I returned, I couldn't believe my eyes. There, on the kitchen floor, were all my saucepans. They were in a line from the smallest to the largest, their handles all pointing in the same direction like a line of soldiers on parade. At the head of them all, standing like a sergeant major, was my wok!'

When a fire broke out in the adjoining Chinese take-away, some men out in the street thought they saw the faces of two children peering from the first-floor window above the corner shop. The men were so convinced that they tried to break the shop door down, thinking the children were in danger from the fire spreading. But the only people in the building were Mr and Mrs Farris, asleep on the floor above. Nevertheless, the noise woke the couple up, saving them from potential danger. Was this intended?

SPONTANEOUS PSYCHOKINESIS?

As early as 1930, parapsychologist Hereward Carrington wrote: 'An energy seems to be radiated from the body . . . when the sexual energies are blossoming into maturity . . . it would almost seem as if these energies instead of taking the normal course . . . find this curious means of externalisation.' Most modern researchers conjecture that the poltergeist is a physical manifestation of inward emotional energy. The famous Swiss psychologist Carl Jung made a similar statement when discussing UFOs: 'When an inner process cannot be integrated it is often projected outwards.'

He heard violent knocking sounds coming from the headboard, and saw a linen chest rise slightly off the floor and travel eighteen inches before returning.

Proponents of this theory believe that in the majority of cases there is an obvious focus, which invariably turns out to be a young woman at the onset of puberty. While we believe this is too sweeping a statement, it does sometimes seem to be true. A case in point was investigated by Professor George Owen in 1961.

During the autumn of 1960, an eleven-year-old child called Virginia went to live with her elder brother and his wife at Sauchie in central Scotland. After going to bed on Tuesday, 22 November, she was disturbed by a 'thunking' noise reminiscent of a bouncing ball. Virginia went downstairs to complain, and the curious sound followed her into the living room. During tea the following day, her relatives were amazed to see the sideboard move several inches from the wall, then back again.

A local clergyman, the Reverend Lund, was called to the house at midnight on the Wednesday. Virginia was in bed but awake. He heard violent knocking coming from the headboard, and saw a linen chest rise slightly off the floor and travel eighteen inches before returning. With both phenomena, the Reverend Lund detected vibrations emanating from the affected objects. When Virginia slept, nothing occurred. A Dr Nisbet was there the next evening and heard knocking and sawing noises. He also observed a curious rippling pass across the girl's pillow, where it twisted to one side.

The phenomenon even followed the girl to school. Miss Stewart, her teacher, noticed that Virginia seemed to be pressing down unusually hard on her desk. When she released the pressure, the lid opened of its own accord. This happened three times. Later, a vacant desk close by lifted slightly into the air. Miss Stewart investigated at once, and found no evidence of trickery. Investigator Malcolm Robinson recently interviewed one of Virginia's former classmates, who attested to the levitations.

When the phenomenon showed no signs of abating, Virginia was transferred to an aunt living nearby. But the rappings and agitated knockings followed her there, too.

Once more back in Sauchie, things quietened down until 1 December, when all the usual happenings resumed. Although attempted filming of these effects met with failure, a tape recording was successfully made of knocking and harsh rasping noises. Afterwards, prayers of intercession were made, and eventually the phenomenon died out altogether.

It is easy to see how cases like this have been linked to the theory of spontaneous psychokinesis (PK) – an alleged ability in some people to cause inanimate objects to move by some unknown energy directed from the mind. Poltergeists, according to this reasoning, are nothing more than spontaneous psychokinesis – an anarchic, unconscious and uncontrolled demonstration of inner hysteria.

Scientists Hans J. Eysenck and Carl Sargent had this to say: 'So what can we learn from the poltergeist? It would be surprising if we got a neat reliable, coherent story. The one thing we do learn is that there is a core of cases in which the evidence for PK is very strong.'

POLTERGEISTS AND LIFE AFTER DEATH

Are poltergeists evidence for survival of death? Although they are considered to be different phenomena, there does seem to be a link with ghostly apparitions. Certainly when entities communicate, as in the Enfield case, they appear to be low-life spirits hanging on between this world and the next. Ghost hunter Terence Whitaker told us of his investigations into the eerie Hobstones Farm at Foulridge near Colne in Lancashire.

It seems that the name derives from a long tradition that elves and hobgoblins played on the stones. Local children's songs handed down through the ages refer to this.

During the seventeenth-century Civil War a battle occurred on the ridge when the land was owned by a fanatical Royalist sympathiser. This violent event seems to have left its mark and, as Whitaker discovered: 'A phantom cavalier in various states of undress has been seen in one of the bedrooms.' Also a troop of roundheads have been reported marching across the moors.

Has the specialness of this area trapped images from the past, or the

During a poltergeist attack at Hobstones Farm all the white eggs in a tray were smashed, but the brown ones were left and arranged in the shape of a cross.

actual surviving souls of slaughtered soldiers? The possibility is enhanced by the fact that another ghostly presence has been witnessed. It was first reported in 1950, when the farmer who then owned the building was in his outside brick toilet. Terence Whitaker reported: 'Suddenly the door burst open and there stood a little monk holding his own amputated arm. It cured the farmer's constipation!' Although the farmer initially thought this was a practical joke, the monk was later seen again inside the house. The farmer soon sold up and moved away.

During the 1970s the new owners saw nothing, but experienced many other phenomena. It was as if the ghostly apparition had transformed its energy into poltergeist activity. More than twenty windows were wrecked in a peculiar way. The evidence showed that they had been pushed outwards from inside the building – so they could not have been smashed by vandals.

One day the owner's wife went upstairs to make the beds and was suddenly deluged by boulders and rocks apparently falling from nowhere. There have also been occasions when rocks have been thrown against the outside of the house, making a terrible noise. This is an interesting 'coincidence', given that the farm's name links 'hobs' (or playful demons) with 'stones'. Perhaps the most unusual poltergeist incident at Hobstones Farm occurred when a washing machine was thrown across the kitchen by an unseen force. Terence Whitaker reports: 'On top of the machine was a tray of eggs with white eggs and brown eggs. All the white eggs were smashed but the brown eggs were left in the tray in the shape of a cross.'

After this, the local vicar brought in an exorcist and the activity died down. Nothing has occurred for a long time; the present owners will not allow any investigation of the property, and appear to have seen nothing unusual.

DEMONIC SPIRITS FROM THE AFTERLIFE?

Unfortunately, demons are not very popular with today's parapsychologists. They prefer a more scientific approach with a credible scientific hypothesis. Certainly psychokinesis is attractive as an explanation for cases like Virginia's. But the theory does have its drawbacks. In many cases, there is no young person involved going through puberty. The witnesses can be of any age and either sex. If an uncontrolled energy was really being unconsciously released, then surely the end result would only be destructive? Many of the incidents put down to the poltergeist seem to demonstrate some sort of orderly intelligence. As an umbrella explanation for the phenomenon, spontaneous psychokinesis leaves a lot to be desired.

What is undeniable is that usually one individual seems to be the focus for the poltergeist. Hauntings tend to break out, then die down for a period before starting up again. Perhaps certain types of people under stress in some way are capable of triggering off the effects? Could it be, as discussed in the Enfield case, that genuine spirits from the afterlife need this nervous energy in order to manifest? Do they 'feed' in some psychic way on fear and hate?

A poltergeist 'who broke all the rules', according to investigator Paul Eno, manifested around a new housing estate in Bristol, Connecticut, built on land which had formerly been occupied by an old hilltop farm. During a week in July 1975 John and Susan Sanford and their two sons, aged ten and twelve, were to be the first of the new residents to fall victim.

Opposite the Sanfords in an old brown house lived a Mrs Hobbes and her fourteen-year-old son. Susan felt very sorry for the middle-aged woman, as the other children taunted her son that his mother was a witch. In an act of kindness, Susan invited her across for a coffee. During a somewhat stilted conversation, she asked Mrs Hobbes why some workmen had stopped demolishing a shed.

According to Mrs Hobbes, the workmen abandoned the job when one of them had felt cold, invisible hands around his neck. The following day, Susan was invited to the brown house for tea. While seated in the gloomy

lounge, she was astounded to see an ashtray rise from the coffee table and float across the room. Her hostess flippantly remarked: 'Oh, that's only the ghost.' Susan left.

Not wishing to seem discourteous, Susan asked Mrs Hobbes over to her place again. This was her last visit, she told Paul Eno, because Mrs Hobbes brought the thing with her.

As soon as the woman left, all hell broke loose. By the time the rest of the family had come home, crockery had been smashed, furniture moved and pictures knocked off walls. This continued all the following week. The family also heard animal-like growls and saw terrifying red eyes at the window. At the end of that week, Susan saw a huge, anonymous black form move across a field and disappear through the wall of the semi-demolished cottage where the shed was situated. The Sanfords then learned that the occupants of four other houses were experiencing loud knocks and moving objects.

While taking site photographs, Paul Eno encountered a strong electrical field which made his hair stand on end. As he drove away, both car doors simultaneously burst open, sending the contents of the vehicle on to the road. When the film was processed, two prints appeared to depict anomalies. One had unusual shapes on it, and the other showed a bearded face at the cottage window. Investigators discovered that the cottage had been notorious in the 1920s for prostitution and bootlegging.

STRANGERS IN THE HOUSE

'If your loved ones emigrate you do not stop communicating. Passing to the next sphere of life is just the same. Why should you cut off all contact with them?' So says Mrs Edith Fern of East London when she tells us of her own strange experiences with the unseen world.

At the age of just fifteen she and her family knew they were not alone in their house. One day she came out of the dining room and saw that the light was on in her brother's bedroom. She switched it off and went upstairs. The light switched itself back on again. This continued several times, until on the final occasion Edith left it on. She had no choice – a voice booming 'Thank you very much!' issued from the room.

Obviously, she concluded, her brother must have been in the room, although she had seen nobody. But moments later she entered the front room across the hall and there he was. There was no way he could have reached that room before her, and there was nobody else in the house.

As Edith grew older, these experiences got stranger and stranger. Eventually she had a daughter and then a grand-daughter. All three went

Left: Damage caused by a poltergeist attack in the cottage belonging to Ken Webster (see Chapter 10).

to stay at a farm cottage one week, and at breakfast her daughter told Edith the oddest thing. 'The wardrobe in our bedroom purrs,' she reported. Apparently it would make this peculiar noise, and if she argued with her daughter (Edith's grand-daughter) it then began to shake as if there was an earthquake. This behaviour, not unnaturally, was disturbing them both, even though Edith was by now used to poltergeist activities of this sort.

A couple of days after this episode it was raining and Edith idly ran her fingers over a line of books in the farm cottage, picking one out at random. It was a collection of travel tales from South America, and towards the end she read a most astonishing story. The author claimed he had stayed in a room where the wardrobe purred when he drank water, then began to shake when he drank alcohol, and fell on the bed when he took a girl back to his room!

Edith wonders what guided her to this book. She says; 'It could not have come from my mind, so it obviously came from a mind outside of my own who knew what was in those books. There must have been fifty or more of them.'

As a result of her lifetime of meaningful encounters such as these, Edith Fern has concluded:

The body is just an overcoat. If you take off your overcoat you do not cease to exist.

'Very few people know the great amount of influence that is brought to bear upon Earth dwellers from outside agencies, namely the spirit world. This body that we have on Earth is equivalent to the space suit you would have to wear to visit the moon. It is not the person . . . . Survival of the spirit after death of the body does not depend on whether you are good or bad, it doesn't depend on whether you are religious or not, it is a universal law. All survive the death of the body because the body is just an overcoat. If you take off your overcoat you do not cease to exist . . . . Your memory, your intelligence, all you have learned on Earth survives death.'

She believes that we are all in contact with these spirits on a constant basis. They feed us information which we detect as 'intuition', and can affect the material world in ways in which we regard as poltergeist activity.

'There is a well-known saying that the spectator sees more of the game then the players . . . . We are the players, those in the spirit world are the spectators. They can see ahead and they can see back. We can only see back. They have already experienced all that we are going through now and they desire to help us. They must not interfere, and may only try to give us guidance . . . . People talk about communicating with the dead. There are no dead. Communication is with people . . . . There is nothing spooky about the spirit world. They were people. They still are people. But they are now people with a greater ability to help us than they had when on Earth.'

THE EVIDENCE AGAINST

Old houses can be very noisy at night when they are 'settling down' as the temperature drops, and in more than a few cases individuals have been caught throwing things across a room, when they thought no one was looking, to enhance the supernatural nature of what is going on. Although there are photographs and tape recordings allegedly depicting poltergeist phenomena, these are easy to fake as all they show are things flying through the air – not *how* they flew, or what made them fly. Less easy to discredit would be a video film of objects levitating, for instance, but, despite the growth of video camera ownership, as yet there is a dearth of such evidence.

Many poltergeist cases involve children, and it may be that some of them are seeking attention or using the supernatural as an excuse to mask their own mischievous spirit.

THE EVIDENCE FOR

Biologist Dr Lyall Watson, author of many fine books including the bestseller *Supernature*, told us that he had travelled the world investigating poltergeist outbreaks. Dr Watson has witnessed first hand such a variety of phenomena that he now sees no reason to pursue any more cases. Poltergeists, as far as he is concerned, are so common they are almost boring.

Such a lot of cases have been attested to, by so many reputable witnesses, that it is hard to believe that the phenomenon is nothing more than fraud, natural causes and imagination. Tape recordings of demonic voices and other unnatural sounds demonstrate the objectivity of the phenomenon.

In instances where people have been observed throwing objects, the obvious conclusion that they were perpetuating a fraud is not necessarily the correct one. Once investigators and the media become involved, sincere witnesses often come under intense pressure to produce manifestations. There could also be another reason.

Researchers Nandor Fodor and William Roll discovered that sometimes witnesses threw things without being aware of it. Roll secretly observed a 'suspect' throwing things, yet a lie detector test 'proved' that he was telling the truth in denying he had done so. Some researchers speculate that in these instances the poltergeist has temporarily taken control of the witness and used them to further their bizarre activities.

Finally, poltergeist activity has occasionally been seen as acceptable grounds for councils to move tenants from affected houses on the evidence.

YOUR VERDICT : A SUMMARY

AGAINST SURVIVAL

- Natural explanations can be found to explain most poltergeists.

- Individuals have been caught cheating.

- People subconsciously seeking attention could be causing the phenomena, and no paranormal explanation need be involved. Mental stress could cause them to 'forget' what they have done.

- Despite the physical nature of poltergeist acts, no one has been able to present unambiguous evidence of their paranormal origin.

FOR SURVIVAL

- People sometimes cheat, even during genuine poltergeist activity, because they are put under pressure by investigators to produce results. Alternatively, tests suggest that witnesses become possessed by the poltergeist.

- Over the last 150 years the phenomenon has been intensively investigated by many scientists, who have become convinced of its paranormal origins.

- There are hundreds of photographs and tape recordings of levitations and strange noises. Many witnesses to the effects are seemingly completely reputable.

Haunted Houses

———◆———

Can strong emotions linger on a site across time?

The major difference between haunted houses and poltergeist outbreaks is one of focus and duration. In the former, it is primarily the building or place which seems haunted; in the latter the phenomenon is often more dependent on an individual and may go with them elsewhere should they decide to move on.

In truth this definition is loose and relies on tradition. Indeed in some key respects ghosts, poltergeists and haunted houses display interrelated features. However, haunted houses tend to have a reputation going back over many years, sometimes centuries. Different people at different times often describe the same apparition seen in them as if 'locked' into the environment. In poltergeist cases, the phenomenon is more sporadic and fitful (see Chapter 6). Sometimes a poltergeist attack beds down in a house and changes character to the haunted house variety when new occupants move in.

Even when a building earns a reputation for being 'haunted', manifestations do not occur all the time. There may be a gap of several years when nothing is reported. In some instances it seems that certain individuals may set off the phenomenon, as if there is an emotional empathy between it and them. Perhaps during times of inactivity at a haunted place the phenomenon is there but dormant.

Could it be that such places lie at a point where the veil between our world and the next is finer, allowing easier access for spirits and demons? Such places could be conceived of as 'gateways'. Perhaps unconsciously, psychically gifted people have the ability to open these 'gates', allowing entry from the other side.

Another theory for haunted houses is that some great emotional tragedy in the past has somehow left its imprint on the building. In this sense, observations of ghostly phenomena are simply like a playback of audio or video 'tape' of scenes from long ago. This idea works best when hauntings are associated with a terrible accident, murder or a battle. Can strong emotions linger on a site across time?

THE ROMAN SOLDIERS OF YORK

A typical example would be the experience of apprentice plumber Harry Martindale in York during the early 1950s. He was installing pipes in the cellar of the Treasurer's House, halfway up a ladder, when he heard the sound of a trumpet. He heard it again and it sounded nearer, and yet again, until suddenly a horse bearing a Roman soldier came through a wall. Shocked, the young man fell off the ladder and watched in amazement as weary-looking foot soldiers appeared behind the horse. None of them seemed to notice Harry as they disappeared through the far wall. It was discovered later that they were following the route of an old Roman road.

The 'video recording' theory is particularly relevant where the witness describes no interaction with the apparition. It acts out its role like an image projected on to a screen. In old buildings which have been modernised apparitions have even been observed walking with their feet disappearing into the carpet, as if following the level of a centuries-old lower-level floor. This may also account for apparitions seen walking through solid walls at a point where a doorway once existed.

If true, this theory suggests that some hauntings may be natural events we do not understand, rather than actual visitations by spirits of the dead. But there are numerous cases on file where the phantom has reacted as if it was very well aware of human observers. That would be impossible if the apparition was a mere 'recording' imprinted on to the environment. If these 'reactive ghost' cases can be verified then some hauntings may well offer good evidence for survival of a conscious, reactive entity beyond the point of death.

THE ANCIENT RAM INN

In the depths of Gloucestershire lies the country town of Wotton-under-Edge, which contains a historical and archaeological gem. The Ancient Ram Inn was built in 1189, and over the intervening eight hundred years very little has been done to change its basic structure. When John Humphries bought the building in 1968 for £3,500 it was in a dilapidated state. With just train driver's wages and a few extra pounds earned through bed and breakfast, John set about making the run-down building habitable. He tore off the corrugated roof that some uncaring philistine had nailed to the ancient rafters of the adjoining barn and began researching the Inn's history.

The Ram Inn, John discovered, had a very colourful past. He uncovered a priest's hole and a bricked up tunnel which once led to the church opposite. Two of England's last highwaymen hid out in the Inn, and the building was notorious for several murders. Perhaps this explains the Ram's plethora of hauntings – terrifying experiences attested to by dozens of visitors over the last two decades.

John Humphries dug deeper into the past, and discovered that the Norman foundations hid macabre secrets. Indeed, during excavation work in one of the rooms a grave was discovered. A local dowser, using his skills at detecting hidden objects, had reported that he sensed bodies beneath the foundations. With the help of a local archaeologist John dug up the floor of one of the rooms and recovered the bones of several children, along with two broken ceremonial daggers.

From an ancient Saxon map, John discovered that the Ram had been built on a circular area of land bounded by huts. Close by are a number of steps carved into the side of the hill. At one time these terraces were used by monks for the cultivation of vines, although they are much older than that. These were a feature of pagan times in many countries, especially in Egypt, from which many mystical traditions found their way into western Europe.

The Ancient Ram Inn, at Wotton-under-Edge, has a plethora of hauntings, attested to in writing by dozens of witnesses.

The image of a stairway to Heaven remains strong in many cultures. In the Old Testament Jacob had a vision of a 'ladder' climbing up towards God. In Egyptian times the soul of the departed king or shaman would rise up a staircase on to a higher plane. Steps were also a feature of pagan sacrificial altars.

A 'ley' – said by some researchers to be a line of natural earth energy which passes through ancient burial sites and places of worship – cuts through the Ram, adding to its magical significance. John Humphries believes that the area within the circle was an ancient sacrificial site, and that the victims were children.

That was not unusual. Dating from the Roman destruction of the city of Carthage in 146 BC to the eighth century BC, thousands of urns have been discovered containing the calcined bones of small children who had been sacrificed by fire. There is ample evidence in the Hebrew scriptures that at one time the ancient Israelites sacrificed their first-born. The story of Abraham (Genesis 22) is a graphic example: his faith is tested when God orders him to take his son, Isaac, and sacrifice him. Just as the sacrifice is about to take place, God calls it off, and instead Abraham sacrifices a ram caught in a thicket of thorns. Does this biblical account have a direct connection with the name of the Ram Inn and the unholy ground it was built upon?

If ever a place should be haunted, it is the Ram. Just to look at it gives that impression, and its colourful history compounds the feeling. Inside, it is like stepping back in time. The building is heavy with a dark, brooding atmosphere. John Humphries has had many experiences, both alone and with witnesses. He has seen things happening to other people – and dozens of guests have signed declarations to the things which have happened to them.

Included in the plethora of phenomena experienced over the years are:

1. Items found moved from one place to another.

2. Objects observed 'floating' about rooms.

3. Electrical equipment, such as light switches, a television set and radio, operating 'by themselves'.

4. People, in front of witnesses, thrown about the main sitting room.

5. Whispering, disembodied voices.

6. Sudden temperature drops.

7. A strange 'mist' (ectoplasm?) forming inside the building.

8. Apparitions.

9. One instance of two men who ran out into the street – whereupon footsteps followed them for some distance.

10. Several people who experienced 'something' crawling into bed with them, and felt 'something' wrap itself around them.

11. Strange balls of light seen in the building.

Here is a statement by a woman who stayed for several nights in the Ram with her partner in November 1984.

'At around 12.20a.m. in the Bishop's Room, whilst Steve was out, I was aware that something strange was about to happen. I was drawn towards the fireplace where I saw a wispy white mist which developed into the outline of a man. I was so frightened I pulled the covers over my head. I did not look again until Steve returned, by which time the apparition had disappeared.

'Nothing else happened until later in the night. Then I felt a presence all around me. I tried to move my arms and open my eyes but I couldn't. Someone or something was trying to pull me out of bed. I started to shout which woke Steve who then grabbed me, and the presence disappeared.

'In the early hours of the following evening I awoke in a terrible sweat, as if I had been in a hot sauna. Later I awoke several times with my pulse racing for no apparent reason, except I had an impression that the sheets were being pulled towards the foot of the bed.'

In many respects these are the bedroom visitor types of experiences (see Chapter 5), but set within a classic haunted house.

Peter Hough visited the Ram as part of an investigation team from the Association for the Scientific Study of Anomalous Phenomena (ASSAP). Highly sensitive recording equipment was installed and photographs taken, and every room was 'staked out' overnight.

A weekend in such a place is not really long enough to prove whether evidence of survival is to be found there. However, strange events did occur: some smoky images appeared on a photograph taken by Lyn Tungate, and several investigators, including Peter Hough, independently experienced a sudden temperature drop in the Bishop's Room, allegedly the most haunted spot within the Ram and the place where the haunting entity has been frequently encountered by intrepid visitors.

Such sudden drops in temperature, known as 'cold spots', are a common feature of haunted houses and the temperature can fall by anything up to 20°C. They often directly precede the appearance of other manifestations, such as apparitions or rapping sounds and it is speculated that heat is absorbed from the room by the spirit entity to be used as the energy that fuels these paranormal phenomena.

In the Ram they seemed to coincide with crackles on the recording equipment in the Bishop's Room. As he entered this room soon after, Mel Turford had the sensation that someone opened the door for him from the inside. The room was empty in the physical sense. But did it contain an unseen and yet surviving phantom?

THE BULL'S HEAD

Unlike the Ram, the Bull's Head does business as a public house. Situated in Swinton, near Manchester, it is run by managers appointed by brewers Tetley Walker Ltd. Strangely, there is no documentation of a history of haunting, although when things started to happen in 1985, previous incidents began to emerge, and staff and subsequent managers have experienced things since. We have on record reports of several different apparitions.

The building dates back to the sixteenth century, but was rebuilt in 1826. Opposite stood a small chapel, but in 1869 the much grander St Peter's church was built here. The pub is on the corner of Station Road, originally known as Burying Lane – named because it led directly to the graveyard in front of the church. In the nineteenth century members of the 'watchers' club' kept vigil from an upper room overlooking the graveyard for body snatchers.

Susan and Donald Flint moved into the pub with their two young sons in January 1985. Just a month later, the first inexplicable incident occurred.

The accounts office is safely situated in a room off the cellar. Made of solid stone and brick, it has just one entrance. It was after closing time on a Saturday evening. Susan was sitting alone in the room, to one side of the doorway, checking some figures. In the deathly quiet, a loud scraping noise abruptly disturbed her concentration. When she turned round to face the back wall, she was astonished to see a small stool moving across the stone floor of its own volition. It moved several times – a foot to the left, then back again, a foot to the right.

She dashed upstairs to their first-floor living accommodation to tell her husband. Susan tried to convince herself it was caused by vibration from the road, but at that late hour traffic was light. Subsequent investigation by one of us ruled out this theory, even at rush hour.

After this first incident, the couple heard of other strange things from several members of staff and customers. All was then quiet until a dramatic and almost fatal episode during the Easter weekend.

On Easter Sunday, 8 April, the couple held a party. Susan invited her mother, Joan, and stepfather, James Kilroy, together with a family friend, Andrew Cameron, who was an electronics technician in the Royal Air Force. Late that night, gathered round the bar, someone brought up the subject of the pub's resident 'ghost'. There was much talk of 'cold spots' and the sighting of an apparition in the cellar. These stories were taken in a light-hearted vein, and two of the men in particular, James Kilroy and Andrew Cameron, were highly sceptical.

Someone challenged them to spend the night in the cellar. They readily agreed. Later, when the pub was quiet, they settled down on the stone floor of the cellar with sleeping bags, opposite a bricked up alcove. Susan and Donald switched off all the lights and retired upstairs. The men, still treating it all as a joke, chatted for a while and then dozed off.

The Bull's Head – a modern source of haunting. In one instance, a man had to be hospitalized for a head wound.

Not long afterwards, James was awoken by the sound of Andrew shouting hysterically. There, framed in the alcove, were several orange and red lights. They hung like a row of vertical three-foot fluorescent tubes, the light dancing and flickering. Suddenly there was a flash like lightning, and the cellar was plunged into darkness once more.

Andrew jumped to his feet, screaming. In the adjacent room the sound of beer barrels knocking into one another could be heard. Andrew stood petrified as the swishing sound of a broom moved around him. James Kilroy had had enough. He decided to make a dash for the cellar steps. Just as he was about to move, a hand gripped his left shoulder, and a voice whispered harshly in his ear: 'James....'

The swishing stopped, and Andrew felt something thrust into his hands, just before the lights went on. Alerted by the bedlam, the Flints and Mrs Kilroy had rushed down into the cellar. What they saw struck them dumb with amazement.

Andrew Cameron was crouched in a defensive posture gripping the long handle of a broom like a rifle, a look of terror on his face. James Kilroy lay at the foot of the steps, blood gushing from his head and staining the floor. He was rushed to a nearby hospital where he received eight stitches for a nasty gash over his right eye. In the darkness, he said, he had become disorientated, panicked and tripped over something, hitting his head on a barrel. There was no way he was going to share with doctors and nurses the terrifying reality of the phenomenon in the cellar.

But the scars bit deeper than a head wound. Kilroy, formerly sceptical and outgoing, was a changed man after the experience, according to his wife. He is now quieter and more introverted. Even several years later he would not discuss the incident, despite encouragement from Mrs Kilroy. Andrew Cameron got off more lightly, although he will not go down into the cellar again – even during daylight.

Of course, we cannot know what is happening within this typically haunted building. Strange forces of some description are clearly at work. Tradition links these with a restless spirit who has not quite made it into the afterlife and is occasionally making its presence felt here on Earth.

As scientists struggle to find a better, more rational solution we are teased by this possibility. Perhaps Andrew Cameron and James Kilroy did have contact with another world. Did they see what can happen when a conscious mind is trapped in limbo between heaven and earth, unable to find peace and incapable of leaving a dwelling place that it once called its own?

BORLEY RECTORY

A look at haunted buildings would not be complete without mention of controversial Borley Rectory, dubbed 'the most haunted house in England' by its colourful investigator in the 1930s, Harry Price. He contributed greatly to the literature of the paranormal, but his obvious love of the limelight and flirtation with the press did not go down well with other investigators who adopted a less flamboyant style. They criticised his methodology, accused him of fraud, and even claimed that Price was responsible for the creation of a myth.

That he courted the media cannot be denied, and evidence that he exaggerated and sometimes cheated to hype up the hauntings at Borley seems fairly substantial. However, to claim that Price invented the entire mystery is at odds with the long history of bizarre happenings at Borley, and seems more like 'sour grapes' on the part of some individuals in the British Society for Psychical Research. Indeed, as late as 1986 two visitors in the village experienced ghostly footsteps.

As late as 1986 two visitors in the village experienced ghostly footsteps.

The village of Borley is about two miles from Long Melford on the Suffolk/Essex border. Much of the land was owned by a family of parsons called Bull. Henry Bull built the rectory in 1863 on the site of a much older rectory belonging to the Herringham family. There is some indication – although not much proof – that the building supplanted a Benedictine abbey. Opposite stands Borley church, which dates from Saxon times. It, too, has been the source of many strange occurrences. Objects have been displaced, and heavy coffins were discovered moved in the crypt.

When Henry's son, Harry, died in 1927, many witnesses claimed they had seen his ghost walking the corridors of the rectory. For the next six months about a dozen clergymen and their wives visited the house with a view to taking up residency, but all of them declined. This probably had more to do with the primitive state of the building rather than anything supernatural. There was no gas or electricity, and the cellar was so damp that newts and frogs made it their home.

During the nine months that the Reverend Eric Smith and his wife spent in the house during 1928 and 1929, they complained of many things. These included the doorbell ringing on its own, footsteps heard, keys vanishing, voices, and the appearance of a phantom horse-drawn carriage on the driveway. It was at this point that Price got involved. He had already earned a reputation exposing fake mediums.

Incidents in Borley had been recorded as far back as 1885, including many features of the classic haunt. In 1900 the four daughters of Henry Bull had a daylight sighting of a nun in the rectory grounds. The same

Borley Rectory in June 1929 before the disastrous fire which razed it to the ground. Often called the most haunted house in England, it was home to countless reports of phantoms and poltergeist activity for half a century.

phantom featured later during Price's investigations: buried bones were discovered, and during seances cryptic messages were received alleging that she had been strangled on the site three hundred years before by a member of the Waldegrave family.

Although sightings of such previous dead residents abounded at Borley, establishing this as undoubtedly a haunting, there were also poltergeist events. These centred around Marianne, the young wife of the Reverend Foyster, when they moved into the rectory in 1929. Guy L'Estrange, a Justice of the Peace, wrote an account of his visit to the Foysters in 1932. Here is an extract.

We were all startled by a loud crash in the hall. 'They're at it again!'

groaned the Rector. I hurried to the door and found the floor outside littered with broken crockery. The Rector looked miserably down at the wreckage. 'These things come from the the kitchen dresser. You can see how impossible it would have been for anybody to fling them down here and get out of sight so quickly.'

He was right, but I was not yet convinced that trickery was out of the question. We came back to our seats after the mess had been cleared away, but an appalling series of crashes soon took us back to the doorway. The sight we witnessed made me wonder for a moment if I were dreaming.

Bottles were being hurled about in all directions in the hall, though nobody could be seen throwing them. Appearing suddenly in mid-air, they would hurtle through space and smash to pieces on the floor or against the wall.

'Where on earth are they coming from?' I gasped.

The rectory mysteriously burned to the ground in February 1939, and with it all sightings of the ghostly nun suddenly stopped. This demise had been foretold during a seance eleven months earlier.

THE EVIDENCE AGAINST

Sceptics believe that the haunted house is a myth often created unwittingly to fulfil a basic need in our mental make-up. That 'need' is a belief in survival beyond the physical. The 'fact' that different people at different times have experienced 'supernatural phenomena' reinforces this belief. If a place has a reputation for being the playground for spirits, visitors arrive *expecting* something to happen, and the slightest sounds reinforce the belief. The haunted house syndrome flies in the face of science, but that is often its attraction. People like to see know-all scientists put in their place, and want to believe there is something far greater than mankind.

We also need haunted houses as part of our diet of entertainment. They make good stories in tabloid newspapers, books and television documentaries. It does not matter whether you believe in them or not: they fulfil the function of creating good-natured debate in the public house or around the dinner table. The haunted house is one of our oldest literary devices and folklore motifs. It intrigues us and frightens us, and is as familiar as storytelling itself. Certain places lend themselves to the rumour of supernatural phenomena. Old houses surrounded by trees, isolated and exposed to wind, stir the imagination.

Sometimes a haunted house myth is not created unwittingly. Deliberate purpose is involved. Rumour can be built upon by individuals out for notoriety, money or both. Harry Price took a photograph of Borley Rectory during demolition which, according to Price, shows a brick suspended in mid-air after levitating from the ground. However, according to a witness the brick had merely fallen from a wall and had been frozen in the frame before it hit the ground. Price was also charged with the suppression or distortion of facts regarding Borley. Certainly in his first book on Borley, *The Most Haunted House in England*, but not the second, he speculates strongly that Marianne Foyster was responsible for some of the occurrences.

In more modern times the haunted house myth was used to great effect and reward in the late 1970s with the publication of *The Amityville Horror* by Jay Anson. This was eventually turned into a blockbuster film with several sequels. The book itself spent eight months on the bestseller list, and sold in excess of three and a half million copies. One reason for its success was simple – *Amityville* was claimed as a true story.

It told of the experiences of the Lutz family after they moved into a three-storey Dutch Colonial building in Amityville, Long Island, New York State in December 1975. *Amityville* describes the ultimate haunting experience: overpowering stenches, green slime, swarms of flies, temperature drops, levitation, cloven hoofprints and demonic entities. All of this was allegedly connected with the (quite factual) brutal slaughter of a family who had lived in the house before the Lutzes. A man named Ronald DeFoe was arrested for the murders, and a financial motive was proposed.

The Lutzes' story possessed all the key ingredients for success, but under investigation it was shown that, if the house was haunted at all, the manifestations were limited compared with the way they had been presented via all the hype. Key characters in the book's story claimed that some of the events reported had never taken place. Sceptics mounted powerful attacks suggesting that a simple story had become gradually embellished. The family were in financial trouble at the time they met William Weber, DeFoe's attorney, the sceptics argued. Weber was interested in establishing that the house was haunted so as to prove that the murderer had been controlled by a malevolent force. The debate still rages over what really happened in Amityville. But certainly factors other than the supernatural often need to be taken into account when assessing a haunting.

The modest council house on the edge of the Pennine hills in Lancashire, where convicted 'Moors Murderer' Myra Hindley lived in the 1960s during the period when the murders took place, has proved rather difficult to

The house on Ocean Avenue in Amityville, New York, which was the scene of several gruesome murders and a later best-selling book and hit movie about the horrific psychic happenings which followed. But was all this true to life?

lease. Presences were said to have been detected by occupants, even if they did not know its recent history. Yet other councils have grown wary of requests to move residents who allege their home is haunted. At times, they suspect, this is just a ploy to jump the queue for better accommodation.

THE EVIDENCE FOR

Even though there must be cases where hauntings have been exaggerated or even invented, and incidents where natural phenomena such as underground streams or creaking timbers have suggested a spectral presence, some cases do stand up. A building like Borley Rectory, the Ram or the Bull's Head would not be able to sustain its reputation for being haunted across years or even centuries unless genuine manifestations were regularly reported.

In some cases the same apparition (the Borley nun, for instance) was reported across many eras and by people who claim they had no knowledge of this phantom's previous appearances. If they did not see a real ghost, how could they describe the same thing?

Many witnesses to events in haunted houses are above suspicion, and have no obvious motives for fraud. In some cases there has been more than one witness, as at both the Ram and Bull's Head.

More specifically, haunted houses can now be 'staked out' by parapsychologists with modern equipment such as video recorders (see Chapter 10). Sudden drops in temperature, unaccountable noises and apparitions have been recorded on many other kinds of sensing equipment. Unaccountable knocks were taped at Chingle Hall, Lancashire (see p.168–170). Physics professor John Taylor installed devices for measuring electrical and magnetic fields near the font in Borley church. Both Taylor and his companion, John Pickford, 'felt' something odd in the building at the same time as they recorded anomalous movement picked up by their equipment.

This is a field which is gaining strength all the time as technology improves. Modern ghost hunters use sophisticated surveillance monitors to try to trap that elusive spook. So far evidence has been disappointingly limited, but as time goes by they expect more successes and rightly point out that the registering of phenomena on pieces of equipment rules out 'imagination'. Measuring devices do not suffer from hallucinations, either. Gradually this work is giving the haunted house a semblance of reality which may take us closer towards the objective proof so rightly demanded by science.

YOUR VERDICT : A SUMMARY

AGAINST SURVIVAL

- People want to believe a place is 'haunted' and imagine or invent things.

- Strong indications of conscious fraud have been found in several famous cases.

- Under investigation some hauntings can be traced to underground streams, uneven floors and mice.

- Even if some hauntings are genuine, they do not necessary present proof of afterlife. Some ghosts could merely be an imprint, or a recording of an event into the environment.

FOR SURVIVAL

- A reputation is built on solid foundations – not on imagination and exaggeration.

- Many witnesses are of impeccable character.

- Hauntings have been recorded on electrical equipment and film, proving their objectivity.

- After seeing an apparition, witnesses accurately described former residents of houses.

ANIMAL HEAVEN

◆

Some cultures used to bury pets with their owners so that they might accompany them on their eternal journey.

If human beings survive death, is this something spiritually unique or do other life forms also go to Heaven? The answer that nearly all believers in life after death would offer is 'yes'. Indeed, some cultures used to bury pets with their owners – such as the cats so beloved of the Egyptians – so that they might accompany them on their eternal journey. However, there is an attendant problem that is rarely addressed.

Whilst it is easy enough to conceive of an afterlife for cats and dogs and such 'advanced' or domesticated animals, we know of no reports of surviving whales and dolphins (arguably mammals that are as advanced in their intelligence as human beings). If they are 'souls' and 'free' of the chains of their body, ought there not to be a sphere in Heaven where these intelligences now reside and perhaps somehow commune with human spirits?

Moreover, where do we draw the line with regard to animal survival? If we assume a pet hamster goes to Heaven, then what about the cockroach we remove with disgust via our boot or the countless ants we mercilessly tread on every time we take a walk outside? Once we start to analyse the make-up of animal Heaven, we see the difficulties that the concept brings.

Of course, in a strict philosophical sense it might be said that only 'spiritually evolved' creatures such as man possess a soul. Religions differ markedly in their interpretation of this question. Some, such as Islam, elevate humans to a unique status, while others, such as forms of Christianity, are tolerant of animal survival but less than clear about its precise nature; cultures which adopt reincarnation often suggest a 'group soul' for lower animals and individual soul survival only for the more advanced.

Yet from a scientific viewpoint it is hard to comprehend. If there is to be survival, then many feel it should require our self-awareness or consciousness which outlives the bodily shell in some form. Therefore would not most forms of life be conscious and so survive?

This instantly leads us into deep and unfathomable areas of speculation. For now, we can only point out the problems and concentrate on assessing what actual evidence there is for animal survival.

'IT WAS JIP – NO DOUBT!'

During the 1980s Margaret Coolidge from Pennsylvania had a pet spaniel she loved dearly. It went by the name of Jip. The dog was apparently very distinctive, with a reddish tinge to its coat, and had the ability to leap quite high when it saw its owner. Sadly, Jip contracted a disease and Margaret had no alternative but to follow the vet's advice and prevent further suffering by having the animal put to sleep.

About six months later she was returning home from a trip. As she walked up the drive to her home she saw through the window the unmistakable form of Jip jumping up as usual.

Margaret was not concerned by this. Indeed, she did not give the matter any thought other than to smile inwardly and open the door. Instinctively she stooped down to greet the dog and it was there. She felt its hairs, heard its yapping bark and was pleased that he was well. At no point did it dawn upon her the dog ought not to be there at all.

Momentarily she turned away, and in that instant it struck her that Jip was dead. The thought hit her like a hammer blow. Looking down, she expected to see her beloved pet somehow resurrected. Of course, as you might guess, there was absolutely nothing there.

Margaret said, quite matter-of-factly, 'I know this story is absurd. But it was Jip – no doubt! He was real as real could be and I *know* he was there. He had come back to see me.'

Not surprisingly, she has taken this as a sign that Jip survived in doggie Heaven and had somehow engineered a brief visit back to see his mistress.

Note, however, that Mrs Coolidge was in that idling state of mind that we have noted so often before in apparition cases. She was also lulled into a semi-expectation of seeing Jip as she reached her door. Can we be absolutely sure – as she is – that the mind is incapable of creating a vivid hallucination to match such an expectation? The fact that the dog vanished as soon as 'reality' took hold may be a very significant clue.

That said, it is unlikely that logic would ever persuade Margaret Coolidge.

SENSATIONS OF MITZI

As with human beings, apparitions of animals can affect all the senses. Debra, from New Hampshire in the USA, tells of a common occurrence that many pet owners have reported.

She owned a Siamese cat named Mitzi, who sadly died from pesticide poisoning. One night Debra felt a pressure on her leg and side as she lay

A group of ladies having tea during World War I in the village of Tingewick, Buckinghamshire. When Arthur Springer, a retired Scotland Yard detective, took this photograph nobody saw a dog in the garden.

in bed. Nothing was visible, but it was the exact sensation she used to get from Mitzi. On other occasions she had 'felt' the animal jump on to the bed as she used to do.

Of course, many amputees feel a 'phantom' sensation of their lost limb for months or even years afterwards. It seems that nerve sensations are 'learned' and can be triggered into a chain of activity reminiscent of the feeling one got previously (not unlike a physical form of the déjà vu sensation). Is it possible that the same thing can give rise to these common accounts of the persistent sensation of dead pets around the house?

NANA APPROVES

Lois Bourne had a similar story to tell about her cross-breed dog Nana. After she died, the bereavement struck home deeply. But both Lois and her husband claim to have seen the kitchen door nudge open, without any breeze to cause this, in just the way the dog would open it in life. Other sounds heard included her 'wheezy breathing' and the cracking sound of the wicker basket in which she slept. Again we must wonder how far these sensations are reality and how far they are based upon the familiarity of the sounds when the dog was living.

But Lois Bourne's oddest experience relates to the time when she adopted a new black labrador puppy and felt great trepidation about how her beloved Nana might react to the new dog in her owner's affections.

One day Lois was visited by a friend who professes to be psychic. She amazed Lois by telling the puppy that she knew she would be a lovely dog because Nana had told her so! Allegedly, the women had had a vivid 'out-of-the-body' dream (see Chapter 12) in which she had 'met' Nana in Heaven and had telepathic contact with the dog. Nana conveyed her acceptance of the new puppy and, so the psychic claimed, was often in Lois's home watching over the puppy like an auntie!

Both Lois and her husband claim to have seen the kitchen door nudge open, without any breeze to cause this, in just the way the dog would open it in life.

'TINA, LITTLE TINA'

This case is interestingly similar to the story of Jip from Pennsylvania. But, as you will see, it develops beyond the point where that one might be interpreted as hallucinatory.

In 1979 Joan Heartside from West Yorkshire lost a twelve-year-old dachshund named Tina. Some time afterwards she returned home at twilight and through the glass panel on the door clearly saw the deceased dog wagging its tail in anticipation.

Joan opened the door, saying, 'Little Tina. Hello, little Tina', and let the dog fuss about her as usual. Then she went to a cabinet across the room where she used to keep small chocolate treats to feed the animal. By now her realisation was dawning that Tina was not really there. It hit home when she saw there were no longer any chocolate drops in the cupboard.

Tina jumped on to the armchair playfully, exactly as she used to do when she was appealing for the chocolate. But Joan reluctantly had to explain that there was nothing to offer. As if this acted as an incantation to remove the spell, the apparition faded away.

As in other cases, this was only one of a number of occasions when Tina's presence was noted – although it was the most vivid. More often the sound of the dog's paws on the landing could be heard, and both Joan and her husband would frequently hear the familiar 'clicking' of Tina's long nails on the metal strip on the door whenever it was left open during the summer. They used to say to one another, 'Tina's come in', as if it were an everyday occurrence not to be thwarted by death.

Obviously, these experiences 'really' happened so far as Joan Heartside and her husband were concerned. The question remains as to how we should interpret them.

ANIMAL MEDIUMS

Some animals seem remarkably sensitive – or psychic, as we might otherwise term it. They are well known, for example, to react to an imminent earthquake and in some cultures, such as China, they are regarded as a better indicator than any science can offer. It could also be said that they are more likely to see a ghost than a human being is. Unfortunately, unlike Lois Bourne's psychic friend we cannot interview them about what took place!

Lois does claim a story from another friend about two dogs that were inseparable in life. At 5p.m. one night one of them, resting in its basket, gave out two bloodcurdling yelps that frightened the owner, then returned to normal. Was the dog dreaming, perhaps? About two hours later a phone call revealed that the other dog – some distance away – had died. The event occurred at the same time as the surviving dog had uttered those cries, making us wonder if it somehow knew.

In his book *Psychic Animals* Dennis Bardens reports a case which occurred in 1920 and was first told to the London *Daily News*.

A man went to work in Romania, leaving his dog Micky at home with his wife. Tragically, a couple of days later the dog was struck by a car and killed. The animal survived in the woman's arms for a time until a vet arrived to put it out of its misery. Her husband was under great strain so the woman decided not to break the news until he arrived back in Britain.

A few days later the wife received a letter from her husband who had now reached Romania. He described a remarkable occurrence on the train as he made his journey across country. A girl had entered the same carriage and asked in accented English if the small, white English dog (a perfect description of Micky) was his. He looked around bemused, but saw nothing where she pointed. He then fell asleep and awoke to the sound of scratching – noises that appeared to be exactly like those that Micky would make when outside the bathroom door at home.

Again nothing was seen, but the man was sufficiently perturbed to say in the letter (which his wife had kept): 'I could have sworn it was Micky. Is he all right?'

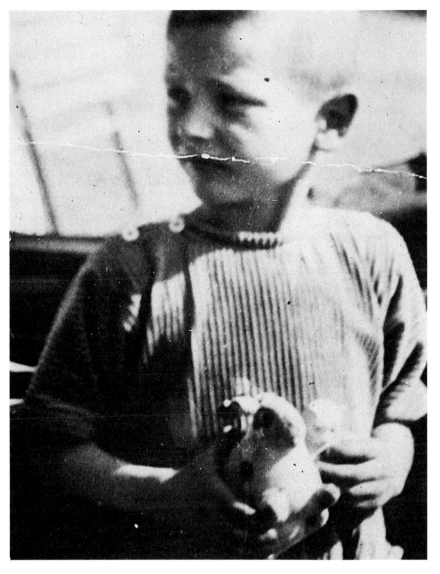

Ghosts of deceased animals often appear mysteriously on photographs when they are developed, even though nothing was seen by the photographer or those being photographed when the picture was taken. In this 1925 snapshot the kitten in the boy's hand was not 'really' there but was later identified as a family pet that had been killed by a dog.

This incident occurred on the very same night that, many hundreds of miles away, the dog *did* lie dying in the arms of its mistress. Had it somehow produced a crisis apparition, exactly as with some human beings on the point of death?

THE RETURN OF PETE

One of the most remarkable stories of animal survival is the tale of Pete, a mongrel owned by a man named John Simpson who was a Confederate spy during the American Civil War.

The couple were found by enemy soldiers, and Simpson was sentenced to be shot at dawn the next day. He asked for his dog to spend the final night with him, but permission was refused. Indeed, immediately afterwards, and out of earshot, the Union colonel issued an order to kill the dog. It was beaten to death.

As Simpson was led out for his execution he asked the escort if Pete was all right. The soldier lied to him, said that he was, and promised to look after the animal. The spy went contentedly to his fate.

He was tied to a post and awaiting the gunfire when he looked down at his feet and cried out that Pete had come to see him. 'I knew the old fellow would come to say goodbye,' he exclaimed. The men, who all knew the truth and could see nothing was there, were bemused and blindfolded Simpson. They assumed that he had simply gone crazy with fear. Then they saw the colonel staring at the same vacant spot, ashen white and clearly also seeing the ghost dog.

Unable to order the execution, the colonel stayed the guns and walked away shocked. That night Confederates attacked the camp and the colonel was killed. John Simpson was freed, and apparently argued to the end of his days that he had seen his dog and that Pete's ghost must have returned from the afterlife to save his master.

We cannot prove that dogs or cats have minds, let alone souls.

THE EVIDENCE AGAINST

Many of the arguments which suggest that apparitions might occur in the mind seems to apply with ghostly animal encounters. However, there is an added complication. We cannot prove that dogs or cats have minds, let alone souls, and yet they still seem to be involved in a two-way communication.

In the case of the man on the Romanian train you might suggest that it was he who detected the death of his dog and the dog's spirit therefore need have had no role to play. However, the fact that the apparition was seen by a stranger, and not the dog's owner, might be significant. Further, when a dog 'senses' danger, or the passing of its master, or the death of another dog (as has occurred on plenty of occasions) this seems explicable only if the animal has consciousness or a mind of the same order as a human being.

Most apparitions of dogs and cats are very transitory, and often do not feature any response by the animal to its owner. One of the best cat survival stories on the files of the Society for Psychical Research has the animal seen three times on one day after its death and chased across the garden by its owner and servants. Yet the cat walks blindly past, following a route that it might have done in life, and pays no heed at all to its pursuers.

Perhaps this evidence best suits the idea that animal ghosts are at most a form of video replay of the life energy of the creature, still reverberating faintly like the sound of a gong that was struck some seconds before.

THE EVIDENCE FOR

Spiritualist philosophy does try to overcome some of the problems expressed about the survival of all life forms. It claims, from the messages allegedly sent by surviving humans, that in the afterlife only the souls of animals who were bonded by love to a human can survive as discrete entities. They are the privileged few of the animal kingdom who have progressed upwards on the spiritual ladder of evolution. Those who are not yet at that stage and from the lower life forms do not possess individual surviving consciousness but exist within a group soul for the entire species.

Presumably this means that when an ant dies its essence returns to the group life force that is the ant, not unlike water in a rain puddle returning to the clouds when it evaporates. This may reflect an interesting feature of the natural world that such creatures exhibit during earthly existence: they act as if part of a community. Ants seem to have the same sort of 'hive mentality' as do bees and termites. The life and death of a few creatures appears incidental to the survival of the group: they are freely sacrificed and never mourned. There is evidence that each individual creature is part of a group, not a discrete entity as each human being is.

One wonders, though, how far down the evolutionary chain we can take this concept. Are plants conscious? Do they have a group soul? Does any of their essence 'survive' death? What of microbes? Again, very primitive organisms such as algae and coral exhibit the same sort of group mind patterns of behaviour that Spiritualist theory discusses. A neat order seems to emerge from these contemplations.

It is also clearly possible to interpret the many cases where dogs and cats are witnessed by their owners after the pet's death, or the crisis apparitions such as Micky on the Romanian train, as being evidence of animal survival. This may well be what is happening.

In addition there are a few photographs which depict animals – usually dogs – at some point after their deaths. These have turned up unexpectedly – normally unseen by the camera operator whilst they were filming something else. Can we account for all of these by illusion or hoax?

YOUR VERDICT : A SUMMARY

AGAINST SURVIVAL

- Ghostly animals rarely interact with humans, who see them behaving more like inanimate 'films'.

- Only certain animals seem to appear as ghosts – the ones that are the closest to humans as 'pets' or companions.

- No consistent evidence exists about which animals survive and why.

FOR SURVIVAL

- There are some cases where animals appear to their owners and (possibly) each other at the time of death.

- Some ghost animals are three-dimensional and reactive, seeming to exhibit purpose.

- There are a few photographs which purport to show animals after death.

ELECTRONIC VOICE PHENOMENA

————◆————

For many years research has been carried out into a little-known phenomenon – contact with the dead, not through a Spiritualist medium but via the use of electronic equipment. The voices of discarnate entities have not only been heard, but recorded too. Electronic voice phenomena (EVP), as the concept is known, has been around since electricity was harnessed and used to power radio equipment.

As far back as the nineteenth century, scientists toyed with the idea of electronic communication with spirits of the deceased. Thomas Edison, inventor of the phonograph and electric light bulb, proposed such an apparatus. He failed to perfect his machine, but since then others have claimed success. One of them was Swedish film producer Friedrich Jurgenson. It all began in 1959.

VOICES FROM SWEDEN

That summer, Jurgenson was out in the remote countryside near his house, recording birdsong. Later, when he listened to the playback, he was bemused to hear not only the sound of birds, but voices actually discussing the birds sounds! He was certain that no one else had been present at the time, but speculated, despite the coincidence of subject matter, that perhaps his portable tape recorder had picked up a stray radio transmission.

Jurgenson repeated the procedure, and the voices appeared again. Only this time they addressed him personally, and claimed to be the spirits of dead friends and relatives. This spurred him on to carry out many more experiments, and in 1964 he published the results in a book entitled *Voices from the Universe*. Not surprisingly, the book attracted a lot of attention across Europe, including that of scientists liberal-minded enough to want to put Jurgenson's claims through rigorous experimental study.

Professor Hans Bender, a German psychologist and director of a state-run parapsychological laboratory at the University of Freiburg, and Dr Konstantin Raudive, former professor of psychology at Uppsala

He was bemused to hear not only the sound of birds, but voices actually discussing the bird sounds!

and Riga universities, cooperated in an attempt to replicate Jurgenson's experiments.

With the help of physicist Dr Alex Schneider and electronic engineering specialist Theodor Rudolph they appeared to be astonishingly successful. Around one hundred thousand inexplicable voices, uttering sentences that were often hard to hear or interpret and which were little more than short phrases, were produced on tape! In a scientific paper written by Professor Bender, he said: 'An extensive examination with better technical equipment in May 1970 made the paranormal hypothesis of the origin of the Voice Phenomena highly probable.'

But not everyone was convinced. David Ellis, a Cambridge student, received a grant under the Pierrot-Warwick postgraduate studentship for psychical research, which enabled him to carry out a two-year study into EVP between 1970 and 1972. He concluded that the phenomenon could be explained in terms of heightened states of imagination, and announced that, at least in six cases, Dr Raudive might have recorded voices from Russian radio broadcasts.

In a more recent article, British researcher Gilbert Bonner made this comment about Ellis: 'He made no attempt himself to try to record these voices, but merely observed the methods of Raudive whom he met in Germany and on this and other interviews with other researchers he based his conclusions.' Other critics have also commented that most of the so-called voices are so hard to make out they could be nothing more than normal background hiss upon which people *want* to hear words and sentences.

Dr Raudive published his results in book form, and this attracted the attention of British publisher Colin Smythe who was interested in purchasing rights on it. But he was not prepared to endorse the book blindly: he demanded fresh objective proof. Following Dr Raudive's instructions, Smythe produced a voice himself, which a colleague named Peter Bander recognised as that of his dead mother. *Were* people merely hearing what they wanted to hear?

With the sponsorship of the *Daily Mirror*, a series of controlled tests were planned; they were to be verified by independent scientists. Chief electronic engineers Ray Prickett and Keith Attwood, of Pye Ltd, carried out the first experiment. Full precautions were taken to screen out stray radio signals and to ensure that nothing could impinge on to the recording heads of the four tape recorders – nothing *normal*, at least.

Everyone in the room was astonished. Over a twenty-seven-minute period more than two hundred voices manifested, twenty-seven of which came through very clearly. They spoke in various languages what were usually faint, hard to decipher and even whispered phrases. In one case the

Most of the so-called voices are so hard to make out they could be nothing more than normal background hiss.

voice of Winston Churchill was reputedly detected, saying, 'Mark this!'; although such an identification was, of course, subjective.

Even more astonishing was the fact that some of the voices seemed to address individuals in the room. As Colin Smythe told us: 'We were all amazed. The evidence was very clear – there was no way the voices could have been produced except by paranormal means. The engineers who supervised the experiment began with an attitude of healthy scepticism which changed to one of conversion.'

Further tests were carried out in the laboratories of Belling & Lee by Peter Hale, an expert trained in the suppression of stray electrical signals such as radio emissions which can sometimes create difficulties with scientific equipment. Some had thought this might account for the picking up of such a strange miscellany of voices as the EVP work was recording. Afterwards, Hale commented: 'From the results obtained ... something is happening which I can't explain in normal physical terms.'

Dr Raudive's book, *Breakthrough*, was published in Britain in 1971. Without a doubt these recordings, independently verified by experts, were a breakthrough of some sort in the field of parapsychological research. But an even bigger leap was on its way, if its proponents could somehow convince a disbelieving world.

SPIRICOM

On 27 October 1977 a rich American inventor called George Meek claimed a huge breakthrough: he had designed a machine to allow two-way conversations between the living and the dead. The instrument used complex electronics to pack small bundles of radio frequencies alongside a single constantly generated tone. A communicating spirit was then expected to change any or several of these frequencies and thus superimpose a message on to the background noise.

The equipment seemed to rely for some of its effectiveness on the psychic ability of Bill O'Neil, who operated it. O'Neil eventually recorded many conversations with two alleged entities known as 'Doc Nick' and 'Dr Mueller', both dead.

Some of the recordings were very clear indeed, although the spirit of 'Mueller' spoke with a sort of synthesised electronic voice. This caused some critics to suggest that O'Neil might be using an artificial larynx – the sort of device that patients are given to enable them to vocalise after surgery for throat cancer. But Will Cerney, who had helped Meek in his original design plans, had tried various ways to duplicate the voice, including the use of an artificial larynx and other filters. He reported no success.

'The engineers who supervised the experiment began with an attitude of healthy scepticism which changed to one of conversion.'

Mueller provided background information about his earthly existence, most of which checked out. He also suggested ways in which the equipment might be improved to give better results! Meek called the project 'Spiricom', and was prepared to give his designs to anyone who wanted to build similar machines to replicate his work. Certainly he did not seem to be involved in a moneymaking scheme and he theorised that, if survival after death was proven, then people would improve their attitude to one another and to the environment.

John Fuller, renowned for his high standard of investigation of other paranormal mysteries, became embroiled in the controversy. Ultimately he wrote a book called *The Ghost of 29 Megacycles*. Right from the first page it is obvious that Fuller is uncomfortable with his material. Yet he is very impressed with both Meek and O'Neil. If it was a hoax, what was the point? Neither man sought publicity. O'Neil, although poor, did not want money, and Meek seemingly did not need any. In fact Meek poured thousands of dollars of his own money into the project.

If everyone is being honest, this is almost certainly undisputed proof of life after death.

However, Fuller must have been aware that there are certain groups in America and Britain who will stoop to highly elaborate hoaxes in order to expose the fallibility of psychical researchers, and thus cause scepticism amongst scientists in the viability of paranormal phenomena.

During his background research for the book Fuller travelled to England to met British EVP expert Raymond Cass, who told him:

'I've gone over the tapes time and time again, as an audiophonic expert. There's one thing I'm certain of. There are two different voices. In other words, O'Neil is not holding a conversation with himself. Other voice tests are still being made by Meek, but I'm confident they'll show the same results. Those of us who know Meek and his track record are convinced that there is no fraud on his part.'

Is electronic voice phenomena truly a communication with beings in the afterlife? A large number of scientists and technical specialists think so – the Spiricom project attracted the favourable attention of an officer attached to the US Air Force Electronic Security Command. Of course, there will always be sceptics.

Listening to the Spiricom voices is an eerie experience. On the one hand one is conscious that one might be the subject of a giant leg pull. Then again, if everyone is being honest this is almost certainly undisputed proof of life after death.

In fact George Meek himself makes no bones about that. In his published material he assures us that: 'For the first time in mankind's history it has been proven incontestably that death is merely a door to continuing life. It is now certain that individual consciousness – what we often refer to as personality – continues to exist in a disease-free and pain-free environment.'

If Meek were lying about the integrity of his contacts, this would be a wicked con trick performed on the weak and vulnerable. Assuming that he is telling the truth – and we see no reasonable evidence that counters this at present – then the consequence is apparent. There seems little likelihood that he is being hoaxed or is misinterpreting the situation.

However, despite the scientific training and the technical talk about perfecting Spiricom and moving on to Vidicom (the next step – planned visual contact with the dead!) – the snatches of conversation from these spectral voices still seem oddly banal. In describing his passing, Dr Mueller says: 'When I got over here it was like waking up in the morning and not knowing where you are at.' He also offers a few philosophical points such as remarking that he is not aware of time (after disturbing his Earth contact at 4a.m.!). Interspersed with this are some seemingly trivial conversations, for instance one about carrots!

After a disappointing series of communications the dead doctor apparently moved on to a new spirit dimension where contact through Spiricom proved impossible – an event he had warned would happen. One wonders why the rulers of eternity did not let him stop a little longer after establishing this promising link with Earth.

Frankly, to some people this quick exit of the chief communicator may appear a convenient cop-out, but of course it could merely be the way of the cosmos. An experiment such as this might seem very momentous to us, but in fact be utterly subservient to the personal spiritual development of Dr Mueller if 'he' really does still live on in some other realm.

We take no stance on Spiricom, but merely offer you the facts to judge for yourself. It is, however, worth presenting the comments of Alex MacRae. As an EVP researcher himself, he travelled from his home in Scotland to the USA to see Meek. MacRae reported in the objective journal *Common Ground* that he was impressed by the team's efforts but not altogether convinced by their results.

He cited a contact via Spiricom with a person who appeared to 'drop in' on the link with Dr Mueller. This was a man who gave his name as Fred Ingstrom and said he had died in rural Virginia in 1830. Firstly, it is slightly curious that if time and space mean nothing in the afterlife all the contacts reported via Spiricom in the USA should be from deceased Americans. Why nobody from other lands? But perhaps this judgement is a little premature on so small a sample.

Fred used terms like 'OK' and 'Oh, boy,' which would hardly be habitual language in a rural community 160 years ago.

However, MacRae noted from a linguistic point of view that some of the comments by the deceased Fred Ingstrom were a little puzzling. For example, he was told 'You sound like a robot' and fully understood the meaning of that expression, even though the word 'robot' was not invented until a hundred years after his alleged death.

Of course, this really establishes nothing. If learning goes on in the afterlife, why should he not be familiar with a robot? After all, he was claiming to be familiar with the use of a Spiricom machine.

More intriguing is that, as MacRae notes, Fred used terms like 'OK' and 'Oh, boy', which would hardly be habitual language in a rural community 160 years ago. Both these expressions are commonly found amongst the language of the Earth-bound communicator on the more mundane end of Spiricom. Naturally, Fred might have picked them up this way – but remember this was a one-off 'drop-in', not the regular communicator Dr Mueller.

Having said that, Alex MacRae does admit that the equipment designed for Spiricom is very interesting and offers no reason to suspect the integrity of the people behind it. We shall have to wait and see whether more results emerge and whether Vidicom ever becomes reality.

THE MESSAGE ON THE ANSWERPHONE

Electronic voice phenomena keeps pace with the technological progression of recording equipment. With the increase in sales of answerphones over the last few years, it was inevitable that something should eventually turn up on one of these machines.

Manchester businessman Bryan Lynn returned home on 9 September 1991 and played back the tape on his machine. Amongst the usual messages from business clients and friends was something that made his flesh crawl. At 4.42p.m. precisely, a voice had spoken on to the tape which can only be described as 'demonic'. It had to be heard to appreciate its awfulness.

The voice sounds inhuman, and it is impossible to state with accuracy what it is saying, due to distortion. Mr Lynn contacted us with the tape, and it was examined by a recording studio. There it was both speeded up and slowed down. Bryan thought he could make out the words 'force me to use' in the middle of the ten-second message. Others think the words 'I hate you' appear at the beginning.

Of course one immediately wonders if the whole thing is an elaborate hoax, but Bryan assures us that none of his friends or acquaintances would have pulled off such a stunt. Even if he was picked at random, what would be the motivation? No one has ever admitted playing such a prank. The tape is still undergoing investigation.

THE GHOSTS OF ROMEO FOXTROT

Romeo Foxtrot 398 is the code name of the only original Avro Lincoln bomber still intact. If legend is to be believed it is one of the most haunted places on Earth, generating now famous audio recordings and offering what seems excellent evidence of life after death.

The Lincoln was designed as a successor to the world-famous Lancaster but entered service after World War II. So Romeo Foxtrot 398 was mostly used on equipment testing missions and was withdrawn in the 1960s, later going to Cosford Aerospace Museum near Wolverhampton where years of loving restoration work began. It was during this period that the haunted nature of the bomber (which had never fired a shot in anger) was to become apparent.

One restoration worker told how obscure materials needed to fix the plane would be handed to them out of the blue or 'appear' in the hangar overnight. This gave the workers at the Cosford Museum Society a sense of being aided in their quest.

After various impressions of a presence inside the aircraft one worker allegedly saw the ghost; his experience was followed by that of another man who reported a dim figure sitting in the flight engineer's seat. They regarded the spectre as friendly, and reporter Hilda Baker noted the sense that they were being protected, citing an instance where a member of the Society fell from the wing on to a concrete floor but escaped completely unscathed.

The belief seemed to be that the ghost came from another aircraft which had crashed in 1943, and the possible reason for its presence was that an engine from that plane was in the hangar alongside the Lincoln. The various stories attracted the attention of the Paranormal Research Bureau in Derbyshire, who soon decided to launch an investigation.

We are grateful to member Michael Hicklin for his detailed account of these enquiries, which began on 1 September 1985. Several group researchers detected 'cold spots' (see p.139) in certain locations.

The oddest experience was that of Michael's wife Linda, who heard a noise in the gun turret and saw a small handle rotating on its own. The group then left several cameras and two tape recorders running on the locked aircraft and departed the scene. Upon their return they found one camera opened, despite the fact that the keys to Romeo Foxtrot had never left the possession of the supervising museum staff.

Linda heard a noise in the gun turret and saw a small handle rotating on its own.

On 20 June 1987 permission was granted to conduct an overnight experiment to monitor the aircraft and hangar. Six people took part, including Ivan Spenceley who had recently joined the group. He had a plan to tape the ghost and wanted to set up his expensive machine, whose microphones were so sensitive that they would pick up the slightest movement. As the team would have to sit about doing nothing, this made them feel redundant. So they compromised by leaving the tape, which was wired into the cockpit, unattended for two one-hour spells. The ghost hunters stayed inside the plane for the rest of the night.

After the first hour they returned to find the tape tangled up in the machine. Michael Hicklin claimed it had done this before 'on every occasion it had been used'. Ivan Spenceley disagreed and felt that something more unusual had occurred. But he succeeded in getting the recorder working again for 1.05a.m. Later that night a handle turned on its own and the taps in the hangar toilet did likewise.

Two weeks later Spenceley told the group that on analysing the second tape he had heard faint noises – Morse code blips, Merlin engines, voices

Ivan Spenceley prepares his recording equipment which he believes has measured the strange sounds emanating from aircraft Romeo Foxtrot in its haunted hangar at Cosford Museum. Were these recordings proof of survival or was there another explanation?

on an intercom and hangar doors opening and closing. They were too faint to hear words amidst the static. Hicklin says that, despite asking several times, the tape was never replayed for him as it was reported away being analysed.

Then, on 17 July 1988, the *Sunday Express* carried an article by Graham Bell which described Spenceley's experiment. The museum administrator claimed that he had personally ensured that the hangar was empty and had locked the doors behind the test. Michael Hicklin disputes this, alleging that no staff members were with the group on 20-21 June 1987. He also points out that the team heard only a brief extract from the tape played to them in the hangar that night and which was later aired on television. Hicklin says this sounded to him just like the metal panels of the hangar 'clicking' as they cooled down.

After July 1988 Spenceley made further media appearances. He featured on a TV show about UFOs with Jenny Randles, telling of a strange close encounter. She debated this with him, but at the time she was unaware of his link with these ghostly recordings which were not mentioned on air. His UFO case featured in a 1989 book written by Tim Good. Despite the fact that it had taken place in January 1988, Hicklin claims that Spenceley never mentioned his sighting before he left the group.

On one visit to the hangar, Spenceley had seen a wartime pilot opening Romeo Foxtrot's door.

We take no sides on the thorny issue of group politics. But Ivan Spenceley's tape is of potential importance, so any major disagreement about its content has to be pointed out. It seems feasible to us that the story about the museum staff locking the hangar doors may refer to a later solo visit by Spenceley after June 1987. Hicklin again seems to dispute this possibility, based on what the museum curator told him. Alternatively the press report may just be inaccurate.

A new account in the *Sunday Mirror* on 19 March 1989 contained a claim that on one visit to the hangar, Spenceley had seen a wartime pilot opening Romeo Foxtrot's door. But the most recent presentation of the case is a big colour article in the Sunday supplement of the *News of the World* on 27 October 1991. This tells of his first visit with the Derbyshire group in 1987. The incident that Michael Hicklin says was simply a tape jamming is told with a more inexplicable air and Spenceley relates twenty post-1987 trips to Romeo Foxtrot (including eight full nights spent in the darkened cockpit). During these visits he has made further tape recordings – including one during broad daylight.

Three former crew members from the plane have reconstructed their in-flight checks, and the tape of these is – according to Spenceley – identical to those picked up from the spook aircraft. This may add credence to his claim about the supernatural origin of the sounds.

Spenceley seems to think that pieces of crashed aircraft grafted on to Romeo Foxtrot may be a possible reason for an 'energy replay' haunting. But there is also a legend about a pilot who reputedly said he loved the plane so much that after death he would haunt it.

We have no desire to suggest that either Hicklin's or Spenceley's version of the story is inaccurate or untrue. We present the conflict in their views only to show that even the most impressive evidence needs careful consideration. If all that Spenceley says is ultimately verified, it forms prime evidence. But a paranormal researcher who was present that first night has mundane suggestions to explain two of the key incidents. Whilst Michael Hicklin may not be correct in his evaluation the situation shows the need to beware of taking evidence at face value.

CHINGLE'S CHRISTMAS SPINETINGLE

Chingle Hall at Goosnargh, on the moors to the north-east of Preston in Lancashire, can lay claim to being northern England's most spook-ridden building. It dates back over seven hundred years, and its most frequented spot is the small room where priests hid to escape persecution. Here and in the adjacent wood-floored corridor many people have heard knocking sounds and creaking boards late at night. There have also been visual phenomena such as blue flashing lights not unlike lightning bouncing off the wall and occasional partial apparitions of a figure alleged to be a monk or priest.

'Whether it is just a gimmick or it will actually work we'll find out tonight.'

Possibly the most remarkable experience occurred in the hour between 11p.m. and midnight on 25 December 1980 when Gerald Main, a reporter with BBC Radio Lancashire, set up a 'ghost hunt' with psychic researcher Terence Whitaker.

Terence had taken along a device he jokingly termed the 'spectre detector', which issued a continuous, high-pitched note. Any slight change in the local electrical field of the area – for example, if an unseen figure should enter the room – would alter the pitch of this sound. As he said before the night's proceedings: 'Whether it is just a gimmick or it will actually work we'll find out tonight.'

As the night progressed the two men were joined by a Spiritualist, Colin Church, who claimed to 'feel and sense' the presence of a figure in the nearby bedroom. They left the spectre detector in the priest's room and suddenly experienced a dramatic plunge in temperature. Colin called it 'a psychic breeze', and even the hardened reporter was a little fazed.

They brought the spectre detector back from the priest's room, and at 11p.m. the temperature dropped again. As it did so, the note on the

machine increased markedly in pitch in gradual stages. Colin Church talked calmly into the tape recorder, describing events as they happened: He said: 'Whoever he is, he is standing right here [between us].'

As the trio recovered from this experience they were joined by Fred Knowles, the Hall manager, who had been in the living quarters downstairs watching a movie on TV. He told them of a skeleton being excavated, but his story was rudely interrupted by the ghost!

Suddenly, there were several very distinctive loud knocks – clearly picked up on the tape. Gerald Main noted that at first he thought that Fred must have kicked a wooden chest with his foot. Fred said not, stepped back and announced as calmly as anything: 'I am exceedingly glad that intervened, gentlemen – it was the ghost.'

The old building at Chingle Hall at Goosnargh, Lancashire, is regularly visited by researchers who have been attempting to procure solid evidence. Both tape recordings and visual images have been captured which some allege may relate to the ghost of John Wall who once lived in the house. Wall was a Roman Catholic martyr who was executed in 1679.

By 11.52p.m. they were back in the priest's room contemplating what had happened, and Terence Whitaker and Fred Knowles were swopping stories about footsteps heard echoing over the floorboards. Suddenly three more distinctive loud knocks came again. Everyone stopped talking at once. Several more isolated bangs followed, seemingly progressing from the priest's hide and out into the corridor. This time all three men were standing away from any of the furniture. There was no doubt in anybody's mind that the sounds started *inside* the wall.

It was once again freezing cold. As Gerald Main struggled to move his equipment for a better recording, Colin Church reported feeling cold air brush past him and Terence Whitaker briefly saw the ghost go around the back of the door. It was 'an indefinable shape'.

As midnight struck and their ghost watch ended, the radio presenter was left struggling to insist to his listeners that what had occurred was no set-up. What the tape had recorded was very real.

This is by no means the only time that similar sounds have been recorded in this chilling location.

PHONING HOME

Lucia Randles (no relation to the co-author of this book) had a quite remarkable experience which defies all logical understanding. It occurred in the summer of 1949 when she was in her mid-thirties, married to a former British soldier, now an office manager, who had rescued her from the devastation of her German homeland and brought her to England.

Early one evening there was a fierce thunderstorm and the air was charged with static. Being extremely sensitive to atmospheric electricity, Lucia was acutely aware of this. But she struggled to ignore it by doing a large pile of ironing, her thoughts wandering as she waited for her husband to return.

She knew there was a wages payroll that day and so he was going to be late. It was therefore no real surprise when the phone rang: perhaps he was apologising for being particularly late. She idly picked up the receiver with her left hand and carried on ironing with the other. She was not looking at the phone, but concentrating on not burning the clothes.

It was indeed her husband, but he sounded very faint. She heard him say, 'I love you so', and she was puzzled by his tone.

'Where are you?' Lucia asked.

He replied, in a voice that trailed away into nothingness: 'I am so far, far away ....'

The entire experience had only lasted a few moments, and Lucia was sufficiently concerned to put the iron down and stare at the phone – or rather try to stare at the phone. For in that instant she realised the horrible truth. Her hand was cupped as if holding a receiver, but in fact it was clutching thin air. They did not even own a telephone!

Lucia, being a very practical person, chastised herself for daydreaming. Obviously she was worried by the storm, and in her state of reverie during the repetitive chore of ironing she had simply imagined the phone call. Pure wishful thinking. She tried to brush away the experience – until one hour later there was a knock at the door. It was a policeman. He told her that her husband was dead.

He had disturbed a car thief on his way from the office. The man had shot him at point-blank range in the head and he had died almost immediately, the inquest later reported. The time of death was more or less exactly that when Lucia Randles had received her non-existent phone call on a telephone that simply was not there.

Three weeks later, while she was in a state of deep depression, there was another hot and oppressive day. This time there was no storm, but Lucia was acutely aware of the static charge. Suddenly she got an urge to communicate with her husband and decided to try holding the imaginary phone again and talk into the air as if it existed. This time she knew there was no phone and nothing happened.

Suddenly, there was a flash of light as if lightning had struck the windowpane. A crackling, buzzing sound filled the room and her fine, long hair stood on end as if attracted by an electrical field. Right in front of her was a strange white ball of light – tugging her hair towards it.

The ball had no shape, being just an amorphous mass, and after a couple of seconds it disappeared instantaneously. But Lucia felt much better now. She saw it as a sign from her husband, and regarded the experience as advice to get out of her depression.

This is not the only known example of phantom phone calls – although they are usually received on real telephones. Whether we consider it genuinely inexplicable, or hallucination tied in with Lucia's sensitive awareness of her husband's plight at the exact moment, it is no less extraordinary.

To us it can never be more than an anecdote or story. To Lucia it was all the proof she would need that we do survive death.

Her hand was cupped as if holding a receiver, but in fact it was clutching thin air. They did not even own a telephone!

THE EVIDENCE AGAINST

Once you have heard some of the recordings made during EVP research the problems are immediately apparent. You have to strain very carefully to hear anything at all. Even then you are picking out what seem like voices from the background hiss of the tape. It is more than possible that at times you only think you hear a message. In fact you hear what you expect, or hope, to hear. The pattern or order is created by the mind, not by the ears.

This is evidenced by an experience in the early 1960s when people throughout Europe detected a message on short wave radio. It was debated for months, but its wording was agreed by all. It was even heard by Jenny Randles who picked it up on her old radiogram. The message quite distinctly said that it was coming from a transmission station that is 'situated in outer space'.

Many years later the truth was revealed. This was not, as had been supposed by some, contact with a secret satellite or even with extraterrestrials! It was a ground telecommunications station in Romania which used an unusual transmission method. This severely distorted the sound unless very sophisticated equipment was used. As a result, words such as 'out of phase' could sound exactly like 'outer space'. Hundreds who thought that the message said 'outer space' would have taken an oath in court. In fact they were all wrong.

On the other hand, the Spiricom messages are a definite step upwards. Once you get over the peculiar modulation and Dalek-like effect of the voice you can distinctly hear what is said and get some semblance of a two-way conversation. However, nothing startling seems to be said. It is disappointingly mundane, given that this is supposedly contact with another sphere of life where (presumably) some of the greatest minds that have ever lived now reside.

None the less, Spiricom seems to offer a stark choice. It is likely that the messages are either what they purport to be – contact with the dead – or a hoax by persons unknown. There is no obvious evidence or motivation for hoax, but unless or until the experiments are duplicated by sceptical scientists elsewhere this work will never be widely accepted as proof. Sadly, as is often the case with this great debate, it comes down to a matter of whom to believe.

THE EVIDENCE FOR

The most positive thing that can be said about these experiments into electronic recording of the dead is that they are relatively simple to duplicate. Anyone can leave a tape recorder to run in an empty house and listen to what results. Of course, faint sounds that may well be detected have many possible sources – from children playing in the distance with their cries caught on the wind to a radio in a house next door picked up through conduction across the floorboards.

However, there are claims that some successes have been achieved in this way, and inexplicable voices have turned up through such do-it-yourself experimentation. With fairly limited modification of the microphone system some screening from routine noises can be achieved, or for even better results a sound-proofed room might be available. Considering how easy it is to carry out such research, the truth or fallacy of the EVP argument should be simple to establish.

As for Spiricom, its startling results make the extra cost in building the equipment worthwhile to research groups worldwide. As the developers seem perfectly willing to share their methods and encourage such duplication, this appears to be positive evidence (would a hoaxer risk obvious failure in this way?) and should be taken up more eagerly than at present.

This is one field of the paranormal where the sceptics should put up or shut up. They have no real excuse for not doing so. There are real difficulties in finding alternative solutions to successful Spiricom results – other than, of course, an outright hoax. We think that scientists should attempt this research as soon as possible and report on what they find one way or another. If they do not even try to conduct such a study, what are they afraid of? That it might work?

YOUR VERDICT : A SUMMARY

AGAINST SURVIVAL

- Electrical equipment can pick up all sorts of stray signals such as radio messages. These might produce spurious 'communications'.

- There are usually possible logical explanations – such as the tape jamming, floorboards creaking or hangar panels contracting in the cold night.

- Cases such as that of Lucia Randles appear to occur in the mind of the witness, whatever their stimulus in the first place.

FOR SURVIVAL

- There are a growing number of cases where seemingly reliable evidence has been tape recorded. Can they all be explained away?

- In the Spiricom experiments, either someone is not the telling the truth (for which at present there seems no evidence) or real contact has occurred.

- Even if phantom phone calls are by definition imaginary, the experience contains clear paranormal overtones which are hard to explain in any way other than some form of communication made at the point of – or immediately after – death.

GHOSTS ON VIDEO AND COMPUTER

———◆———

There is no doubt that some apparitions are subjective, at least in the sense that witnesses need to be 'sensitive' to 'see' them. On record are cases where just one person in a group saw an apparition. Whilst he could describe it in vivid detail, the others were completely oblivious to the phenomenon. However, there are many examples where groups have shared a sighting, lending weight to the belief that ghosts are objective – that they possess a reality of their own. If apparitions are actually 'seen', using the apparatus of the eyes, then there is no reason why they should not be recorded on film.

We have already discussed ghosts which have appeared on still film in Chapter 5. Strangely, most of these were not seen at the time the picture was taken! Perhaps film, like certain individuals, is sensitive to the presence of ghostly phenomena. In that case, whether or not an apparition is visible to the eye, if it moved down a corridor before disappearing through a closed door – and there was a video camera present – you would expect it to be recorded. And if it was, it must be an objective phenomenon rather than subjective imagination.

LIKE A THIEF IN THE NIGHT

This perplexing case was investigated by Peter Hough with the assistance of a young man called Ian Topham, under the auspices of the Association for the Scientific Study of Anomalous Phenomena (ASSAP). The location is Butterflies night club in Oldham, Lancashire. The manager, Cameron Walsh-Balshaw, told us what happened in the early hours of 27 October 1991.

'John Reid – the assistant manager – and I locked up the club and set the burglar alarms. Every Saturday night, after work, we usually go down to his house, have a cup of tea, a laugh and watch a video. Then I travel home to Doncaster.

'When we checked the video, we found we had filmed someone coming down the corridor, who turned and walked through the closed cash office door.'

A still from the security camera film taken at Butterflies nightclub in Oldham, Lancashire at 4.32a.m. on the morning of 27 October 1991. This unique film seems to depict a ghostly figure which walked through a wall at exactly the moment when the alarm bells were set off in this same part of the locked and empty premises. Police found no evidence of a break in – at least not one carried out by an intruder from this world!

'At around four-thirty, the police phoned to say the alarms were going off. We came down to the club, but there was no sign of a forced entry, so the police came in with us to check the interior. Everything was okay. The alarms had been triggered from inside the cash office, but this was still securely locked, and there was no one inside.'

The men checked the security camera which films the corridor outside the cash office. 'When we checked the video, we found we had filmed someone coming down the corridor, who turned and walked through the closed cash office door. The door was shut; indeed the video showed it shut, yet the figure seems to go through the door ....'

The film is timed and dated. At 4.32a.m., something in a short-sleeved shirt walked into the cash office and triggered off the alarms. The system works by sending out a fan of infra-red beams. If one of them is interrupted nothing happens, but when two in succession are blocked, the alarms sound. It does not need anything substantial to break the infra-red beams. Even particles of smoke can achieve this.

Like many Victorian buildings, Butterflies has its fair share of ghostly happenings. Several staff have experienced strange things over the years. When the story received some local publicity, a man called Derek Lloyd came forward and speculated that the ghost might be that of his father who tragically died in the building whilst carrying out renovation work in 1936. In that same year, another man was electrocuted to death during work on a sub-station situated outside.

We interviewed some of the staff at the *Oldham Evening Chronicle* who had examined the film. Photographer Darren Robinson said: 'I was very impressed when I first saw it. The manager came across as sincere, and I have no reason to believe it was a hoax. However, someone suggested it might be a double exposure. Perhaps a previous image was not erased properly when the tape was reused.'

Is this possible? Could a previous image of the corridor with the office door open and someone walking through it, have only been partially erased during re-recording? Further, could it have been a deliberate hoax? Separate recordings mixed on to one tape could have created the same effect. After all, double exposure – both accidental and fraudulent – has accounted for many ghostly images in the past.

Mr Balshaw poured cold water on the first explanation: 'That can't happen. All our tapes are demagnetised before they're used again. It's part of our insurance agreement. We have a bank of tapes, but what we start off with each night is basically a brand-new tape.'

What of the possibility of a hoax? We learned that there was a simple test for this. If there is more than one image on videotape, then there must be more than one 'signal'. The tape was tested by BBC technicians using an oscillator. Dave Hulme of the BBC verified to us that there was only one signal on the tape. It was a genuine image of a figure walking down a corridor and passing through a solid door ....

Roger Bryson wrote two newspaper articles about the case for the *Oldham Evening Chronicle*. He had confirmed with the police that the alarms had gone off that night, and at that time. Roger explained that as a journalist he would always have reservations, but when he learned that the image could not be due to double exposure he added. 'If that's the case, it is a very startling video.'

THERE'S A GHOST IN MY COMPUTER!

Computers are now a part of everyday life. Most offices have one – as do many homes. It is hardly surprising that ghosts have started to manifest on them.

We have come across some strange stories. One man, a highly gifted technical artist, found his home invaded by a poltergeist. This did all the usual things that a spook like this tends to do, such as moving shoes about and lining up coat hangers on a bed with remarkable precision and symmetry. However, it also did something else a little more adventurous.

The man was a computer buff and liked playing the screen-based version of the word game Scrabble. For this you have to use letters you are 'dealt' to spell out the longest word possible and build these into a crossword grid against words played by your opponent. The computer can take the role of 'opponent' if you do not have a dedicated partner. It was straightforward enough until this man started to battle his computer. Then, apparently, something took over the controls and would not play fair.

Normally the computer selects from its huge inbuilt vocabulary whichever word will score the most points. But this computer started to play words which were directly related to the man's life. On several occasions, he says, when faced with a problem, the artificial intelligence began to play words in turn that spelt out the answer!

Of course, this is rather subjective. We wonder if it might not work like other so-called divinatory systems, such as Tarot cards. In other words, it is not the cards themselves which mean anything. They merely act as symbols (as do tea leaves in the bottom of a cup or ink blots in a psychiatrist's surgery) on to which the subconscious mind grafts images that carry inner relevance.

In fact, this is not unlike dreams. The only difference is that when we are asleep the mind builds pictures around symbols to form a semi-coherent story. When awake, we may not notice the process so easily.

Perhaps the words that the computer played in the Scrabble game were exactly the ones it was programmed to play. The apparent meaning read into them may have evolved from the way in which they triggered associations in the mind of the human player. So were they used to express something that his inner mind had been trying to tell him all along?

THE EVIDENCE AGAINST

Computers are sensitive electronic equipment. We know that human beings are filled with electrical energy, as evidenced by those who experience incredible static charges which can cause shocks when metal objects like car doors are touched. There are well-attested cases of individuals so full of such natural energy that they cannot use many pieces of equipment, from vacuum cleaners to irons. They simply overload the circuits and burn them out.

'Jinx' employees can scramble the screen making it look as if a ghost is in the computer.

With a computer the situation is more delicate. Many offices tell stories about 'jinx' employees who scramble screens and cause them to malfunction. It seems likely that these are individuals carrying high static charges who accidentally affect the sensitive electronics in such a way as to damage functions. The result looks like a ghost in the computer – if the screen churns out gibberish – or if a program does not behave the way expected because of an unseen technical fault that corrects itself as soon as the 'haunted' operator is no longer sitting by the screen.

What we do not yet know is whether there are some situations where people with psychic abilities (if these exist) can affect computer screens in a manner akin to poltergeist activity, unconsciously controlling them by 'playing' with the electronics and creating more meaningful messages. We also do not know if this can be extended to video images; although the principle might not be too different.

If it is possible that psychokinesis can cause a human mind to turn a light switch on and off (as some researchers contend) – then why not scramble a computer to print messages on screen? If this can occur, it would explain the graphic designer and his Scrabble words. Presumably these emerged from within his own mind and perhaps he – or the agent responsible for the other poltergeist events – was able to alter the output of the computer.

At this stage that idea must remain debatable, but it does require deeper investigation and some scientists are already researching the way in which humans and machines interact. In our modern world, increasingly dependent on technical equipment for life and death decisions, that is a very wise precaution. For if this is merely possible we cannot afford to ignore its consequences.

THE EVIDENCE FOR

One extraordinary story that came our way was from a man in Swansea, South Wales. He reported that his TV set was tuned to a station after it

Right: Beside another of the 'Tomas' communications sits the computer which became the focus of the strangest contacts of all – reputedly transmitted across four centuries by the long-dead Tomas Harden. Ken Webster attempts two-way exchange of information by writing a reply on the VDU screen.

had gone off the air for the night. As a result he experienced a sea of static, hissing noises and black and white dots filling the screen, just as we might expect.

Yet – remarkably – before he could turn off, there on the screen was something else. For a few seconds he had the unmistakable sight of a dog. It was his dog – his *dead* dog – that had passed on to the 'afterlife' some months before.

Without evidence we can do no more than take him at his word, but wonder if it is possible that electronic signals can be manipulated in this way – either by the human mind or, just possibly, that of someone or something beyond the point of death.

This opens up some fascinating experimental ideas. Can a video recorder be used to try to 'tune in' to the other side, just as is alleged by the supposed audio-only version of the EVP phenomenon?

There is a simple way to test this. If enough people can join in our revolutionary experiment then we will soon know if it is possible or just a pipe dream.

All you have to do is tune your video to a station that definitely does not operate during the night – or, better still, to a space on the frequency dial well clear of any known station. Then set it to record at 3a.m. (this seems a good time, based on our experience of when paranormal phenomena are often reported). Tape half an hour of what should be nothing and replay it when you have the chance.

Of course, the odds are you will see and hear exactly that – nothing – except static and hiss. But if you try this a few times then who knows what the result might be? If you do pick up anything unusual, then please let us know!

The Websters' Acorn computer started to display messages on screen during occasions when it was left unattended.

THE GHOST IN THE MACHINE

Certainly the most dramatic story yet told of a video ghost comes from Ken Webster in his book *The Vertical Plane*. When Ken had moved into an old cottage in Doddleston, on the Cheshire/North Wales border, poltergeist events began. These ranged from furniture being suddenly piled up by unseen forces to messages being scrawled on walls by persons unknown.

Then the Websters' Acorn computer started to display messages on screen during occasions when it was left unattended. For about two years around three hundred such messages appeared, attested to by several of Ken Webster's friends and visitors. Some have since confirmed their belief in the integrity of this story direct to us.

The messages appeared to come from various sources, including one

Tomas Harden who had reputedly lived in the same cottage in the six-teenth century. Somehow he had a vision of a 'leems-boyste' (seemingly his word for light-box, which is presumably how he describes a computer). As a result he was somehow (not really explained) able to transmit his messages across time and turn up on the screen four centuries later.

The story gets very complicated before the contact ends. Other messages appear bearing the inscription 2109 which some people interpret as coming from time travellers. Visionary phenomena also manifested. But what does it all mean?

To be fair, Ken Webster never tries to impose any view. In response to a critical review in the paranormal magazine *Magonia*, he wrote in January 1990: 'I am not claiming anything other than having written down what happened. On that basis I don't need evidence ....' He adds, however, that the Society for Psychical Research investigated the matter, as did a North Wales UFO investigator called Gary Rowe. Both were apparently impressed, judging from their continued study.

Some minor confirmation of the historical accuracy of people and places in Tomas's messages emerged, but a lot more needs to appear before the sceptics will be converted. Already there have been suggestions that a sophisticated hoaxer 'hacked' into the Websters' computer, which was then a very common type popular with schools. This seems a reasonable suggestion, as hacking is an art beloved of intelligent teenage youths.

However Webster disputes that, on the grounds that the messages use language that was correct for the period in question according to historical sources he has consulted. The person also knew details of the cottage, which a trickster would have had difficulty coming by.

Of course, if he could establish through contemporary sources that the language used seemed appropriate then so could a relatively clever hacker with a desire to pull off a good wheeze. On the other hand, Ken Webster does not hide the fact that some of the messages appear to contain references to events that are not historically accurate. For example, Tomas expresses fear that his missing lover would be burned as a witch, when no such actions occurred in the era in question. Webster says they tried to reassure Tomas of this fact, but the message in reply claimed that unofficial mob burnings did take place which our history has failed to record.

This is a case that seems to be both inconclusive and unconcluded. We may yet hear more from it. Also, it may well represent a type of phenomenon that will be on the increase in future years. Indeed, there has already been one story from a software company that one of their computers has been video filmed switching itself on at night, despite being clearly

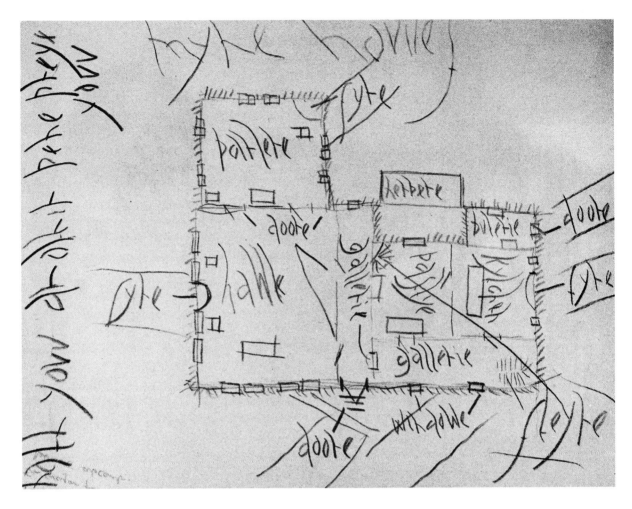

unplugged! Serious attempts were made by experts to discover if freak bursts of energy might be able to 'power it up', but nothing was found before the haunted machine was taken away. Who would use a ghostly VDU?

Perhaps, if there is an afterlife, the spirits there are as intrigued by new technology as the living seem to be.

A plan of Ken Webster's cottage attributed to one 'Tomas Harden' from the 16th century showing how the dwelling had looked in his day. Weird messages and pictures appeared on the walls and floor of the cottage. Ken Webster tells this strange story in his book *The Vertical Plane.*

YOUR VERDICT : A SUMMARY

AGAINST SURVIVAL

- Little hard evidence exists, and these cases are mostly anecdotal.

- Video recordings can be distorted and computers can be hacked into.

- Since electrical equipment can be scrambled by electrical fields and some people are known to possess a lot of body electricity, rational solutions may yet be found for some cases.

FOR SURVIVAL

- These reports are increasing as technology grows more sophisticated, perhaps suggesting that contact is being attempted.

- The intelligence behind messages, if not hoaxed, is hard to explain.

- If EVP can work in an audio sense there is no reason why more sophisticated contact cannot take place.

PAST LIVES

———◆———

A thread often running through the concept of past lives or reincarnation is that our actions on Earth build up a 'karma' – a sort of debit and credit book of good and bad deeds. This determines our next lifetime in an Earth body. New problems will be set as a result of how well we coped before, and through these earlier experiences we can grow and evolve as both a spiritual entity and a physical human being. The beautiful efficiency of this system is easy to see. It offers solutions to many problems that some religious doctrines struggle to accommodate.

Why do we not possess sure knowledge that life is eternal? We speculate about the will of God. Reincarnation suggests that conscious knowledge during life would defeat our spiritual progression. Decisions would not be down to our innate character but forged from self-motivation about an easy life next time around. The suicide rate amongst those in difficult circumstances might well sky rocket.

How can God justify a baby born with crippling injuries or a life snatched away before it has barely begun? With the idea of reincarnation, persuasive answers appear. It may be necessary to have such a tough life to learn certain things for that soul's progress – or an early demise may help others, such as the parents, develop by coping with the adversity.

Equally, if every child born is a new soul wouldn't Heaven be overcrowded by now? Assuming that there are a finite number of souls and that when population booms they simply return to Earth with a faster turn around than before, past lives would offer a ready solution to the dilemma. Indeed, the idea of having past lives transforms any examination of spiritual questions. Not that this makes reincarnation true, of course – only attractive.

There is a parallel with scientific knowledge. Energy cannot be created or destroyed – it can only be changed from one form into another. When you add heat to water it changes form to become steam. This can turn a wheel round and generate a new form of energy – electricity – which can be used to heat a wire and thus create light. But in all of this transfer the basic energy that existed in the system remains – it just manifests in a variety of ways.

Therefore, reincarnation may provide a spiritual analogy. The energy of

If every child born is a new soul wouldn't Heaven be overcrowded by now?

our mind or inner selves would continue to exist in differing forms, animating new bodies when they are born.

So, if alongside the physical body there is also a spirit or mind energy that goes 'elsewhere' after death, it would presumably continue to form part of the sum of energies that exist within the cosmos. If it were subsequently to become part of another physical body, it would not be doing anything unexpected by science. Indeed, it would in many ways be following the constant cycle of nature that is best exemplified by rain.

Rain falls from clouds on to the ground, is evaporated as moisture by the sun's heat, and rises into the air to form a part of the cloud system. From here it will eventually fall to Earth once more as rain, probably on some other part of the Earth's surface. Then the cycle will begin all over again.

It takes little imagination to conceive the parallel between human life and reincarnation as demonstrated by a raindrop. We see one of these being 'born' as an independent entity from out of the atmospheric clouds, briefly 'living' a life and then extinguishing itself, or 'dying' as a separate entity as its 'essence' evaporates and rises back to be absorbed into the mass of clouds that cloak the Earth. Then – when the time is right – a new raindrop forms from this mass and begins the cycle over again. It may be different, but it contains the essence of that earlier raindrop which 'lived' and 'died' in a former time somewhere else on Earth.

So – strange as it may seem to those of us unfamiliar with the concept – reincarnation as a philosophical system has a great deal to offer the search for truth about life after death. Which leads to the inevitable question – aesthetics aside, does it have any real evidence to support it?

WHAT DID YOU DO IN THE WAR?

Such a question would seem wholly inappropriate to ask about World War II of a man born in England sixteen years after it had ended. But Paul Catlow, from Norfolk, does ask it of himself and often. The reason is that he has had a series of incredibly vivid dreams in which he has constantly experienced his 'death' in the horrors of those battles.

In fact, 'his' death was actually that of a German soldier named Karl Schumann – an unremarkable person, not the stuff of a Hollywood fantasy. And yet pure-bred Englishman Paul Catlow seems to know him very well.

He 'knows', for example, that Karl was born in Hamburg. He also knows that he was killed fighting on the Polish front on 23 October 1944. He knows because he has seen, felt, smelt and *lived* through the experience of being hit by machine gun fire from the Russian army and then finding him-

He has seen, felt, smelt and lived *through the experience of being hit by machine gun fire from the Russian army.*

self floating in an out-of-the-body state (see Chapter 12) above the corpse, now free of all pain.

These visions – for they are really too powerful to be called mere recurring dreams – are awesome. But they were not the starting point of Paul's peculiar obsession. When he was a child the war had a fascination for him and – more than that – when playing with toy soldiers he always discarded the British and American ones in favour of the Germans and the Russians!

The now adult Paul is certainly not taking to the concept of reincarnation with any undue ease. He told us: 'If I could accept the notion that I haven't lived before and that my memories of having done so are an elaborate self-hoax, I'd be very much happier.'

But there are problems. He has never dared to check whether a real Karl Schumann did die on 23 October 1944 – although he knows this would prove nothing even if it were true. For, if the record exists somewhere, then it can always be claimed that he read it or was told about it, although he does not recall that ever happening. Still, he recognises that as a valid criticism.

More puzzling is the German uniform he wears in these dreams. Paul's experience of war films on TV suggest that a German soldier would have been clad in the standard grey uniform and jackboots. But this is not at all what he sees Karl wearing in these visions.

Yet Paul's dreams speak the truth. As the war was grinding towards inevitable German defeat, and more and more old men and teenagers were drafted to defend the fading Nazi cause, it became impossible to produce the proud standard uniform for them all. Instead, the peculiar green clothing that Paul sees his alter ego wearing was precisely what the soldiers on the Polish front did wear during late 1944. Again, he could always be said to have known this inside his mind somewhere, but he has no conscious recollection of it.

Paul Catlow does, however, have an interesting point to make *against* the idea of reincarnation. If his dreams do reflect a real past life when he was a German soldier just sixteen years before he was born into this present existence, then how come he finds the German language almost impossible to learn? Would not some innate aptitude be 'handed on' along with the memories?

Experiences such as Paul's are thought by many researchers to be spontaneous recall of past lives. The claim is that we all have these locked away inside our heads but normally do not have ready access to them. However, they can emerge in dreams – such as here – or with very young children who seem to be in closer contact with these vestigial memories.

OUT OF THE MOUTHS OF BABES

There are a remarkable number of stories of children between the ages of three and six who amaze their parents with statements such as 'When I was alive before' or 'When I was an old man'. Parents tend to dismiss them as fantasies or 'role play' games – all part of the learning process. Children of that age do have very vivid imaginations, of course. However, when more heed has been paid to what the children say there have been some major surprises in store for their bemused parents.

One young English boy of four gave a graphic account of being killed by a Red Indian in the American West. Of course, he could have based that story on something he had seen on television, but is it not more likely that he would have given a romanticised account of killing the Indians – not of being killed himself?

Indeed, it is the death scene to which almost every supposed past life story reverts automatically. Why? If just a fantasy were being produced, then would it not be more likely that a pleasant or heroic deed would be the source of whatever tale is dredged up out of the mind? On the other hand, if the account is a real memory then the death of the being that 'we' once were is bound to be one of the most vivid experiences.

Only real memory seems to account for this anomaly in recall. Fantasy flounders in the face of it. Indeed, it is even true that peaceful deaths (such as those occurring in one's sleep) are rarely the first thing remembered – although they can be retrieved if probed for. Violent or sudden deaths, on the other hand – certainly the most memorable if these are indeed true recollections – tend to be the starting point of a past life recall.

In one notable case two young girls from Northumberland were killed in May 1957 by a car driven by a depressed woman who was trying to commit suicide. She slewed off the road at speed and struck them as they walked down the pavement. The girls and another child died instantly.

A few months later the girls' mother became pregnant. Her husband – who, we stress, believed in reincarnation – insisted that she would have twins and that the girls would be reborn. Both the mother and the doctor doubted this: there was no evidence of two babies in the womb, or any history of twins in the family. However, in October 1958 twin girls were indeed born to the Pollock family.

Even more extraordinary was the fact that these children were said to be spontaneously behaving like the dead sisters they had never known. One even had a mark on her head which allegedly coincided with a scar left after one of the dead girls had fallen off her bicycle at the age of two. When they were first shown the dolls that the dead girls had owned, and

When the Pollock twins were shown two dolls which had belonged to their dead sisters, they immediately took to them. The names they unwittingly gave the dolls were the same as those given by the previous little girls. Were the twins indeed the reincarnated spirits of the fatally injured sisters?

which had been stored away for several years after their deaths, the twins immediately named them exactly as their 'other selves' had done.

The 'spell' broke at about the age of six when they lost all memory of this past life. But this was not before an incident when they suddenly screamed and were found arm in arm clutching one another and crying, 'The car! The car! It's coming at us!' Someone on the road had started a car engine, and the vehicle was pointing towards them at the same angle as the car that had killed their sisters some years before. They would be very unlikely to know this, even if they must have known how the girls had died.

Of course, the tie-in with the father's unusual but firm belief in past lives is curious, and suggests to some people that he may have subconsciously and unintentionally encouraged some of these events to occur. Yet they did happen, and they require some sort of explanation. Can this glib evaluation suffice to account for all their puzzling aspects? If not, it is remarkable evidence.

If it were unique, this case would be intriguing enough. However, it is very far from unique. Stories like this are actually quite common all over the world in societies that both believe and disbelieve in reincarnation. It seems to make little difference, except maybe to the parents' attitude. Some listen to what their children say; others take it to be no more than imagination.

PAST LIVES AS PSYCHOTHERAPY

One of her patients had terrible psychosomatic head pains and was terrified of the colour red. In a regression she described witnessing her own murder.

Californian psychologist Dr Edith Fiore says in her book *You Have Been Here Before* that 'whether the former lifetimes that are "relived" are fantasies or actual experiences lived in a bygone era does not matter to me as a therapist – getting results is important. I have found past life regression consistently helpful, often resulting in immediate remission of chronic symptoms ….' She argues from her case files that, by putting a person suffering from a phobia into a hypnotic state and regressing them past birth to another lifetime, it often emerges that an incident (usually linked with a death scene in that previous existence) is the source of the phobia in today's personality.

As an example, one of her patients had terrible psychosomatic head pains and was terrified of the colour red. In a regression she described witnessing her own murder – she had been hit over the head with a club, and blood was spurting everywhere. There are countless similar cases on record.

On the other hand when British hypnotherapist H. W. Hurst was doing experiments for his book *The Thousand Year Memory* he found something that might contradict this. He conducted a battery of psychological tests on people when they were regressed to a previous existence and again when they were their normal waking selves. His results were significant. He said: 'Wherever each past life may come from or whatever its cause may be, it really is a totally different person we are talking to.' When he later had the results studied in detail by two independent psychologists, they reported that on average there was only a 23 per cent similarity in psychological traits between the present personality and the one supposedly found in the past life.

This in itself proves little. It is quite likely that a similar study of the lives of separate 'minds' in a multiple personality patient would show such patterns. However, it does beg the question as to why a past life event should have an extreme effect on the present life personality if that 'self' is so substantially different.

More than that, it makes one wonder if reincarnation – even should it be proved an incontrovertible fact – could legitimately be called survival of death. After all, if most of us never know anything of our earlier life, and if our present personality is significantly different from the 'us' that lived before, then in what sense have we survived – or, more specifically, what part of 'us' has really survived? Is the 'soul' just 23 per cent of the personality – the other three-quarters being the product of the present-day environment?

Such questions worry American therapist Dr Margie Reider, who has been involved in a remarkable recent case. She has regressed some thirty-five people in a small Californian town, who all claim to have lived past lives *together* in a town called Millboro, Virginia. This was during the Civil War of the 1860s. Only three of the group say they have ever been to Virginia, and yet under hypnosis the various members reputedly told interlocking stories and described buildings and other landmarks that are either there now or were present at the time.

Of course, critics will always claim that this might have been set up by the subconscious minds of the regressed people that were tuning into knowledge they possessed but had forgotten all about. Perhaps the group were deluding themselves as the story snowballed in complexity, confirming one another's tales without consciously intending to do so.

Whether you treat the claims sceptically or as evidence of a real phenomenon, Dr Reider's opinions of it are interesting, because she does not seem to favour the view that we really have lived before. Rather she supports an idea along the lines of the 'collective unconscious', as suggested by the psychologist Dr Carl Jung. He argued that all mental imagery enters a pool of collectiveness into which at some deep inner level we can all potentially dip our minds and fish out pictures or symbols. It is the source of myths, inspiration and creativity and – here perhaps – of access to real information from the past.

Of course, if this is what occurs, it leaves wide open questions such as how and why it works through the medium of past lives.

EXPERIENCING OTHER LIVES

Jenny Randles has taken part in a past life experiment with Surrey therapist Mary Cherrett, who specialises in discovering how psychological patterns in this life might relate to hidden past life memories. Only a light hypnotic state was induced, and Jenny was fully aware of what was happening. She 'saw' pictures pop into her mind and described these in a sort of 'free association' to which she was guided. Jenny notes: 'I have no way of knowing where the images came from. They could have been fantasy or they could have been dredged from my subconscious memory. Certainly they were often unexpected and took on the form of a living dream or film unfolding before my eyes which I could watch and report to others.'

Initially, Jenny was taken back to a period in childhood of which she had no conscious recall – before the age of two. She was living in rural Lancashire and described looking at the village school longingly. Asked to explain this odd reaction, the taped record shows that Jenny said: 'A great adventure is coming …. But I know that because of what has already been.'

Later, Jenny's mother admitted that when her daughter was only one year old she had had an odd ability to replay stories and nursery rhymes as if she was a tape recorder. She also used to nod at passers-by in such an adult way that some were reportedly frightened. When she started nursery classes the teachers expressed worries about Jenny's behaviour to her parents, who were urged to discourage these unusual habits.

Does this imply that Jenny had spontaneous recall of a previous life when very young, but that this was 'trained' out by teachers who regarded the result as abnormal? How often does this occur with young children?

Jenny described her own birth in a manner which, her mother says, was close to reality. Even then, Jenny claimed, she had a job to do linked with communication. Her words were: 'I didn't want to be here. But now I am I must make the best of it …. I'm settling down now.' As here, almost all reliable past life stories obtained under hypnosis are offered by the witness in the present tense.

Jenny also noted how this recollection triggered repressed memories from childhood where she had nightmares of entering a pipe, cave or underground burrow head first and getting stuck. Mary Cherrett said that she had often come across this before, and that such nightmares were caused by the trauma of a difficult birth. When Jenny asked her mother, it was confirmed that her birth had been unusually protracted and difficult. Jenny may well have absorbed this information at some point during her life without realising it. Even so, the confirmation of these two consciously unknown circumstances via the regression was intriguing.

Taken back next to before her birth, Jenny regressed to the scene of a cottage in a wood: 'There are trees all around it. Branches are hanging around. The door is open, as if it is never closed. It's dark inside. Everywhere is old stone – like straw, or hay, or twigs, probably all of them in this round – no, it's not round – rectangular whitish stone. And there's a wooden table with one leg that's shorter than the other ….'

Jenny says that she now 'recognises' this cottage. It is one she has seen in vivid dreams throughout her life. But was this dream cottage a fantasy trigger for the 'past life' scene, or were 'past life' memories buried deep inside occasionally to peep through the mental barriers as dreams? Either option seems equally likely.

A full past life memory emerged to Jenny of a woman named Mary Reynolds, and the location was the Forest of Dean in Gloucestershire between 1766 and 1782. She was raised in Bristol at a place called Church Lea and married a man called Frank in 1759. ('He had a beard and whiskers down the side of his face and he used to stand with his hands in his pockets', Jenny or 'Mary' says, describing the man from her vantage point in the cottage years after he has left her to fend for herself after blaming her for having no children.)

Asked to describe Frank, 'Mary' can do so vividly:

'He has got a hay fork and he is sticking it in the ground and shouting at me. He's taking it out on me what he's feeling. I accept that. He's not really taking it out on me. But he's directing it at me. He wanted to do things … but he can't …. He's picking something up in his hand and [laughs] – he's saying 'that's mine, that's all that's mine. That's all we have to show for all these years' …. It looks like a clock ….'

In the Forest of Dean 'Mary' existed by cooking food in a great open pot and selling it for a pittance to passing stagecoaches – in a sort of prototype motorway service café! She saw the name of this place as Alferinton (up-dated later to Alvington) and described how Mary had gradually become weak through some debilitating illness and was visited by an 'apothecary' ('He's not a doctor …. He was very kind. He can't really do anything. He knows that and I know that but he helps …. I used to think that if I get up again it will be a miracle. But I did.') Eventually she died in 1782, aged forty-eight, of this slow wasting disease which had no name.

A fantasy invented for effect? A tap-in to some collective unconscious or a real memory of a previous existence? Who can say? Certainly, Jenny cannot. She notes only: 'I have passed a few miles from the Forest once years ago on a train and spent about three hours in Bristol city centre one day. Otherwise these are two locations which I do not know at all. Maybe my attraction to the Bristol area is relevant to some fantasy, or maybe the love of the area is a result of some inner memory.'

The story was given to Ian Wilson, a noted sceptical researcher into past life claims. By chance he lived in the Bristol area. Wilson noted that Mary Reynolds was the name of a well-known case from Pennsylvania in 1811. 'She fell into a deep sleep for twenty hours and when she woke up had assumed a different personality.' Jenny admits it is virtually certain she had read of this case somewhere in the past and, as Ian Wilson said, the choice of name may have been the result of her mind playing games. Similarly, Jenny could have read a story about the Forest of Dean, now long forgot-ten by her conscious mind. This is always the trouble with past lives. Wilson did not try to establish whether Church Lea or Frank and Mary Reynolds ever existed, but he did say: 'Any number of houses around here have that sort of name.' He had no knowledge of a place called Alvington.

However, careful study of large-scale maps shows that there is indeed an Alvington (which might have derived its name from an older form,

A section from a large-scale Ordnance Survey map showing part of the Forest of Dean. Alvington is situated on the southern edge of the Forest to the west of the Severn Estuary.

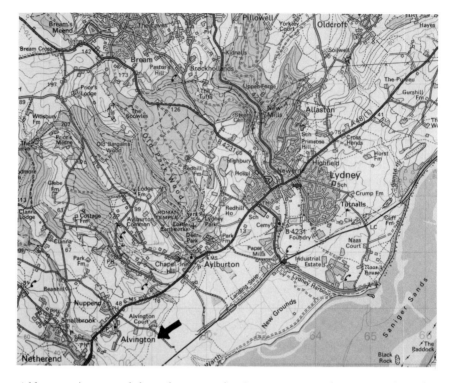

Alfrington) situated directly across the Severn estuary from Bristol on the Welsh/Gloucestershire border. It is a tiny village on the edge of the Forest of Dean. Jenny has certainly never been there. But had she read about it long ago? The mind has an incredible capacity for remembering.

CRYPTOMNESIA

Neurologist Dr Wilder Penfield made a remarkable discovery during his research. Since, on account of its lack of pain centres, it is possible to operate on the brain with the patient still awake, he electronically stimulated certain parts of the tissue and found to his surprise that patients suddenly regressed to a 'memory'. This could be of a conversation, a sound, a smell – indeed, rather the same as what occurs during past life recall.

So far as we know, these memories always related to the present life (a potentially significant negative finding, although some images were untraceable). But many referred to events that had been long forgotten by the patient – exactly like the imagery triggered by regression hypnosis.

This is just part of our evidence for what is called cryptomnesia – a process by which memory (whatever that is and wherever it is located in the brain

– science does not yet know) stores every trivial detail that enters the mind. Ninety-nine per cent of this is blocked from conscious awareness; otherwise there would be an overload of information that would be impossible to endure. Indeed, it may well be that a breakdown in this process is part of the explanation for the illness of schizophrenia, where data flows into the mind all the time from mental sources.

Whilst on the positive side this possibly opens the door on some past life theories, it has major negative consequences for the belief in reincarnation. Literally everything we have ever come across in any form (from a conversation in the same room as our pram was situated to an article in a magazine we skimmed through whilst sitting in the doctor's waiting room, is potentially accessible. If asked whether we knew anything about a certain subject we could honestly say 'No' and that would be true in a conscious sense. But in the deeper recesses of the mind we may well be able to find data that we claim to know nothing about.

In the deeper recesses of the mind we may well be able to find data that we claim to know nothing about.

As a result, if we come up with a past life memory and refer to things we can legitimately state we were unaware of, we can never be certain that it does not depend upon something accessed through cryptomnesia. This is why checking for past life facts to confirm stories of other times proves nothing. If the facts have been recorded somewhere we *might* have come across them and just forgotten all about it.

Of course, the more obscure the record, the more difficult it is to track it down and the less likely that we might have come across it previously. But it can probably never be stated with absolute certainty that it was impossible to have known the information offered up in a past life story.

In 1976 researcher Jeffrey Iverson wrote a book and made a TV programme based on the work of past life regressionist Arnold Bloxham. He seemed to have overcome this problem with one woman who some years before had been regressed to life as Livonia, wife of a tutor to the Roman Emperor Constantine c. 286 AD, and to Rebecca, a Jewess, massacred in 1190 in the crypt of St Mary's church, York.

The two lives seemed impressive because the Roman facts fitted what we knew but added to our understanding of the situation with details that might be historically accurate, although they were not known to be fact when the regressions occurred. The second case was important because, although the massacre was historical fact, the church in question had no known crypt. One was later discovered around the time the book was published. However, important as this looks, sceptical researcher Melvin Harris did a lot of detailed study and later came up with quite startling conclusions.

With Rebecca's story he was less than impressed. There were problems with her description of the relevant area of York, which seemed to involve modern misconceptions rather than historical accuracy. He also found that St Mary's church had not been specifically identified by the regression, only one like it, and he claims that the underground room subsequently uncovered at this site was more likely to be a small vault well post-dating 1190. It is none the less ironic that a debate over a crypt should lead to the damning evidence that Harris found which seemed to prove that this woman's memories were the result of cryptomnesia!

Even the book's fictional characters were incorporated into the past life.

He traced two novels by Louis de Wohl, the most important being *The Living Wood*, published in 1947 – well before the regressions occurred. We can never know if the subject had read these books, but it seems almost certain that the novels are the source of her Roman past life memories. Virtually all the characters and details in her account can be found there, based loosely around accepted fact. Indeed, even the book's fictional characters (including, it seems, Livonia, – the source of the 'memory' itself) were incorporated into the past life.

Jenny Randles may also have seen cryptomnesia in action during her third past life experienced through Mary Cherrett's help. It was decided to regress to the source of her morbid dread of water, which manifested as real phobic terror even as a very young child.

Jenny found herself describing a 'little wooden jetty' in a lake in the grounds of a house near Chester. A member of a well-to-do family, she saw herself as eighteen-year-old Robert Dale in a 1937 death scene which involved the jealousy of her brother Alan, who was then 16. Because Robert would take over the family business and Alan did not think him worthy of it, he pushed his older brother into the water off the jetty. Robert got caught up in something and was trapped just under the water's surface, unable to escape. Alan did nothing to assist, and the whole thing was written off by the police as a terrible accident.

Jenny kept saying things after 'drowning', like 'Why would he do that? He was my brother.' Then she would answer herself: 'He pretended to be nice, but when we were on our own he wasn't. He didn't hate me. He didn't know what he was doing half the time.'

A search was made through several months' editions of the *Chester Chronicle* for 1937 but there was no mention of the Dale family or a drowning. However, in order to rule conclusively that the incident never occurred more research is needed. Indeed it is even conceivable that Alan Dale is still alive – if he ever existed. However, Jenny believes there is more than a distinct possibility that this was a fantasy based on cryptomnesia. Certainly, it readily explains the water phobia. Even more intriguing is that after the hypnosis Jenny had a vivid dream in which the drowning was 'relived' in all its terror in what she says 'was such vividness that it is almost impossible not to regard it as a real memory'.

However, equally true is this fact. When the regression occurred, Jenny was on the verge of moving some twenty miles to a new home in an area she barely knew. But she had been there once, some weeks before the regression, to view the property. She had looked at the local map at the time. Only after she moved did she spot that, just a few hundred yards from her new home, there was an Alandale Road! Had this been part of the trigger for the 1937 past life 'memory'?

''TIS CALLED BLUNDERBUS'

We know exactly what a 'blunderbus' is. According to Wilfred, a coachman on the London–Bath road in the early 1800s, it was a concoction of ale, rum and a touch of gunpowder into which a hot poker was deposited! Supposedly it was a speciality of the Swan Inn at Didcot near Oxford, but nobody has established the historical existence of this wicked brew.

Jenny Randles heard about it from 'Wilfred' thanks to hypnotherapist Joe Keeton. The man was, of course, long since dead – if he ever lived – but he was reliving a terrible drunken stupor, moaning 'I can't get up … I'm ill' in a thick West Country accent through the lips of Ray Bryant – one of Keeton's star regressees. The acting was superb, if (subconsciously) that is all it was. Of course, for Ray, the life and times of Wilfred are something more. But what?

Blunderbus was a concoction of ale, rum and a touch of gunpowder into which a hot poker was deposited!

Aside from this delightful character, Ray has also 'become' a peasant – Robert Swayer – living in Essex around the turn of this century but who has never been traced, and two females – one a rich little girl who died at the age of five, and the other, Elizabeth, a cleaning girl, born just after Wilfred had 'passed on'. Again the existence of neither has been traced. These lives are perhaps marked by their mundanity, which is not entirely true of Ray's major 'past life' – that of Reuben Stafford, of whom a very great deal has been extracted through Joe Keeton's hypnosis.

Stafford was born in 1822 in Brighthelmston (which Ray Bryant commendably admits he consciously knew was the old name for Brighton in Sussex). Reuben moved north, joined the army in 1844, married a Lancashire woman called Mary Smith, and fought in the Crimean War. He was wounded in 1855 and reached the rank of colour sergeant in a Lancashire regiment. He then moved to London after being invalided out, and had a fairly uneventful later life working around the docks, into which he subsequently jumped to end it all.

Jenny was able to engage in another remarkable conversation with the seemingly authentically accented 'Reuben' (via the hypnotised mind of a decidedly non-Lancastrian Ray Bryant). He described being cared for by nursing staff following his wounding in the Crimea.

> *JR:* 'What are you doing?'
> *RB:* 'My 'and is hurting.'
> *JR:* 'What did you do to it?'
> *RB:* 'I was shot.'
> *JR:* 'Who by?'
> *RB:* 'The enemy.'
> *JR:* 'Who is the enemy?'
> *RB:* *[Puzzled]* 'The Russians.'
> *JR:* 'Who is looking after you?'
> *RB:* 'The ladies.'
> *JR:* 'What ladies?'
> *RB:* 'Florie's ladies.'
> *JR:* 'Where do they come from?'
> *RB:* 'Eh? … Out from England.'
> *JR:* 'What is she doing over there?' *[This meant in the Crimea]*
> *RB:* *[Taking it literally as 'over there' in the room]* 'She's tending. They're lovely ladies. Lovely ladies all of 'em.'

And so it goes on. Ray (or Reuben) describes the medicines used by Florie's ladies (Florie of course, being Florence Nightingale) and his aspirations afterwards – 'I'll go back to my regiment, I 'ope' – and talks of life back home in his cottage on the Preston Road out of Ormskirk 'near to t' cross'. Again we must ask if this is remarkable innate acting ability, storytelling by the inner mind, or something deeper.

One curious thing is that Joe Keeton's cases always involve British subjects regressing to British past lives, whereas other researchers do not seem to have the same results (one of Jenny Randles' three lives was French). Is this a sign of what is called the 'experimenter effect' – in other words, have the results of these experiments varied because of the person who was conducting them?

Certainly, in Reuben's case parts of his life have been confirmed by research (not conducted by Ray Bryant). His army record was found at Fulwood Barracks in Preston and his death certificate traced (see right). Using these (without Ray seeing them), he was questioned under hypnosis about small details. He made mistakes, but in general was accurate.

Without knowing that the death certificate existed, Reuben relived this scene. It matched what the coroner described. This was the turning point for the sceptical Ray Bryant.

But what does he believe the experience means? Surprisingly, his response is not that reincarnation is true in the strictest sense. Ray says it is like watching yourself on TV: 'You are taking part in one mind and watching it in another …. It's rather like dreaming but knowing that you are dreaming …. The person in the regression is giving answers that you (consciously) know are wrong but you are powerless to stop it. Yet later, often these answers turn out to be reasonable – better than the answers you would have consciously given ….'

As for his interpretation of the phenomenon, Ray says:

'I don't think Ray Bryant was Reuben Stafford. I think there are bits of him in me. It's made me look upon the soul and death more in the scientific sense as the leaping of a life force from one body to another rather than a spiritual thing. I believe that – whatever the mind is – part, at least, does survive death. I am not the least afraid of death now, and I used to be. But now they can do what they like with the carcass. That's not me. It's just a case to carry me around in.'

The death certificate for Reuben Stafford.

CERTIFIED COPY OF AN ENTRY OF DEATH

Given at the **GENERAL REGISTER OFFICE, LONDON.**

Application Number 41864

| | REGISTRATION DISTRICT | Poplar | | | | | | | |

1879. DEATH in the Sub-district of Poplar in the county of Mid

No.	When and where died	Name and surname	Sex	Age	Occupation	Cause of death	Signature, description, and residence of informant	When registered	Signature of registrar
Columns:— 1		2	3	4	5	6	7	8	9
97	Found dead Second April 1879 Millwall Dock	Reuben John Stafford	Male	52 yrs	Waterman	Violent suffocation by drowning How caused not proved Millwall Dock	Certificate received from John Humphreys Coroner for Middlesex Inquest held Fourth April 1879	Tenth April 1879	Abraham Purdy Registrar

CERTIFIED to be a true copy of an entry in the certified copy of a Register of Deaths in the District above mentioned.

Given at the GENERAL REGISTER OFFICE, LONDON, under the Seal of the said Office, the 13th day of October 1983

DA 769509

THE EVIDENCE AGAINST

As you will have gathered, much of the evidence for past life memories emerges from hypnotised subjects. This in itself provides a major flaw.

Hypnosis is known to be an altered state of consciousness in which the subject is highly susceptible to influence. Even the slightest cue from the person questioning him or her can provoke a response. The subject feels a great need to please the hypnotist.

Of course, in circumstances where hypnosis is used to come up with a past life there is already an expectation of this. Certainly the person under hypnosis is very unlikely not to *want* to relive something (the fascination factor alone will be sufficient motivation). Given that the hypnotist will also probably be expecting or hoping for it, this is in effect playing right into the trap that hypnotic regression introduces.

The hypnotic state enhances creativity, fantasy and memory.

Experiments have shown that, if you regress a person to an event they cannot consciously recall but which can be checked for accuracy against existing records (for instance, the order in which pupils sat in a classroom at school), then sometimes remarkable accuracy does occur. But just as often inaccuracy (probably nothing more than imaginative guesswork) is the result. In addition, it has also been shown that a hypnotised person regressed to the night of a bogus shooting incident, for instance, can be implanted with a false memory that they did hear the shot that in reality never took place.

In other words, the hypnotic state enhances creativity, fantasy and memory in about equal proportions – with the result that you can never be sure what you are getting in any specific instance. This is why hypnotically retrieved testimony is hardly ever admitted as significant evidence in a court of law.

Coupled with the very real problems of cryptomnesia (and given the good chance that this ability can be enhanced in the hypnotic state) there are very real problems with accepting most past life testimony as a valid recollection of a life that actually took place. Since in some cases (such as that of Livonia) we apparently know the source and feel sure that the story must just be a fantasy, why should this not be true for most – or all – of the others?

THE EVIDENCE FOR

Of course, not all past life memories emerge through hypnosis. Paul Catlow's did not. The children described earlier had spontaneous recall in their early years. Studies carried out by an American parapsychologist at the University of Virginia, Dr Ian Stevenson, found countless cases which he published in great detail. These involve children from many countries around the world (mostly those that accept past lives readily), whose memories of previous existences came naturally. These *seem* to reflect what Stevenson cautiously terms evidence 'suggestive of reincarnation'.

Possibly there are other explanations available here. Maybe cryptomnesia works in dreams and childhood imagination better than at other times, and so the 'past life' generating scenario is a natural one at such a point. But why would anyone feel the need to 'relive' a fantasy past life and dredge information from the deep subconscious to help in doing so?

With Stevenson's cases there are sometimes good reasons. A child born to a poor family, say in India, may gain advantage by claiming to be the deceased relative of a richer family that lives nearby. Certainly it has been noted that in such cases the life is almost always a recent one, almost always occurs in the same country (indeed usually within a few miles of where the child currently lives) and hardly ever features a life that is worse off than the present one. However, that does not apply in every case, and there is a growing body of testimony that bucks this trend.

Another problem is illustrated by the Livonia and Rebecca story. Here the lives – especially the girl who was in the court of a Roman emperor – do seem very colourful and fantasy-like. It is no real surprise that they were shown to be such. However, such recalls are very few and far between. Researchers are wary of anyone who relates a tale of life as a princess of ancient Atlantis or some historically known character with a rich and dramatic lifestyle. The truth is that 99 per cent of all past life memories are nothing even remotely like that.

Researchers are wary of anyone who relates a tale of life as a princess of ancient Atlantis.

The typical past life is dull, routine, with little of great importance – hardly the stuff that fantasies or daydreams are made of. It also often reflects the violent life, poverty and early death of people in the past – not what you would expect anybody to conjure up for amusement.

An experiment carried out by Jenny Randles, with the help of noted past life hypnotherapist Joe Keeton, demonstrates this well. The subject was a BBC producer who had never been hypnotised and was selected as she had no previous interest in or beliefs about the subject one way or another.

This young woman was regressed over a series of recorded sessions and interviewed under hypnosis by Jenny. She described an unenthralling life as a pig farmer's daughter at some period far in the past that could not be placed. Indeed, that girl (Jill Leadenoak) had very little knowledge about events beyond life on the farm and the tiny nearby village. She would happily tell us the names of her pigs and how they matured the local cider in some disgusting – but we later found historically accurate – manner involving dead rodents! Other than that she was as uncommunicative as might be expected for a poor peasant girl from a few hundred years ago. Certainly it was not like it is in science fiction drama, where the time traveller meets a yokel and immediately has a free and easy conversation. It would have been easier talking to one of Jill's pigs!

The question is – if this was a fantasy, why was the imagined scenario *not* like it is on TV? Why was a dull, routine life communicated in such a stuttering, yet logical, way? Brilliant acting? The unregressed woman flatly refutes that. But at the same time as we struggled to obtain details Jill spoke in an incredibly broad rural accent utterly unlike the one used by her twentieth-century mouthpiece. Indeed, she – the BBC producer – was clearly embarrassed when she first heard the tapes of Jill's earthy voice coming out of her own lips.

We were never able to find Jill Leadenoak, which even if the story was reality is no surprise. But we later traced some clues in her story to Hertfordshire. This was not the county we expected to be looking at, but we later discovered it was appropriate to the accent back in medieval times.

This is very much the way it is with tens of thousands of regressions that have been carried out. The contrast between what you get and what you might expect to get is very marked. If it does not point to real access to some actual past life it requires another, as yet unrecognised, explanation.

POSSIBLE EXPLANATIONS

A number of ideas have attempted to explain the problem in terms other than actual reincarnation or some form of fantasy. Here are the main contenders.

Multiple Personality

Perhaps in an altered state of consciousness, such as hypnosis or deep reverie, a person can 'tap' inner layers of their psyche which have been structured into other individuals for some psychological reason. One speculation is that this is a mechanism to keep 'in hand' missing traits from one's own persona if needed in an emergency. Thus an inherently cowardly person may have inner strengths of courage built around a core personality deep within; this is tapped during regression and cloaked as a past life simply because that is what is expected to emerge in this circumstance. The idea is a far from proven theory that seems to have real problems accommodating the unsavoury and mundane features of past lives, or the sudden recollections of early childhood when personality is far from developed.

Clairvoyance

Information might be detected in the mind from a deceased personality rather in the way that mediums claim to obtain it, but if so, a false assumption is made. Rather than treating the data as coming from another 'dead' person, it is recognised as forming an 'internal' image and so presumed to be a past life experience from within oneself. If this is true it presumes life after death, but has another more serious problem. Why do past life recalls never feature 'messages' being given by the deceased person – only straight-forward recall of the trivia of their lives?

Genetic Memory

As a scientific theory this looks attractive to some. Unfortunately it is the one idea we can completely rule out. The suggestion is that, just as genes pass on behaviour and physical characteristics from parent to child, so too may memory be transferred down the racial or ancestral chain. In other words, each of us might contain fragmented memories of our ancestors' life experience within our genetic make-up.

There are two decisive blows to this hypothesis. Surely, no memory of events after the birth of the child from which you are ultimately descended could possibly be involved. Yet past lives frequently feature death scenes as their strongest feature. Death clearly must post-date the birth of your ancestor, so how could memory of it be passed on to you? Even more damning, there are many cases of childless past lives. Mary Reynolds, the eighteenth-century life described by Jenny Randles, was one of these. If there are no children, no genes can be passed on. Whatever else such experience may be, it is not genetic memory.

Collective Unconscious

Jung's idea was that all mental activity enters a kind of collective pool, and as we are all part of this pool we can 'tap' into it and produce past lives. But why do we get the same past lives each time and not new ones every session? Occultism has adopted from Hindu tradition the idea of the Akashic record, storing everything that everybody has ever done and which is available to people in deep meditation. In his book *A New Science of Life*, biologist Dr Rupert Sheldrake suggested that all life-forms are moulded by an energy field. Habits and evolutionary trends are passed on in an unseen universal 'consciousness' to hone and shape the template of this life field, using individual contributions from each living entity. He uses this theory, for example, to explain why, if rats are taught to perform a task in a laboratory in New York, not only do future generations bred there from that stock perform the task more rapidly (conventionally explained as the passing on of inherited genes) but, far more inexplicably, rats on the other side of the world with no direct links seem to learn the trick as well! Perhaps human beings are a consciousness within a greater consciousness, and we have bits of earlier humans within our 'selves'.

YOUR VERDICT : A SUMMARY

AGAINST SURVIVAL

- The hypnotic state is notoriously capable of stimulating fantasy.

- Cryptomnesia can almost never be ruled out as a source of confirmed data.

- A few cases have almost certainly been shown to be imaginative in nature.

- In Third World countries, where children recall past lives, they invariably describe recent lives with wealthier families; so there are possible motivations for conscious or unconscious fraud.

- Why should all Joe Keeton's British patients always relive British past lives? There are almost no cross-racial past life transfers.

FOR SURVIVAL

- There are quite a few consciously recalled past lives which utilise no hypnosis and can emerge in very young children unaware of reincarnation.

- Sometimes quite obscure details can emerge which require very extensive checking to trace and prove accurate.

- There have been a few cases where skills such as previous languages have been passed on under hypnosis; and deep level regressees, or regressees of several sessions, often adopt a seemingly natural relevant accent.

- Past lives as the opposite sex are not uncommon; although the split does seem to be less than 50/50 (but is more than in multiple personality cases, where only around 10 per cent or less of personas are not of the same sex).

- Past lives tend to be very mundane and display poverty and violent death in proportions unlikely to occur in fantasy; these are consistent with the substantially worse lifestyles of earlier times.

OUT OF THE BODY OR OUT OF THE MIND?

———◆———

Does the mind exist as an electromagnetic field around the body?

Most rationalists have a simple explanation for why they do not believe in survival after death. A human being is a biological entity ruled by the major organs of the body, notably the brain. When these cease to function – through illness, accident or old age – then inevitably that entity must be said to have 'died'. It is rather like having a radio set which happily plays music until one of its main components fails. If you can repair it, it will come back to life. But if the damage is irreversible, the radio no longer works. It is irreparably dead.

This mechanistic approach to life (treating everything as a machine) is the old-fashioned way of science, fostered during the enlightened era of the Renaissance, proving the trigger for the industrial revolution and much of the fruits of today's technology. However, it is now found to be wanting in many ways. The brain fails to conform to the designs of a machine. Nobody can explain how it stores memory or creates emotions. No one knows why we have consciousness and awareness of our selves. Is this unique to human beings, or shared by other animals? What mechanistic purposes does it serve to have free will and knowledge of self-mortality as opposed to robotic behaviour programmed into the core of our existence?

As a result there are a growing number of scientists, from neurologists to physicists, who say that the brain is *not* the origin of consciousness. Mind is separate and distinct, channelled *through* the organ of the brain. Indeed, some scientists speculate that the mind might exist as an electromagnetic field around the body. They take us back to the mechanistic argument, and remind us that if we dissect a radio set to look for the signal that it broadcasts we will never be able to find it. It appears to come from the speakers, and stops if we do something terminal to the machine. But even if the radio set is smashed to tiny pieces, the signal which seemed to be an integral part of it still exists. We just cannot tune into it any more.

So might it be with the mind. Perhaps it too exists like a radio signal, processed through the component of the brain, manipulating the physical self to alter and control its environment.

If this tempting analogy is accurate, then it opens up the way towards logical and scientific acceptance of life after death. If the 'I' which we perceive to be our 'inner self' is an energy field free in time and space, but channelled through the brain, then it may well not matter whether that brain and its accompanying body stop working altogether. True, that mind will not be able to function *in the material world* without the brain and body. But if we are mind, rather than brain and body organs, our 'spirit' or essence could continue to exist irrespective of the status of our physical host.

This seems a radical, even desperate, concept to some people. But it is actually well supported by the growing knowledge of modern science. Perhaps more significant, it is an idea that seems to have widespread anecdotal support from everyday experience. Surveys show that one of the most common 'paranormal' experiences – shared at some point in their lives by over 50 per cent of the population – is the feeling that the mind has temporarily disassociated itself from the body. Singer Kate Bush poetically describes the sensation as being like a 'kite' tethered loosely to the body, floating freely above. In this state, those who have the experience realise that *it* is the essence of self and the body is just a shell.

Whilst these 'out-of-the-body experiences' – or OOBEs – are clearly a part of life, not death, they point the way towards survival and are a necessary prerequisite. If mind really can detach itself from the body, then it makes survival both plausible and probable. If it cannot, and the OOBE is a delusionary trick, then – whilst not disproving survival in some other form – it would be strong evidence for the mechanistic interpretation.

Singer Kate Bush describes the sensation as being like a 'kite' tethered loosely to the body, floating freely above.

TO BE A KITE

Jenny Randles had an OOBE in January 1971, two days after her maternal grandmother had died and the night before the funeral.

She was staying with a friend, in a strange and unfamiliar house, when she awoke in the middle of the night. She insists that she was wide awake, and yet she was not *in* the bed as expected. Instead, Jenny was floating a few feet overhead, looking down upon her own body as it was sleeping. She saw this unfamiliar room, rather than an image of her own bedroom as happens in a dream.

The sensation was remarkable. At this stage Jenny was a teenager with no experience of the supernatural. This unexpected happening was absolutely terrifying. In the second or two that it lasted she was gripped by an indescribably powerful terror. As if this acted as a catapult, there was a near instantaneous jerk and she found herself back in her body, sitting bolt upright and staring about the room scared witless and sweating profusely.

'Originally you are very nervous about approaching the side of a mountain at 600 mph and so you kind of blink.'

At the time Jenny was training to be a science teacher, and the experience contradicted everything that she was learning. For a long time she attempted to rationalise it. She was told – and wanted to believe – that it was merely a dream. The fact that she had been under intense stress at the time (university exams coupled with the death, which had occurred suddenly and in her presence) were factors that had provoked a temporary disassociation from the horrors of reality. However, being given this explanation, and logically accepting it, are very different from absorbing and believing the solution. This proved impossible for one simple reason.

The very basic and – by most standards – trivial OOBE was intensely and convincingly *real*. Jenny has on many occasions, before and since, experienced flying or lucid dreams of incredible vividness. The difference with this OOBE was that it *felt* exactly the same as being awake. The terror that Jenny felt was that of reality and not that of a nightmare. However, it can only be a personal and subjective judgement.

MIND TRIPS TO THE STARS

A few people have claimed to be able to induce OOBEs almost at will. They have been studied in laboratories, but with mixed results. One such person is American Robert Monroe, who has written a series of books including *Far Journeys* (Souvenir 1986), which presents extraordinary details of his alleged rides, free of time and space. He has developed a comprehensive concept of the various realms in which OOBEs supposedly take place. These have interesting similarities to the various afterlife phases that deceased spirits are said to pass through.

Robert Monroe told us how he brings on an OOBE:

'I become deeply relaxed and then I roll out [of my body] – I don't pull out. Then, having the freedom, I go up and find some beautiful clouds to dive through. It's a lot of fun …. Once you have your courage up by diving through clouds that don't hurt you, you can come down and dive through mountains and houses. Originally you are very nervous about approaching the side of a mountain at 600 mph and so you kind of blink. But after a while you get used to it and it's a lot of fun.'

Robert Monroe believes that we all regularly experience OOBEs during sleep, but do not realise it. He says that 'dreams of flying are a rationalisation of what an out-of-body experience is.... Your left brain – the conscious mind – says there's no such thing – so you had a flying dream .... A falling dream is the re-entering of the physical body.'

Psychologists have different interpretations for the flying dream which most of us experience from time to time. They see it as a product of collected hopes and wishes. But it is rather interesting to note that the sensation of flying in such 'dreams' is quite a puzzle. After all, until very recently nobody has flown by way of free-fall parachuting. So how can the flying dream be so commonplace and ancient? Where did the imagery for the dream experience come from? Apparently, with some exceptions (such as the feeling of wind) free-falling is very like the widespread 'dream'.

Even if they *are* dreams, and not immediate OOBEs, they must take their form from some actual experiences stored in our memories – and that cannot mean memories of actual flying! But could Monroe's OOBEs actually be vivid forms of dreams, unconsciously induced in a relaxed state?

In support of that, we might cite his stories about drifting up to the stars and floating around the solar system. Monroe talks of seeing things on other planets that are later verified by space probe photographs, but could not supply any actual illustrations when we asked. He merely claimed that he had seen craters on the surface of Mars before the orbital missions surprised scientists with the great extent of these structures.

'They go through Mars and come out the other side. It's kind of boring.'

In defence of his apparent inability to prove his argument he pointed out: 'It's rather boring. You'd be surprised. It's hard to keep people in the out-of-body state interested in craters and rocks. They go through Mars and come out the other side. It's kind of boring.'

Nevertheless, if it could ever be established that OOBE trippers to a planet *did* legitimately see surface details before the space probes photographed them, it would be impressive proof. It is surprising that this point has not been seized upon by research scientists. The verified truth of such claims would also disprove much of Einsteinian physics!

Apparently, OOBE trips to Mars occur at many times the speed of light (if not instantaneously). The transition from Earth to another planet does not take many minutes or hours to complete, as it would by the fastest possible physical route. As we presently have no means of knowing how such a faster-than-light feat might even be conceivable, let alone possible, it would add very valuable data to our understanding of the mind, and demonstrate that we *must* survive physical death.

MY MIND IS IN MY BIG TOE

Dr Susan Blackmore is a psychologist and very rational paranormal researcher who seeks – and believes that she has found – non-psychic explanations for phenomena such as the OOBE. However, unlike many scientists she has worked from an objective approach, taking the issues very seriously and not ruling other solutions out of court. She has even had an OOBE herself.

Psychologist Dr Sue Blackmore is one of the world's leading researchers of the OOBE. At the start of her lectures she sometimes tries an interesting experiment. She asks the audience to think about where 'they' are located within their body. This is an odd question to which most of us will never have given any thought, but try it now.

Do you feel that the real or inner 'you' is located in your brain, or above your eyes, in your heart or spread throughout your body? A multiplicity of answers have been offered. Someone once responded with the feeling that 'they' were in their big toe!

Interestingly, nobody ever seems to say that they regard their inner self as being placed outside of the body. We all anchor ourselves within in some way. This creates a difficulty when it comes to determining whether our mind has left the body in an OOBE situation. If we can think that our self is in the head or in the big toe, why not also simply think that it has moved from inside our body to somewhere up by the ceiling? In that sense, can an out-of-body experience be considered real or just imagination?

Sue Blackmore experienced an OOBE when she was a student at university. It was deliberately induced in a state of relaxation. She told of roaming free to gaze disembodied at the rooftops. Later she was able to check and discover that the view she 'saw' in this state was incorrect. To her it was nothing more than a dreamy sort of illusion. Since then she has become a leading parapsychologist, regularly featuring in journals and on TV, approaching the subject from a refreshingly open-minded but sceptical viewpoint.

Dr Blackmore was part of a paranormal research group at the university when the experience occurred. But her prior awareness of the subject does not make her detailed and valuable description of the events any less useful. Nevertheless it does distinguish it from the majority of OOBEs. These are not self-induced, nor do they tend to occur to people with a working knowledge or interest in psychic phenomena.

Of course, that does not mean they cannot happen to such people, as noted by Jenny Randles' experience. But the Randles and Blackmore accounts describe very different types of OOBE. Sue Blackmore's was not unpleasant; it involved her stretching out of her body and being aware of doing so, roaming free around imaginary landscapes and yet still retaining at least a partial contact with her real body and the people in the room around her. Robert Monroe's OOBEs are similar – but these are generally occurring to people who are trying to make them happen.

On the other hand, Jenny Randles' account is much more like the spon-

Mountaineers climbing high peaks such as Mount Teide on the Canary Islands off the coast of Africa often experience a feeling of being disassociated. Is this merely due to the effects of rarefied air on the brain or do they literally leave their bodies?

taneous OOBE that is reported by many who have never heard of the term. There was no sense of separating out (she just *was* out). There was no link with her body or the room in which it was located. She seemed to be gazing impassively at her physical self over which she had no apparent control. And there was no pleasure of any sort in connection with it, only intense terror.

These differences may prove very significant. The fear and lack of any control are more suggestive of reality than are the somewhat dream-like features, self-awareness and pleasurability of the induced OOBEs. Indeed, Jenny Randles has had both flying dreams and dream-like OOBEs as well as her single spontaneous event. They are utterly different in feel. Most OOBEs are akin to lucid dreams. The OOBE that happened unexpectedly when she awoke in the night was so real that it is difficult not to regard it as such. Of course, there may be a gradation between these two extremes. Both may in effect be the same phenomenon in differing guises. But the differences cannot simply be ignored and may be more than just apparent.

None the less, based on her experience and study of the evidence Sue Blackmore is today sceptical of the idea that anything leaves the body. She considers the OOBE to be imaging within an altered state of consciousness.

THE EVIDENCE AGAINST

Undoubtedly there are reports of experiences which are either lucid dreams or flying dreams but which exhibit many or most of the attributes of the

OOBE. When the details are compared with the real world environment, they do not check out. The OOBE occurs in a world which is similar to – but not exactly like – the real world. It is imaginary.

Sue Blackmore noted several major differences in roof tiles and chimneys on top of a building that she 'flew' over in an OOBE state. She had never viewed the building from that vantage point in real life until she went and checked after her OOBE. Then she found those details to be incorrect.

In such situations there can be no doubt that these OOBEs are essentially an imaginary experience. Psychologists quite fairly point out that if some are, why not all of them? Perhaps such descriptive errors occur during dreams that mimic OOBEs. If a man dreams that he is wearing red trousers, and he does not own any red trousers, then would he reject the fact that red trousers existed or that he was wearing trousers in the first place? We realise that the dream was based on two perceptions common in the mind – that the man usually wears trousers, and that red ones exist because he has seen them somewhere else. As with most dreams, an imaginary scenario is created which does not necessarily invalidate the individual elements from which that imaginary scenario is produced.

In other words, we may have flying dreams because we do all occasionally have real OOBEs. They are an imaginative reflection of a real experience. Psychologists would say that this is trying to make the facts fit a theory, but the claim of some researchers is that such a view is needed to accommodate the two types of OOBE – the common imaginary experiences, and the rarer seemingly evidence-based OOBEs.

Sue Blackmore has also pointed out that, even in apparently successful experiments to demonstrate that a person sees 'reality' in an OOBE state, we can never forget the possibility that they may gain the information used for their vision via some form of ESP – without actually going anywhere.

THE EVIDENCE FOR

Surveys show that the OOBE is both a remarkably common experience and a pretty consistent one. This might imply a fundamental reality.

Sue Blackmore has compared four separate surveys which produced almost eight hundred people who claim to have had OOBEs. If we look at an average of their results, they suggest that somewhere in the region of 15 per cent of the population have had what they believe was an OOBE at some point in their lives, making this one of the most common psychic experiences.

In most cases (60 per cent) this was a one-off experience. As many as

In the region of about 15 per cent of the population believe they have had an out-of-the-body experience. Usually this occurs spontaneously, although some people claim they can leave their body at will. Percipients describe being near the ceiling looking down at their physical self.

80 per cent on average saw their own 'real' body from a different vantage point, but very few experienced the actual point of separation from the physical self. There is a common Spiritualist claim that a 'silver cord', like a mystical umbilical cord, links the astral 'body' with the physical one. However, only a tiny percentage (about 4 per cent) actually reported seeing it during an OOBE. Jenny Randles did not; Sue Blackmore did. This may hint at the view that some of the figures suggest – that the cord is less a feature of spontaneous OOBEs than of the more contrived or dream-like ones.

A number of researchers have attempted to test people who claim to have OOBEs by getting them to go 'out of the body' and 'see' a target that would not be visible *unless* they drifted up away from their body towards the ceiling. There have been some positive (if controversial) results.

Dr Charles Tart, in California, made one of the earliest attempts by asking a woman to read a random number written on a sheet of paper and placed on a shelf. As she was wired to a machine she could not physically move without disconnecting these wires. The wires monitored her brain waves, and any disconnection would show up on the resulting graph. The woman was correct in one out of four trials – the only one where she claimed she was able to drift up and read the number. However, on another of the trials, whilst unable to see the paper, she did read a clock that was not visible from her body position. The moment when she read the time coincided with changes in the brain wave pattern consistent with an altered state of consciousness – but *not* with disconnection of the wires.

American parapsychologist Dr Karlis Osis tried an interesting twist on this idea, in which a series of symbols in a box were set up via a complex optical system. This meant that you could only see a pattern form as a kind of kaleidoscopic illusion if you were in a disembodied state up in the air and looking through the hole into the box. From any other location you would observe something different.

Osis claims that his experiment worked and that a subject would successfully describe the scene. This implied he really was looking at it from an out-of-the-body state located somewhere in front of the opening to the box. However, there was criticism of Osis's methods. It was pointed out, for example, that he decided he had scored a hit if any part of the picture was correctly noted.

Perhaps the most sophisticated idea was a 'black box' developed by British engineer Professor Arthur Ellison. He explained to us how this worked.

A random number was generated out of sight around the back of the machine. Nobody ever saw this. The person attempting to read it in an OOBE state would tap in a number, which he or she believed to be the same, via buttons on the front of the box. The computer in the machine would automatically check this 'claim', generate the next number round the back, and move on. At the end of the trial it would record how many times the number that had been 'seen' and tapped into the machine matched the number that had been generated out of sight around the back. Significantly, since neither the experimenter nor his subject ever knew any of the numbers that the machine produced, this theoretically ruled out all obvious forms of ESP – suggesting a real OOBE.

Sadly, results with this black box have been very limited – nothing like as positive as the other tests. Possibly this is because it creates an artificial situation. In order to operate the machine, the subject of the experiment is clearly not in the sort of OOBE state that most spontaneous witnesses report. Jenny Randles remarks from her experience that the act of using the machine would simply be impossible in the OOBE state that she entered. Other reports seem to endorse this view. Perhaps Professor Ellison's clever device is a test of clairvoyance rather than of the OOBE state.

I CAN SEE CLEARLY NOW

There are some remarkable claims of evidential success in a spontaneous OOBE state. Biologist Dr Lyall Watson told us about the time in Africa when he was in a bus that overturned. For a time he found himself out of his body, able to look down at the wreckage where a young boy was trapped. The bus was perilously close to toppling over and crushing the child. When Watson snapped back into his body he was able to escape relatively unscathed from the vehicle and help rescuers release the boy. He really was trapped in the exact position that Watson had seen – a location not visible to him in his position on the bus.

In 1992 Dr Keith Hearne conducted a survey of psychic experiences in Britain. One case was of a woman who, after surgery, had an OOBE in her bed and drifted above the doctor and nurse attending her. In this disembodied state she went to another room and floated over a nightdress. The garment still had its price tag on, and later – when conscious – she astonished its owner by 'predicting' how much it had cost!

Such stories are anecdotal, but they also illustrate the way in which the OOBE commonly occurs in a crisis situation. It is in fact recognised as the first phase of the near death experience (see Chapter 13).

An intriguing case we came across was verified by the witness and the nurse present. It was reported direct to Jenny Randles in August 1984, when she spent several weeks in Arrowe Park Hospital on the Wirral.

Jenny was told by one nurse that cardiac care patients at the hospital not infrequently reported OOBEs. Discussing them was discouraged. Later, the ward sister reluctantly agreed that about twice a year she came across patients who described the phenomenon. Before leaving, Jenny was directed to the following example.

A man in his fifties had experienced a thrombosis. He was injected with the drug heparin and developed a hostile reaction. His skin turned purple and a lung was blocked. At this point, the doctor and nurse had left his side.

The man described how he suddenly found that he was floating about five feet in the air. There was no pain. His mind was clear and lucid and he could see all that went on. But there was a shimmering haze in front of his eyes as if he were looking through a gauze sheet. In this state he saw the man in the next bed react to his condition, climb out of bed, come over and call for help. Then a nurse rushed in and cleared his breathing.

When he was brought back to consciousness he was able to describe all of these actions with accuracy. The man in the next bed confirmed this.

For a time he found himself out of his body, able to look down at the wreckage where a young boy was trapped.

Research into out-of-the-body experiences goes some way to demonstrating that the phenomenon does actually occur. Such 'proof' is a prerequisite to an acceptance of life after death. If we can leave our body while it still functions, it indicates that the two are not one and the same, but the result of some quirky evolutionary symbiosis. Perhaps *mind* existed long before it partnered up with primitive, biological bipeds.

YOUR VERDICT : A SUMMARY

AGAINST SURVIVAL

- The OOBE does feature imaginative scenery, which suggests that it could be a vivid dream.

- Some OOBE witnesses who say they 'saw' things in their out-of-the-body state later checked and found these were incorrect.

- Certain psychological conditions, such as depersonalisation, might explain a feeling of being 'out of the body' during times of stress.

FOR SURVIVAL

- Some remarkable anecdotal experiences seem to suggest that people really can go out of their body and view scenes not visible from the bodily position.

- Experimental data suggests that the self 'sees' from a position above and beyond the body – but how it does so without eyes is unclear.

- If mind is timeless and spaceless, as the OOBE implies, then consciousness may be eternal and could survive death.

THE NEAR DEATH EXPERIENCE

◆

WHAT IS A 'NEAR DEATH EXPERIENCE'?

The term near death experience, or NDE, was coined by American medic Dr Raymond Moody in his ground-breaking book *Life After Life*, published in November 1975. Destined to be a global bestseller, it put a handle on a phenomenon which has probably haunted mankind since consciousness began. Indeed, precedents go back to pre-Christian times, recorded in the *Bardo Thodol* – the Tibetan Book of the Dead.

Moody's research led to scientific respectability for what up to then had been little more than a ragbag of bizarre anecdotes related by embarrassed people who had been brought back by fortune or medical skill from the brink of death. It encouraged many other individuals in the medical and mental health professions to take up the challenge and involve themselves in carrying out their own research into what were formerly known as 'death bed visions'. One of these was Margot Grey, a British clinical psychologist, who succinctly summed up the essential meaning of the term.

'Many people who nearly die, whether in an accident, during surgery or in other traumatic circumstances, subsequently report a remarkable experience while physically unconscious. This event brings with it a profound and permanent alteration of their understanding of the nature of reality. There are many elements, recounted independently by thousands of people, common to all these accounts. These frequently involve an encounter with a compassionate being of light, a meeting with deceased loved ones, and feelings of inexpressible beauty, peace and transcendence, leading to a loss of fear of death, greatly increased sense of life's purpose and a more loving and open attitude.'

Dr Raymond Moody identified the main components of the NDE, which are presented here in a modified form.

THE COMPONENTS OF THE NEAR DEATH EXPERIENCE

A Sense of Being Dead

Initially, subjects do not realise that they are 'dead'. They find themselves floating above the body, looking down on the frantic attempts at resuscitation. When they do recognise the body as their own, fear momentarily takes hold followed by understanding and heightened awareness of what is going on. They can recount in detail medical procedures and whole lines of conversation and other unusual observations. At this point they attempt to intervene physically, by touching or speaking, but this inevitably fails.

Peace and Painlessness

Prior to the experience, people are often in severe discomfort. Once they are released from the body, however, pain is left behind and a genuine sense of spiritual peace pervades.

Out-of-the-Body Experience

The out-of-the-body experience, or OOBE, is a phenomenon which can occur away from life-threatening situations, spontaneously, or in some cases by conscious will. This is also true of the tunnel journey and subsequent meetings with other-world beings (see below). However, these are, with some exceptions, mandatory components of the NDE.

At the point when the subject hears the doctor's pronouncement of death, he becomes aware of himself as an entity separate from the body. yet to himself he still has form, although it is not necessarily an ethereal copy of his physical self. It has been described as composed of energy or light patterns. While in this out-of-the-body state, the subject can move through walls merely by an act of will, and accurately observe things which are happening elsewhere.

The Tunnel Journey

Now that the subject realises he is dead, far from feeling depressed, he is filled by a sense of exhilaration at what lies ahead. He now enters a dark tunnel, sometimes described as a deep valley, at the end of which is a bright light. Occasionally the subject is accompanied by a being, often perceived as an angel, who guides him towards the light. More rarely, the journey is not via the imagery of a tunnel; instead, the subject floats upwards towards 'Heaven'.

Other-World Beings

At the end of the tunnel lies a place of light, variously described as a beautiful garden, a city of light, or the gateway to Heaven itself. Here are other beings, glowing with an intense luminescence. This 'energy' is more than just a visual perception, it radiates a pure love that washes over and bathes the subject. Usually, some of these being are recognisable as the deceased relatives and friends of the new arrival.

The Ultimate Being of Light

The subject then becomes aware of a supreme Being of Light, whom people with a religious background identify according to their beliefs. It is described variously as Jesus, God, Buddha or Allah. The Being radiates such love and understanding that when the subject is told he must return, as it is not yet his 'time', he does not want to leave.

During the Near Death Experience, people describe travelling down a tunnel or through a dark valley at the end of which is a very bright light. Along the way they often meet deceased relatives and friends. At the end of the tunnel stands a supreme Being of Light.

The Life Review

Before returning to his earthly body, the subject is sometimes confronted by a life review. The whole of a person's life is presented before them: every act, every deed – good and bad. The Being of Light guides them through it. But this is not passive observation. Not only does the percipient see the results of his past acts, he *feels* the hurt and love he has generated in others.

The life review can also be experienced by a person on the point of death who does not describe a proper NDE. Many people in such situations have said afterwards how 'my whole life passed in front of me', leading to a well-known 'old wives' tale' trivialising the experience. Sometimes, subjects are given a glimpse into their own personal future.

During an NDE time does not pass in the same way as it is normally perceived; it is greatly compressed, and there is no real sense of passage. Only a few minutes may literally elapse while doctors fight to resuscitate the patient, yet a much longer, and indefinable, period will subjectively seem to have occurred.

The Return from Death

Subjects often re-enter the body at the speed of a bullet through the head.

Many people do not want to return to their physical bodies. There are on record cases where, on being resuscitated, patients have admonished their doctor for bringing them back to life! The return journey is usually much quicker than the journey out. At the point of reanimation, subjects often re-enter the body at the speed of a bullet through the head.

Aftermath of the Near Death Experience

The experience can totally change the outlook of an individual, irrespective of any previous religious beliefs. The experience can make a person more spiritual, many see the shortcomings and irrelevancies of organised religions. Death itself now hold no fears and, incongruously, life becomes more precious. Subjects feel there are now only two things which are important: knowledge and love. Some people go on to develop clairvoyant 'powers'.

Although these are the main components, not many people experience all of them during an NDE. There are small variations, too, although the core experience of death, floating, tunnel, light, beings and return is commonly universal.

THERE AND BACK AGAIN

When middle-aged Derbyshire mum Shirley Wood collapsed one Sunday morning in the 1980s, she though she was dying. 'I was timing the potatoes for lunch when suddenly a sharp pain hit me under my left breast. Clutching my chest and gasping for air, my husband and eldest son guided me into the lounge and on to the settee. I struggled painfully for air for about twenty minutes, then my condition worsened and I drifted into blackness.'

This blackness was not unconsciousness, because Shirley was still very much aware of everything. The pain had gone. Everything was calm and peaceful. She floated out of her body, as light as a feather, and drifted down into a black pit . . . . She heard her 'spiritual' voice say: 'Well, this is it, I'm dying. This must be death.' Her voice sounded so clear and sharp in the black silence, and there was no fear.

Then Shirley was floating upwards again, and a being joined her, taller, grey-looking, gently taking her hand. Only the top half of its body was visible – the lower half immersed in blackness. It had sunken eyes, no hair or ears. It was all shades of grey from almost white to nearly black – there were no other colours at all. Even the eyeballs were grey. The various shades kept changing to make up the contours of the face and to show emotion. Shirley and the grey being began moving through a valley. Suddenly the being became very excited and began singing and dancing, its shoulders and trunk bobbing up and down. 'I have never experienced such joy and happiness,' said Shirley. 'It was indescribable. The being told me we were on our way to Heaven. When we arrived the gates would open and a brilliant light would spill out enclosing us like the warm embrace of a lover's arms. I couldn't wait to get there, never giving my family a thought.'

At last they arrived. They seemed to stand for quite a while. Then happiness turned to disappointment when they realised the gates were not going to open. The grey being became very agitated, and raised one arm, crying: 'The light's not there!' Shirley could tell by its face that it was very upset.

'It hesitated for a moment, as if wondering what to do next. Suddenly we were travelling backwards in a flash of speed. I shouted: "I can't die yet, my family need me!" There was a whistling sound, then I was back in my body, entering at the front of the head. At that very moment I came out of the blackness and heard myself gasp.'

Shirley had been unconscious for ten minutes. Her doctor said the attack was caused by shortage of iron in the blood resulting in oxygen starvation of the brain. This caused her heart to have a 'spasm', as she called it. She admits that the experience has changed her life. 'Although I don't attend church, and neither am I a religious fanatic, I'm sure God allowed me to see Heaven's Gates, so I could tell others. Now it's taken over my life. It's always in the back of my mind and I can't sleep at night. I want to do more things to help other, less fortunate people.'

Our research suggests that other anomalous experiences might pre-date, as well as post-date, a NDE. Shirley Wood had such an experience a full three months before that near fatal Sunday lunchtime.

'This wasn't my flesh-and-blood face, but a grey spiritual replica.'

'One night towards the end of February I had been in bed about two minutes when I began to 'see' things through my right eye. I seemed to be at the back of a brightly lit room and was very terrified. For a brief second I saw my own face screwed up in horror. This wasn't my flesh-and-blood face, but a grey spiritual replica.

I tried to turn my head away, but it was held in a vice, forcing me to see. Feeling a little calmer, I left the body completely and glided to the front of this strange, unknown room. A coffin stood before two curtains. They were heavy, expensive brocade in a beautiful gold colour, slightly patterned with sycamore-type leaves.

The coffin was before me and I noticed the shine on the new wood, similar to pine but not quite as yellow. All at once I realised I was in a crematorium. Then everything went black and I returned to normal.'

At the time, Shirley interpreted the experience as a premonition of the death of her father, who was ill. But since her NDE she sees it instead as a warning of her own possible imminent physical extinction. Perhaps God changed 'His' mind, she suggests.

A BAD TRIP

International clairvoyant Peter Lee has attracted a list of celebrity clients over the years, including Bob Marley, Yul Brynner and Princess Michael of Kent. But it is his own personal experiences which stick most vividly in his mind. Like Shirley Wood, he too had psychic experiences *prior* to his brush with near death, including an out-of-the-body experience as a small child. This is what happened when he nearly died.

'I was in Germany, and up the side of a mountain with some people. Suddenly I fell and was conscious of hundreds of little stones rolling beneath my body. I became aware of a clump of grass, or outcropping of some kind, and realised if I didn't grab it I was finished. Reaching out, I caught it firmly. I was relieved. Then it gave way . . . .

'As I fell, all the events of my life flashed before me like a roll of film unwinding. Then I was aware of a tunnel of light stretching before me. Instinctively I *knew* this was a tunnel of *life*, not death. As I drifted along there were people I recognised who had passed away. Suddenly I was snapped back out of the tunnel, and I remember thinking; "this doesn't feel much like Heaven . . . there's pains in my head . . . my legs hurt . . . I realised I was still alive and on the mountainside. When they picked me up I expected my body to jangle, but by some miracle no bones were broken."'

NEGATIVE NEAR DEATH EXPERIENCES

Although the majority of reported NDEs are spiritually uplifting, a very small percentage are not. These are the negative experiences, where the percipient, rather than having a taste of 'Heaven', feels the heat of 'Hell'.

Initially Shirley Wood found herself sinking into a pit, before rising and making her way along a valley. If she had continued to sink, the experience could have turned into a negative NDE.

NDE researcher and philosopher Dr Michael Grosso relates such a case. A man took a drug overdose in order to kill himself. In the presence of friends he suffered a heart attack and turned blue, entering a critical death phase. A nightmarish NDE followed.

Many of the usual components were missing. He descended into an inferno, where horrific-looking beings clutched and clawed at him. This place was suffocating and claustrophobic. Fortunately, perhaps, medical personnel were able to resuscitate him. Apparently the experience did change him for the better, but through the use of the stick rather than the carrot. Dr Grosso adds a rather intriguing postscript. The audio tape used to record the interview was subsequently found to have erased itself. Grosso remarks that neither before nor since has his tape recorder given any similar trouble.

NEAR DEATH EXPERIENCES IN COMBAT

A special area of study are combat NDEs. These are experiences generated on the battlefield in some individuals during moments of intense stress –

moments when they feel their own physical extinction is imminent. These cases do not follow the precise pattern of civilian NDEs, causing some researchers, notably Raymond Moody, to believe they are a completely different phenomenon.

He recounts the case of a serviceman in Sicily during the invasion of Italy in World War II. This American soldier threw a hand grenade into a German machine gun nest and hurled himself to the ground. The grenade was a dud and failed to explode. He heard the Germans firing at him, although he was not hit. At this point he apparently left his body and travelled to New Jersey, floating over an assembly line of women putting hand grenades together. He pleaded with them to take more care over their work, but of course they could not hear him. Then he was back in his body and threw a second grenade, which destroyed the nest.

Robert Sullivan is a civilian investigator who uncovered forty cases where combat veterans experienced heightened sensory awareness. His work shows that these were essentially the same as civilian cases. However, two veterans reported how they were able to dodge bullets because their perception somehow slowed them down. Another experienced 360 degree vision while running away from some Germans who were firing at him. Sullivan believes these extra-sensory 'powers' are all connected somehow with the core near death experience.

Possibly the most graphic combat NDE of all was that experienced by a soldier in Vietnam and related to American cardiologist Dr Michael Sabom. The victim was very severely wounded and fell 'dead' instantly, but in his out-of-the-body state was able to observe his former comrades searching the corpse which they saw broken and critically injured on the ground. He was taken away to the mortuary and lost consciousness for some hours, only to awaken to full reality moments before death would have been quite irreversible. The mortician was preparing to inject his 'lifeless' form with embalming fluid!

RESEARCH INTO THE NEAR DEATH EXPERIENCE

Serious attention was first given to the process of death in the 1960s with the publication of a book entitled *On Death and Dying* by distinguished Swiss-born psychiatrist Elisabeth Kubler-Ross. She worked with former Nazi concentration camp victims, and became convinced that at the point of death something unexpected occurred.

Dr Raymond Moody was a young philosophy student about this time when he came across the experience of Dr George Ritchie, a Virginian psychiatrist. Ritchie had been pronounced dead of double pneumonia, but experienced a classic NDE when the phenomenon had not been recognised by any researchers as such. Moody collected similar stories into his best-selling book *Life After Life*, which initiated near death research on a worldwide basis.

Gradually many scientists from a variety of disciplines got involved, such as American cardiologist Dr Michael Sabom, who published the results of his work in 1982 in *Recollections of Death: A Medical Study*. Originally a sceptic, he sought medical evidence that such cases were real by checking whether the patient could describe revival techniques which they could not have witnessed unless they were floating in mid-air above their bodies, as alleged.

He and Moody have pleaded with the scientific fraternity to take the phenomenon seriously. Subsequently the International Association for Near Death Studies – IANDS – has become a forum for the exchange of research findings and ideas.

In Britain, an affiliated branch of IANDS was launched following a comparative study by Margot Grey, a humanistic psychologist with a practice in clinical psychotherapy. Margot experienced her own NDE whilst travelling through India in 1976. Her research appeared in the much praised book *Return from Death*.

For many it was Dr Kenneth Ring who legitimised this work in the eyes of the scientific community. Ring showed that religious background, race and age had no bearing on the experience. As a psychologist interested in altered states of consciousness, he only had to hear an NDE story to become scientifically intrigued. That was in 1977, and since then he has contributed greatly to this and associated subjects. It was Ring who founded IANDS.

In 1992 Dr Ring published the results of an in-depth research experiment which compared the psychological profiles of near death experience with people who claim to have been abducted by aliens. This idea seems utterly outrageous, if not absurd. But 'The Omega Project' reveals startling statistics which show that a common trend is clearly present. In both cases the person is in an altered state of consciousness, undergoing extremely similar and extraordinary visionary experiences. Afterwards, both emerge with completely changed perspectives on life and enhanced psychic abilities. Dr Ring believes that such people have a different perception of reality from the rest of us.

David Lorimer, a former Winchester schoolmaster, is the current (1992) chairman of IANDS. He says:

Near death researcher and author Dr Kenneth Ring, who has studied the psychological profiles of those who experience this traumatic phenomenon in what he called the 'Omega Project'. He has found significant evidence of similarities right across social bands.

'Some scientists write off the NDE as pure hallucination because their training has taught them to react in this way. We have many cases on record of NDEs occurring in people without cerebral inoxia [oxygen starvation] taking place. Currently we are engaged in a programme of categorising and rating the many letters we have received from people reporting this phenomenon. We will then begin a scientific study and publish our results in the way of articles in scientific journals.'

Dr Peter Fenwick is a consultant neurophysiologist at St Thomas's Hospital and the Maudsley Hospital in London; he is also president of IANDS. He sees the answer to the NDE puzzle in more esoteric terms. 'The answer depends whether I'm adopting a scientific or world view. Both views might be relevant. Perhaps it's all linked to quantum mechanics. The world view on survival after death might structure the reality of it – and not the other way round.'

A SCIENTIFIC INVESTIGATION OF THE NEAR DEATH EXPERIENCE

In 1980 Kenneth Ring published the results of his study as *Life at Death: A Scientific Investigation of the Near Death Experience*. His system of questioning has since been accepted as the standard method for interviewing potential NDE subjects. He interviewed over a hundred respondents and compared NDEs emerging from accident, illness and suicide. The study showed that NDEs were not dependent on circumstances, and provided a wealth of statistical information.

Researchers from Evergreen State College in Olympia, Washington state examined the near death experiences of forty-nine residents of the north-western USA. The percentage of subjects who recollected each component of the core NDE experience did not match Ring's results. Was this because the sample was smaller?

In 1982 George Gallup Jnr conducted a poll, using the full resources of the famous international Gallup Organisation, and found that 8 million Americans had gone through the NDE experience. The study was conducted over eighteen months, and covered the entire USA. It showed that the phenomenon was more prevalent than had previously been thought, and generally confirmed the conclusions of other researchers based on much smaller samples. But again, the statistical results compared badly with other studies.

For example, Ring found that just over a third of his sample experienced the out-of-the-body stage, whilst Evergreen found twice this and Gallup less than Ring. Below is Gallup's breakdown of respondents who recalled what components made up their NDE. As Gallup based his results on a much larger sample, perhaps his should be regarded as the most accurate data available so far.

	Percentage
Out-of-the-body	26
Accurate visual perception	23
Audible sounds or voices	17
Feelings of peace, painlessness	32
Light phenomena	14
Life review	32
Being in another world	32
Encountering other beings	23
Tunnel experience	9
Precognition	6

British psychologist Margot Grey conducted her own comparative study of near death experiences, and presented the results in her book *Return from Death* which was published in 1985. She was more interested in the humanistic features of each case, such as conscious awareness of external and paraphysical environments. She felt that the NDE raised two fundamental questions. Can consciousness exist independent of the brain, and are NDEs the source of all cross-cultural religious doctrines?

The study backed up many of the results of the previous investigations, concluding that the phenomenon had a subjective 'quality' that was entirely convincing to the subject. While accepting that a neurological basis for NDEs had not been explored thoroughly, Dr Grey felt that the scientific method of investigation might not be fully applicable to the finding of a solution. Grey also highlighted the incidence of subjects who afterwards became endowed with paranormal 'powers' such as precognition and psychic healing.

THE EVIDENCE AGAINST

NDEs are anecdotal – they cannot be scientifically duplicated or accepted as anything other than stories related by people who have almost died. In fact, similar accounts have been related by people who have not been on the point of death (see Chapter 12). How can they be proof of an afterlife?

Another component, the tunnel, can be traced to a subconscious memory of birth. In a time of severe stress, the mind reverts to a vestigal memory of being forced out of the womb.

Some medical professionals believe that the experience may be a sign of disassociation. The cite major psychoses such as paranoia and schizophrenia, and organic brain problems like delirium, dementia and temporal lobe epilepsy. Schizophrenia involves the 'hearing' of disembodied 'voices', and delirium is brought about by lack of oxygen to the brain, resulting in a chemical imbalance and hallucinations. NDEs too seem to arise when the brain is starved of oxygen.

The out-of-the-body component can be explained in terms of 'autoscopic hallucinations'. These involve the mental projection of one's self into visual space. The subject can see a perfectly solid-looking duplicate of himself in the way he would see another person.

Another component, the tunnel, can be traced, according to scientists like American cosmologist Carl Sagan, to a subconscious memory of birth, which is an experience common to all mankind. In other words, in a time of severe stress, the mind reverts to a vestigial memory of being forced out of the womb along the birth canal towards the waiting circle of light that is the 'real world', and where very often strange beings (doctors and nurses) will be waiting and focusing all their efforts on you. The parallels, when looked at in this possibly misleading way, are striking.

This so called 'birth trauma' has been used by Californian English professor Alvin Lawson to explain claims of abduction by alien beings. Our own research into this field supports Kenneth Ring's conclusion that there are undoubted parallels, but not Lawson's.

NDEs may result from a psychological mechanism that kicks into gear when an individual's life is on the point of termination – something to make the going easier. The idea that the mind tricks itself when threatened is called 'transient depersonalisation'.

Sceptics also cite mind altering drugs such as Thorazine, Valium, Demerol and morphine, as being another possible source. These pain killers are often administered to seriously ill and injured patients and could explain medical NDEs, it is thought. In cases where drugs are not administered, the brain can release its own pain killing chemicals – endorphins – which are about thirty times more powerful than morphine. Do these have similar effects?

If NDEs are spiritual journeys, then why are they not *exactly* the same in all cases?

In one case on our files a man in a dentist's chair in Middlesborough in 1964 found himself out of his body observing the scene from near the ceiling. He drifted through the roof towards a strange figure that he considered to be an alien and then entered a UFO! Here he was given a typically glib message about the fate of the Earth and warned that he would have to fight demons that would try to possess his body if he was to return to Earth. Indeed, he was challenged by small ugly creatures, but finally achieved union with his body. The dentist confirmed that the man had undergone an allergic reaction and almost died. As he had re-entered his body, the percipient had observed the doctor banging his chest to the tune of 'Hit The Road Jack' – a poular song of the day. This highly unlikely 'memory' was confirmed to be the truth by the allegedly startled dentist.

Just how does one evaluate this as a factual near-death memory? It appears much more like some form of personalised hallucination built around a common theme with elements that are consistent to most cases.

There is also the fact that none of the subjects in any NDE case are dead, only 'near death'. We believe that the brain suffers irreversible damage after only a few minutes starved of oxygen. Some spark of consciousness must remain even in patients who are pronounced dead, otherwise they would not be able to revive. Does this generate the NDE which is clearly a phenomenon of life, not of death?

THE EVIDENCE FOR

There are cases on record of subjects who met deceased relatives or friends in an NDE state, before they had knowledge of their death. Sir William Barrett, author of the 1926 book *Death Bed Visions*, recorded a case of a woman on the point of death who 'saw' her deceased sister waiting for her, when she was not aware that the sister had died. The news had been deliberately kept from her.

Many people who suddenly find themselves 'floating' do not immediately recognise their own body lying prostrate below. We have an image of ourselves built up from mirrors and photographs – but it is not one in a state of death. If NDEs were nothing more than internal fantasies, then that lack of recognition would not arise.

Subjects claim that, in their out-of-the-body state, they can travel through walls into other parts of buildings. Moody relates a case where a woman on the point of death afterwards commented that her daughter had been wearing mismatched plaids in another part of the hospital. This was verified by a relative. Some subjects have been able to recount whole lines of conversation made by people in the operating theatre, *and* in other rooms, and report observing medical procedures. The literature is full of such cases. Sceptics say their minds 'heard' this and invented the image of 'seeing' it happen.

Very young children also experience NDEs. They have no advance knowledge of what an NDE consists of, can have few expectations of death and almost no self body image. They are relatively more free of cultural conditioning than adults.

For example, in one 1983 case that was reported to us, a child of almost five underwent surgery in order for an artificial heart valve to be put in place. According to the testimony of his mother and a nurse on duty at the time, he recovered from the operation with one pressing question. 'Mummy, why wouldn't the doctors answer me when they put that thing inside? . . . I was up by the ceiling watching.' Not only did the boy relate a procedure which his physical eyes could never have seen, but he also described the artificial heart valve which he was considered too young to have been shown before the surgery.

If this child was simply recounting an hallucination, how was his description such a correct match of reality?

In many cases the subject has been medically certified dead according to our present recognition of such symptoms. The heart has stopped beating, EEG monitors have registered straight lines, and the pupils of the eye have ceased to function. The individual has remained in this state for much longer than the five minutes after which it is presently believed that irreversible brain damage occurs. Sometimes, hours later, the patient has spontaneously revived – with a strange tale to tell.

Sufferers of schizophrenia exhibit depression, despair and hopelessness, whereas NDE subjects are better mentally adjusted after the experience than before.

Although cultural conditioning plays its part in how individuals *label* their experiences, the NDE does not act as religious confirmation. Just as many agnostics and atheists seem to have NDEs as do religious believers. Often the experience will turn a person away from organised religion, as it fails to match the definition of Heaven that the Church imposes.

NDEs are not caused by mental illness. Sufferers of schizophrenia exhibit depression, despair and hopelessness – in contrast to NDE subjects, who are better mentally adjusted after the experience than before. Very few are not positively motivated by the NDE trauma. Indeed, as the NDE seems to prepare a person well for real death in the future (very few emerge from their experience without this positive benefit) there is a case for arguing that it would be an evolutionary advantage. In that sense we might expect the NDE to occur quite widely in later life as a psychological preparation, or always in crisis situations; but there seems no evidence that it is age-related or as widespread as this might suggest.

The symptoms reported by sufferers of temporal lobe epilepsy do not fit the components of the NDE either. The only exception is the life review, which seems only to refer to a triggering of the memory centres in the brain.

Proponents argue that NDEs are not drug-induced fantasies. Between 1971 and 1977 Ronald K. Siegel carried out tests on volunteers, who were given various medical and hallucinatory drugs. Siegel had a mixed response in simulating NDE components: the closest match was with the description of the 'tunnel'. However, as most of the drugs used increased suggestibility in subjects, perhaps this is not too surprising. Siegel eventually abandoned the idea that the phenomenon was purely an organic hallucination, and moved on to other reductionist explanations.

Subjects are unanimous in insisting on the reality and the undream-like quality of the experience. There has to be some electrical activity in the brain for hallucinations to occur, but in the cases where an electroencephalogram has produced a completely flat line (hence the popular movie about NDE research being titled *Flatliners*), and the brain is by definition 'dead', hallucinatory activity is not theoretically possible. However, there are a few cases where the electrical activity has been so low that the machine has been incapable of recording it.

The suggested link between oxygen starvation and NDEs is a nonstarter. Since the 1920s the effects of oxygen reduction to the brain have been well known. Various tests have been carried out on volunteers in air chambers where the supply of oxygen has been gradually reduced. Mental and physical abilities became progressively impaired, resulting in convulsions, slowness in reasoning, and memory difficulties. Hallucinations were not produced. The absolute clarity and reality of the near death experience cannot be a result of oxygen starvation.

Overall, the NDE gives the impression of being a remarkable, widespread, consistent and predictable phenomenon – almost unprecedented in terms of the paranormal. In the recent past it has become the best hope that parascientists have of establishing real proof of survival after death. Even if that objective fails, it seems likely to add to our presently poor knowledge of human consciousness.

As such, the NDE represents the new final frontier of study into that shadowland beyond death.

YOUR VERDICT : A SUMMARY

AGAINST SURVIVAL

- By definition, the percipient is not dead, only 'near' death.

- The 'evidence' is mostly anecdotal – stories told by people.

- Despite a catalogue of components, the experience is not identical in every case – as it should be if it were wholly objective.

- Some people have experienced various components of the NDE when they were not in a life-threatening situation.

- The NDE could be a psychological mechanism to make dying less traumatic.

- Some scientists believe that the experience is the result of mind-bending drugs or psychopathological states.

FOR SURVIVAL

- There are many cases on record where the percipient has been certified as dead, only to revive minutes – even hours – later.

- Percipients have afterwards described medical procedures, lines of conversation and events taking part in other rooms at the moment of death – when physically these could not have been seen.

- The victims of mental disease and mind-bending drugs suffer only negative consequences. NDE percipients become better people. The experience transforms their lives in a very positive way.

- The NDE does not act as religious confirmation. Just as many agnostics and atheists have the experience. In most cases, it drives percipients away from organised religion.

CONCLUSION: ABOUT DEATH

◆

T his is a book about death. But it is not a sad book. Indeed, you might think that it is a very optimistic contemplation of the biggest question each of us must ponder.

What happens *after* our time is over? Do we cease to exist like the little dot on a TV screen when we switch it off, or is the signal still out there – drifting in space, perhaps attracted by a different aerial on a different house, ready to burst into life once again to a whole new set of players, or existing in a form that you and I just do not see?

These are the choices that we face. Often the evidence may point in two directions and it is difficult to know which trail may be the right one to follow. In addition, there appears to be a difference between what is logically, rationally and scientifically correct and what seems emotionally in tune with universal law.

Of course, wishful thinking is a powerful lure. None of us wants to die. So we may yearn to meet once more those whom we have loved and lost. But wanting something to be true is never enough. It has to *be* true. Yet in that inner, almost intuitive, conviction might there not be real insight rather than selfish desire?

Scientists attempt to legitimise this gut feeling as a product of our genes. The basis of life is procreation, they say. Survival is an instinct that has allowed our species to evolve. When hoping for survival, we misinterpret this built-in programming designed to further the race as a belief in our individual survival.

Until we realise that this is typical scientific rationalism it seems a very persuasive argument. In fact, the truth is that science knows no more about reality than you or I do. Scientists are forever climbing the hill to reach the summit of all knowledge, only to discover that the summit is an illusion and more hills just keep on appearing before their eyes.

If gut feelings, beliefs and powerful emotions can indeed be put down to

Do we cease to exist like the little dot on a TV screen when we switch it off or is the signal still out there?

233

chemical reactions or mathematical equations, then of course science will be proved right at some point in the future. At times the supernatural does seem to support this pragmatic view, because its adherents have a tendency to claim too much and do so rather too quickly. So the sceptic understandably goes overboard in an effort to prove the believer wrong.

And yet – if what few things we can say with reasonable certainty about ESP and consciousness are indeed true – then mind is much stranger than a few flickering equations. It can bypass time and space and link together the physically unconnected. Emotion *is* a key to all of this and no scientist has come close to distilling love in a test tube.

When we watch a movie such as *Ghost* – the blockbuster about survival of death – why do we react as we do? You could say it is a nice story of the simplest kind: girl meets boy, girl loses boy, girl finds boy again. It plays on the pseudo-reality of an inner self which scientists allege to be mere biocircuitry designed to propagate Darwinian evolution.

How inadequate you find that as an explanation, you alone can say. But why then do we feel uplifted and call the ending to this movie a 'happy' one? Why did millions go to see it again and again? Why did it make more money than any film in British box office history? For after all, in the end girl loses boy again – and seemingly forever. There is a happy ending only if the entire audience accepts one fundamental premise.

When the character Sam follows the bright light and goes down the tunnel in typical NDE fashion, just as the credits roll, then he 'dies'. If the idea of survival is a sham, that is the end of him and the movie is a tragedy. But it seems improbable that anybody watching this magic unfurl believes for one moment that Sam has crumbled away for good.

No – the movie succeeds because it seems that every sentient human being shares awareness of a truth that no one can prove. Despite what scientists say, despite what some of the evidence may even argue, and despite the number of ways you can come up with to offer more rational explanations – somewhere inside of us is that spark of comprehension that burns so strongly it can never be extinguished. We just *know* that some part of us survives past bodily death, perhaps to go on to fulfil a deeper purpose.

And somehow this knowing is enough to change the world.

We just know that some part of us survives past bodily death.

YOUR VERDICT

If you followed the advice in the Introduction, you should now have a sheet of paper containing your scores for each chapter. Here is your chance to determine your own conclusion to this enquiry. Add all the plus scores together, then all the minus scores, and take the lower figure from the higher one. You will then have a result somewhere between plus 130 and minus 130. Find the section below that matches your score (if it is on the borderline of two, read both) and you will discover what this means in terms of the ultimate question: *Is there life after death?*

More than plus 100

You feel that the evidence is overwhelmingly in favour of survival. What form this takes remains to be seen, but you have concluded that some part of our inner self is in some way eternal, and that the dissolution of the physical body may not be important to its continued existence.

However, very few people will feel able to adopt so strong a position, given the contradictory nature of some of the evidence. Try reconsidering the negative aspects of those chapters where you reached very positive conclusions. Beware the possibility that you made up your mind before you started and never gave the sceptics the hearing they deserved.

Between plus 71 and plus 100

You have realised that there are times when the cautious view is preferable, but on the whole you consider it very likely that we do survive death. Some part of our inner self is in some way superior to the material body.

You may well have been powerfully persuaded by the personal accounts – and these often do seem impressive. But it is perhaps sensible to bear in mind that these are only anecdotal and often rely upon the testimony of one or at most a few individuals who can, of course, be mistaken in their interpretations. Did it necessarily happen in exactly the way that the witnesses assumed it did? On that may lie the crux of your decision.

Between plus 41 and plus 70

On balance you think survival of death is a real possibility, but some of the evidence is not as persuasive as it seems at first sight. There are always alternatives that can be introduced to try to explain away a reported phenomenon, but sometimes at least you are of the view that the sceptics' position is strained and rather less credible than the more straightforward approach.

It is true that sceptics do at times try over-hard to seek explanations – but then ask yourself whether you have always given them a fair hearing. We do seem to have an inbuilt desire to survive death – a driving force deep inside. You may feel this is an instinctive awareness that we have an eternal part – a soul, if you like – which is certainly a valid way of looking at things. But it may also be true that we are blinding ourselves by self-delusion. This is a powerful factor that it is best not to overlook. Wanting something to be true does not necessarily mean that it *is* true.

Between plus 1 and plus 40

Your view of the evidence is a very balanced one. You have found it hard to weigh the facts and reach a conclusion. However, you seem to have erred on the side of optimism rather than pessimism.

There is a famous philosophical axiom about survival. It argues that it is definitely superior logic to believe than to disbelieve. Here is why. If you believe and are proven correct, you can live your life in relative peace of mind and will be prepared when the transition comes. If you are wrong and at death all consciousness is simply extinguished, you are not even going to know that you guessed wrong! On the other hand, if you choose the negative view you will not know you were right and be around to say 'I told you so', and will spend fruitless years without any hope of anything more than mundane reality. Who wins in that gamble?

Between minus 1 and minus 40

On the whole you have found the evidence slightly wanting and the views of the sceptics just a little more persuasive. On balance, you feel it is possible – but unlikely – that we do survive.

It is undeniably true that much of what at first glance looks to be impressive evidence crumbles upon enquiry – or, at least, has rational alternatives to be borne in mind. But as your judgement has seen, the sceptical position is not so strong as to rule out completely all possibility of an afterlife. Consider which aspects of the evidence you found the most persuasive (the chapters with positive scores, or the smallest minus scores) and read into them further. These areas deserve more investigation – just in case that definitive evidence eventually emerges. Don't cut off all your escape routes!

Between minus 41 and minus 70

You feel pretty confident that we are unlikely to survive death. There is usually a better explanation on offer from rational science.

It is true that human beings are fallible. They can make errors of judgement and at times twist the facts to fit what they desperately want to believe.

We would all like to think that we are in some way immortal, but if it is true that this life is all we have, and that what is termed the supernatural is a testament mostly to human gullibility, then your watchword should be to make the most out of what we have got.

On the other hand, some of the evidence was less clear-cut than you might have expected and there are some areas (those chapters with the least negative scores) which deserve deeper study. It is always wise to be open-minded, because humanity does not know everything and science has been proved wrong many times in the past.

Between minus 71 and minus 100

Your verdict is quite clear. Life after death is very unlikely, and the so-called evidence proposed by others to accommodate its possibility has little to offer a rational appraisal. What it does show is that there are a great many deluded people who have made themselves believe, perhaps after losing loved ones and seeking solace.

On the other hand, there were one or two stories that made you stop and think – if only for a moment – that this world is not as cut and dried as we might like to presume. There are still mysteries to be unravelled, and it could be that new facts will emerge that would make you revise your opinion, if only slightly. At least these positive factors should give you scope to be more tolerant of those who profess that they believe in survival. You may now see why some intelligent, rational people have looked at this evidence and come to a different conclusion from you.

Lower than minus 100

There is no doubt in your mind at all. Survival of death is a myth, and a potentially harmful one that has led countless billions of people astray with false hopes and illusions.

But ask yourself how much of your decision was really based on a fair and honest assessment of the facts. Did you genuinely weigh up the pros and the cons, or have you simply tested the evidence against a pre-existing viewpoint? Can you sincerely conclude that none of the evidence gave you cause for wonder or reconsideration?

If your answers to these questions are 'Yes', then fair enough. You are a genuine sceptic – and the world needs people like you. That is particularly so if you are right … but never rule out the remote possibility that you might perhaps be wrong. A nasty surprise could await the unprepared, for in truth nobody knows the answer to this question – even if we think we do. The only certainty is that one day we will all find out.

REFERENCES

———◆———

M uch of the material in this book is the result of our own investigations, interviews and personal correspondence. However, no investigator stands alone. We are indebted to many others and to the great body of work that already exists in the field of afterlife studies. We list below some of the books, magazines and research groups that we have found useful. Should any reader wish to correspond with us and relate their own evidence they can do so, in full confidence if desired, by writing care of 37 Heathbank Road, Cheadle Heath, Stockport, Cheshire, SK3 0UP.

BOOKS AND JOURNALS

Bardens, Dennis, *Psychic Animals*, Hale, 1988

Blackmore, Sue, *Beyond the Body*, Heinemann, 1982

Burland, C. A., *Myths of Life and Death*, Macmillan, 1974

Cavendish, Richard (ed.) *Man, Myth and Magic*, Purnell, 1971

Cavendish, Richard (ed.) *Encyclopedia of the Unexplained*, Routledge & Kegan Paul, 1974.

Collins, Doris, *The Power Within*, Granada, 1986

Costello, Mike, 'Death Trip USA', in *Psi-Eye*, 1986

Eno, Paul F., 'A poltergeist that broke all the rules', in *Fate*, June 1986

Evans, Hilary, *Visions, Apparitions, Alien Visitors*, Aquarian, 1984

Eysenck, Hans J. and Sargent, Carl, *Explaining the Unexplained*, Weidenfeld & Nicolson, 1982

Farmer, Philip José, *The Riverworld Series* (five volumes), Berkley, 1971

Fiore, Dr Edith, *You Have Been Here Before*, Sphere, 1978

Fort, Charles, *The Complete Books of Charles Fort*, Dover, 1974

Fuller, John G., *The Ghost of 29 Megacycles*, Grafton, 1987

Garland, Joanne, *Herald of the New Age*, Grafton, 1988

Gooch, Stan, *Creatures from Inner Space*, Rider, 1984

Grey, Margot, *Return from Death*, Arkana, 1986

Harris, Melvin, *Sorry, You've Been Duped!*, Weidenfeld & Nicolson, 1986

Hough, Peter, *Witchcraft: A Strange Conflict*, Lutterworth, 1991

Hurst, H. W., *The Thousand Year Memory*, Sphere, 1983

Keeton, Joe and Petherick, Simon, *Powers of the Mind*, Hale, 1986

Kubler-Ross, Elisabeth, *On Death and Dying*, Tavistock, 1970

Meek, George: publications available from Metascience (address below)

Monroe, Robert, *Far Journeys*, Souvenir, 1986

Moody, Raymond, *Life after Life*, Bentam, 1980

Moody, Raymond, *The Light Beyond*, Macmillan, 1988

Ortzen, Tony, 'Spiritualism Today', in *Exploring the Supernatural*, April 1987

Price, Harry, *The End of Borley Rectory*, Harrap, 1947

Randles, Jenny, *Mind Monsters*, Aquarian, 1990

Randles, Jenny and Hough, Peter, *Death by Supernatural Causes?*, Grafton, 1988

Randles, Jenny and Hough, Peter, *Scary Stories*, Futura, 1991

Raudive, Konstantin, *Breakthrough*, Smythe, 1971

Ring, Kenneth, *Life at Death*, Coward, McCann & Geoghagan, 1980

Ring, Kenneth, *The Omega Project*, William Morrow, 1992

Russell, Barbara, 'Report on an all night vigil at an inn', in *Anomaly*, 7, 1987

Schatzman, Morton, *The Story of Ruth*, Penguin, 1982

Sheldrake, Dr Rupert, *A New Science of Life*, Granada, 1983

Underwood, Peter, *The Ghost Hunter's Guide*, Javelin, 1988

Watson, Lyall, *Supernature*, Hodder & Stoughton, 1974

Webster, Ken, *The Vertical Plane*, Grafton, 1988

Whitaker, Terence, *Ghosts and Legends of Lancashire*, Hale, 1980

Wilson, Colin, *Poltergeist!*, NEL, 1981

ADDRESSES

ASSAP (Association for the Scientific Study of Anomalous Phenomena), 8 Paul Street, Frome, Somerset BA11 1DX

Fate magazine, PO Box 64383, St Paul, MN 55164-0383, USA

Metascience, Box 947, Franklin, NC 28734, USA

Society for Psychical Research, 49 Marloes Road, London, W8 6LA

The Sceptic magazine, Box 475, Manchester, M60 2TH

UFO Call, weekly news updates on research at 0898 rates on 0898-121886 (UK only)

INDEX